THE DIVINE SCANDAL

FINDING GOD WHEN THE SH*T HITS THE FAN

JORDAN STORMENT

ISBN 978-0-578-67309-7

I dedicate this book to my loving wife Morgan. Thank you for showing me what unconditional love looks like.

I also dedicate this book to my beautiful children, Finley and Sullivan. Daddy loves you to the moon and back.

CONTENTS

SENSELESS GOD

Chapter 1

SENSELESS GOD

This is a story about the greatest scandal in history to ever be covered up. This is the scandal that your Sunday school teacher left out of her curriculum. Those cute little felt boards would give our children nightmares if they revealed the true scandal we find in our Bibles. We must protect our children from the real stories that fill the pages of our Holy Book. Much of the Bible resembles a Jerry Springer episode with a lot more violence. Rape, incest, murder, prostitution, suicide, adultery, orgies, drunkenness, probably weed (but I can't prove that), and the list goes on. All of these heinous deeds were committed by "Christians" in the Bible. If they were alive today, we would lock them up and throw away the key. We have taken the pages of this scandal and bound them in expensive leather. We have censored the stories all throughout scripture to make them suitable for children. We have taken characters from this scandal, such as David, and turned him into some sort of superhero. We have taken this story and created "happily ever after" fantasies where they don't exist. We have hidden the dead bodies that number so many they would pile as high as the Empire State Building. We have concealed the truth with good intentions. Not wanting people to reject God due to the scandal of Scripture, we domesticate the Truth. In doing so, we have alienated the ones whom God is calling. Those meant to be ambassadors for the kingdom of God are passively standing by in shame and isolation rather than welcomed in as active participants in the kingdom of God as the Sons and Daughters they are. The problem is that this Scandal is the very key to unlock our freedom. The Truth is immersed in the scandals we find all over scripture. We must embrace this scandal if we desire to be free.

In Genesis 38, Judah accidentally had sex with his daughter-in-law, Tamar. His wife died, so he did what any reasonable man would do, (can you sense my sarcasm?) and went to proposition a prostitute, or at least someone he thought was a prostitute. It wasn't until after he had sex with her that he realized it was his own daughter-in-law! What? This is insane! "This can't be the same Bible that I read," you might be telling yourself. Don't worry, it gets worse. In Genesis 19:32-36, Lot had sex with BOTH of his daughters and got them pregnant! Yup, that's right. Throw this sicko in jail! His daughters come up with the genius idea to get their DAD drunk and have sex with him to keep the family lineage going! What the hell?!? Yes, this is the same Bible that we preach out of on Sundays. We've all heard the story of Noah and the Ark.

Noah is an action figure. We love to tell our children this story with the cute animals. Yet we skip the part about Noah being a drunk. God says that Noah was the only righteous man on the planet, and he consistently followed God's will and enjoyed a close relationship with Him. That's some pretty high praise coming from the creator of the heavens and the earth. It's not as if Noah did not have a drinking problem before he "met Jesus," and once he invited Jesus into his heart he cleaned up his act for good. Nope. It wasn't until AFTER Noah had powerful encounters with God that we find him literally piss drunk in a tent, completely naked. That sounds like a clip from the movie "Old School" with Will Ferrell, where he gets so drunk he strips naked and goes streaking butt naked through town. This movie is completely inappropriate and I do not recommend anyone watching it (although you will laugh). But yes, this is the same book that you have been told your whole life is the perfect and infallible word of God. What the heck? Like I said earlier, if the Bible were a movie, you would never let your kids watch such filth. Actually, you might not even go see the movie yourself because it's so graphic and revolting. In Joshua 2:1, God uses a prostitute named Rahab to help take the city of Jericho. In Matthew 1:5, He goes out of his way to mention that Rahab is in the lineage of Jesus! How can this be? The perfect Son of God is born from a lineage of prostitutes. Jesus came from the wrong family. God doesn't need a perfect person to accomplish a perfect work. Are you beginning to see a theme here?

Not only do we censor scripture, but we do this in our own lives on a daily basis. When Adam and Eve sinned, brokenness entered the world, and they hid. We've been hiding ever since. When we feel completely exposed our default response is to hide. Adam and Eve hid behind fig leaves, but we hide behind shallow projections of ourselves that we present to the world around us, hoping not to be exposed. Social media is the obvious platform for us to create the best version of ourselves to show the world. We do this all day long in our everyday lives. I think those of us who have been in Christian communities probably suffer from this more than most. Since our Christian communities have an added layer of pressure, there is an expectation to live and act a certain way. When someone who is a part of our community starts "coloring outside the lines," we don't really know how to handle it and we subtly shun and ostracize those who don't look, talk, and act like we do. To be clear, when I reference "coloring outside the lines," I don't mean actual sin. I mean coloring outside the lines of what that group has decided is, and is not, acceptable behavior. Most of the time, the sin that is unacceptable happens to be our neighbor's sin. We downplay and justify our own struggle, yet the sin our neighbor wrestles with is completely unacceptable. We withhold the same measure of grace we demand for ourselves. We project an image of ourselves on social media, at work, on Sunday morning, and sometimes even to our closest family and friends. We could spend every minute of the day with others and still be hidden. Known by many, but truly known by no one. It's common to hear from those who were close to someone who committed suicide that they "were in shock" and "had no idea" their loved one was struggling. How can this be? You spent your whole life around this person yet still had no clue how deep of a struggle they were in. Simple. We only show people what we want them to see. Deep-rooted insecurity and longing for love and acceptance from those around us, we don't trust that if they saw us fully exposed, that they could still love us. We don't even love ourselves. We don't know and trust deep in our bones the One who made us actually loves us. We NEED affirmation and acceptance from everyone around us, therefore we show a version of ourselves we think they can love. Stuck in hiding. Stuck pretending. Some of us have been faking it so long we don't even realize that the version of ourselves we are projecting isn't real. We don't even know who our true self is anymore. We won't find healing for our souls until we let down the facades. Take off the masks. Quit faking it. Quit hiding and let Him in. Just like truth is immersed deep within the scandalous stories in scripture, truth and healing can only be found deep within the scandalous story of your life. Until we find the courage to go deep within our own brokenness, we won't find healing. The very thing we are hiding from is the very thing God is using to set us free. The very thing the enemy has used to try and kill you with is the very thing God is using to redeem you. If it is hard and feels like you are dying, you are headed in the right direction. You are headed to the cross. If you let go of your life, you will find it. God is in the business of resurrection. God cannot resurrect something that refuses to die.

I have begun to fall in love with Scripture. Not because it is "ultimate truth," "inspired," or "holy." I am falling in love with the Word of God because it is so incredibly scandalous. It comforts my soul to witness the perfect Word of God emerge from the lives of imperfect people like me. Stories and lives so screwed up that we would never allow our children to watch such "filth." These scandals fill me with hope that God can work through the scandal of my life. Too many have walked away from their divine calling because they feel unworthy to partake in God's story. If they only knew their personal scandal fits right in with the rest of God's dysfunctional family, they would embrace this call. Self-hatred and shame would no longer paralyze those of us who feel called, but unworthy. We would no longer disqualify ourselves based on fabricated stories and lies that have been fed to us by religion. We would let go of our need to "have it all together" so that God can use us. We would begin to feel the power of God rise up in our weakness. However, when the only part of King David's life that we tell is the story of "David and Goliath," how can we measure up? Lest we forget that Paul was once Saul, how can any of us live up to that standard? Surely I am not fit for this Kingdom. Surely none of us are fit for that kingdom.

What if the Kingdom of God is still in grave contrast to the kingdoms that we have built in the name of God today? God empowered a serial killer named Saul to write half of the New Testament that we uphold as the "Word of God." If this happened today, I'm sure it would cause quite an uproar. We would be offended by a scandalous God that would not only forgive this man and love him, but give him a new name and appoint him as a leader above all of the "well behaved Christians" that have served God so faithfully. These are the scandals we find all over scripture. Like the older brother in the story of the prodigal son that was infuriated when his brother was not merely tolerated by his father after his betrayal, but celebrated. He had been so faithful! He had read his Bible everyday, prayed before every meal, and gone to church every Sunday! Scandalous! How could his father do this! Is there no justice? This Father must be delusional! Possessed!

What if your church appointed an adulterer to be your pastor and leader? Even worse, a murderer?!? Doesn't something deep inside of you cringe at the thought? How could they? I mean, let's be reasonable. I suppose that an infinitely loving God in all of his power might be able to forgive this person. But this person will be no pastor of mine! And yet, we read the "Word of God" everyday, like diligent servants, that was written by the hands of murderers! The blood on their hands stain the pages of our Bible. Their fornication leaps off the pages of scripture like an X-rated movie! How can we embrace these events that took place in scripture and refer to them as "The Perfect Word of God," yet reject them if they happened in our present day? Do you see the contradiction? God's Word is eternal. It is past, present, and future. We cannot accept His Word in the past and deny it in the present day. If so, we are rejecting His Truth altogether. We accept grace in theory, but deny it in practice.

I bring this up because I feel God calling the same fools like me that he has been calling since the beginning of time. "God chooses the foolish things of the world to confound the wise." We need to honestly reflect and ask ourselves if we are seeking out the admirable things of this world or the foolish things to usher in the Kingdom of God. Worldly kingdoms seek the most admirable, beautiful, blemish-free individuals to be a part of their kingdoms. Is this the Kingdom of God we read about in the gospels? Is this the Kingdom we saw Jesus establishing? When Jesus intentionally rebuked the religious elite of his day and called fishermen to "come and follow me," what kind of kingdom was He creating? When God anointed David to be king of Israel, knowing full well that David would abuse his power to seduce Bathsheba, then have her husband Uriah killed to cover up his mess, what in the world was God thinking? Why would Jesus proclaim Peter to be "a rock that he will build his church upon" right after he tells Peter that he is going to deny and betray him? Why would God use a serial killer like Saul to write down His Word that would be read for hundreds of thousands of years to come? This God doesn't appear to be very sensible.

This is the gospel. Period. This is the love story that is written about us all! A bride that has ran into the arms of countless lovers. A bride who has prostituted herself over and over again for cheap thrills. A bride who chooses convenient affairs over the cost of true Love. This is my story. This is your story. This is our story.

I would like to invite you to partake with me in this timeless scandal. Lay down your pride and give in to the still-small voice of our Lover that is calling your name. Sink deep into the reality that you are a whore who is deeply loved by God. It is from these depths that a well springs up of overwhelming joy. Fall into the arms of the One who has loved you senselessly before you were born. Give in. Take off the mask. Get ready to be swept off your feet by a God who is, and has been, pursuing you every moment of your life, no matter how far you run from Him. Every breath you've ever taken has been mercy. This is not a god who loves occasionally, this is the God who IS love. The love that God has for you led Him to a cross where he would be tortured to death for you while you were spitting in his face. This is the passionate lover of your soul.

> "I pray that you, being rooted and established in love, may have power, together with all the saints, to grasp how wide and long and high and deep is the love of Christ, and to know this love that surpasses all understanding-that you may be filled to the measure of all the fullness of God."

Ephesians 3:17-19

OFFENSIVE GOSPEL

Chapter 2

OFFENSIVE GOSPEL

If the gospel does not offend you, I would seriously question whether or not you actually believe the Gospel of Jesus found in the New Testament. The Gospel, at its core, is the most offensive love story in history. It is offensive to our sensibility, our logic, and our shallow perspective of justice. Sometimes I think we forget that Jesus was brutally murdered by humanity. It is as if someone else killed Jesus long ago, and we would have never done such a terrible thing. You do realize Jesus was murdered for preaching the Gospel, right? Which means, in its very nature, this message is so offensive that it led us to murder God. Wow. This Gospel message had to be so scandalous, so offensive, and so heinous that we could not allow Jesus to continue to preach this message. I'm fairly certain if Jesus were alive today and preached the exact same Gospel message today that he did in the New Testament, we would just kill him all over again.

Let's think about that for a minute. It's not as if Jesus flirted with the line of what was appropriate and inappropriate. He violated their worldviews and belief systems so vehemently they could not simply ignore him. He crossed the line way too far. They had to eliminate Him. I feel like there are a lot of crazy and offensive things you can say and people will just ignore you. Apparently going around and telling people you are God is not one of those things. A little bit of free life advice: don't go around telling people you are God, don't tell rich people to sell all of their possessions, and don't tell powerful people to humble themselves. That might get you killed. Take it a step further; if you are extremely offensive, people will just ostracize you. Jesus went further. They couldn't stand it. The gospel made their skin crawl. It made them rage inside. Imagine spending your whole life climbing the proverbial ladder of success in society, and this guy Jesus comes out of nowhere preaching a message that flips the system on its head! You worked your whole life to get to the top and this fool shows up and says the top is now the bottom? I've been stepping on people my whole life to get to the front of the line, and now the first in line are last? Jesus says in Matthew 20:16, "So the last will be first, and the first will be last." I worked really hard to sit in the most honorable seat at the table, and now my honorable seat isn't so honorable anymore? How could he?!? I'm not about to sit by and watch this guy ruin my life's work with this bullshit message that the poor are now blessed and the rich are not! Off with his head! This is the Gospel. Jesus said if we actually begin to follow him and preach this message that the world would hate us. Nothing has changed. Well, actually something has changed. The Gospel we preach has changed.

We have shaped a Gospel more suitable to our lifestyle and the American dream. No matter what point in history or culture the Gospel is being preached, people will still riot against it. Some people will fall so in love with the Gospel of Jesus that they will die for it, but that means someone is on the other end of the sword killing because they cannot accept this message. This is what Jesus promised us. Not much has changed, but so much has changed at the same time.

Jesus didn't just walk around preaching a gospel that made us feel warm and fuzzy inside. Most people didn't like the Kingdom of God that Jesus spoke about. They were pretty comfortable in their own little kingdoms. They did not like the economics of this kingdom, because they had become quite rich from the kingdoms they created. They did not like hearing that the first were last because they were standing at the front of the line. They did not like the dinner table in the kingdom because they were sitting in the most honorable seats and Jesus flipped that paradigm upside down.

The Gospel is a paradox. On one hand it is Good News. This is the foundation of the whole Gospel. The Gospel of Jesus is Good News! But on the other hand, it is really bad news. Here is where the paradox lies: Jesus came to give life and life more abundantly, but in order to find that life you need to die! Wait, what? Did he come to give life, or death? These ideas seem to be at war with each other. How do they coexist? Jesus came to give resurrection life. God cannot resurrect something that refuses to die. Nothing has ever been resurrected without first dying. Unfortunately, you cannot avoid the cross and grave on your way to resurrection life. It is the only way. Jesus did not mislead us when it came to this reality. We must pick up our cross and follow him. Jesus says in Matthew 16:24-26, "If anyone would come after me, let him deny himself and take up his cross and follow me. [25] For whoever would save his life will lose it, but whoever loses his life for my sake will find it. [26] For what will it profit a man if he gains the whole world and forfeits his soul?"

Anyone who hangs on to their life will lose it, but those who lose their life for His sake will find new life. Jesus did not pick up His cross so that I wouldn't have to pick up mine. He promised me that I would have to pick up my cross, that was His command to us. Baptism is supposed to be an outward demonstration of this internal reality. We are identifying with Christ in his death, and being raised to new life. My soul is drawn to the Gospel, but my flesh hates it.

The path to new life is a bloody mess. It is painful. It hurts. It is humiliating at times. It requires nothing less than death to find true life. I must lose my life if I intend to gain it. If this bothers you or offends you, I would suggest that you might have a problem with Jesus, not me. The Gospel is not "stay the same person but try to be a better moral version of your old self." The Gospel is and always has been death and resurrection. True life is only found on the other side of the cross. We will never be satisfied until we experience resurrection life.

You see, my soul longs for the fulfillment of true life, but everything in my flesh squirms and resists the Gospel. My ego scratches and claws for control. In an attempt to make the gospel suitable for everyone, we have slowly domesticated the truth. We have subtly and non-verbally communicated a message that "you can still hold on to your life," "you don't really have to let go of your love of self, money, and all of the other things we worship with our life," "Jesus didn't REALLY mean that, it was a metaphor for something else," "you can just be a good person and come to church regularly and be fine." Quite simply, these things are not true. The enemy does not fabricate elaborate lies that sound absurd to wreak havoc in our lives. He is not dumb. He is not going to try and convince you that unicorns are real. He is going to creep in and subtly manipulate truth just enough that it is void of life, yet appealing enough for us to buy it. Think about it. If I were the devil and my primary objective was to keep people from coming to Jesus for healing, what would be the most effective method to achieve that goal? If my goal were to keep sick people from going to the doctor, it seems like a pretty good strategy to convince all of those sick people that they are well. The very fact that a person could be unaware of their sickness is the very thing that would keep them from seeking healing. Pretty deceiving, huh? Jesus said, "I did not come for those who think they are well but I came for the sick." What if my superpower was lies? I have no actual power or authority; my only power is deception. What would be the scheme of the enemy? If it were me, my strategy would be to convince everyone that they were okay. Above all else, this would be the scheme I would use to keep people from Jesus. What if I could convince an entire nation they were "Christian" just because they were born in America? What if I could trick them into believing that if they attend a religious gathering occasionally, they were no longer sick? What if creating the illusion that people are okay and they don't need Jesus is the most powerful tool of the enemy? Think about it. If you're a good criminal and you're trying to rob people, you're going to create counterfeit that resembles real money as close as possible, yet has no value. Sometimes we believe that Satan is trying to trick us with Monopoly money, not realizing our whole bank account is full of counterfeit, and we are bankrupt.

Most of us think we love the story of the prodigal son found in the New Testament. Yet, much of the time if we are honest with ourselves, we end up being the older brother in the story, not the prodigal son coming home. You mean to tell me that my younger brother can squander his family inheritance on sex, drugs, and rock-and-roll, and the minute he comes home, receives the same reward as me?!? I have been at home all of these years doing my chores, being a faithful son while he was out partying all night. You mean to tell me that I don't get a greater reward? This doesn't seem "fair" to us. Thank God we are not the judge.

Jesus also ran around telling people that in order to find true life they needed to, and I quote: "eat my flesh and drink my blood." What the heck? Is this some sort of cannibal gospel? What in the world is that supposed to mean? Jesus had a knack for thinning the herd! He could take a church of 5,000 and in one sermon sift it down to 20. Maybe preaching wasn't Jesus' spiritual gift. How about this one: unless you hate your father and mother you are not fit for the kingdom of God? So now Jesus has zero family values. What am I supposed to do with that? "I hate you Mom! Sorry, I am just trying to follow Jesus, you understand right?" I'm not sure how that would go over with my Mom.

In Luke 6:27-36, we find the holy grail of sermons from Jesus that are completely ludicrous.

27 "But to you who are listening I say: Love your enemies, do good to those who hate you, 28 bless those who curse you, pray for those who mistreat you. 29 If someone slaps you on one cheek, turn to them the other also. If someone takes your coat, do not

withhold your shirt from them. **30** Give to everyone who asks you, and if anyone takes what belongs to you, do not demand it back. **31** Do to others as you would have them do to you.

32 "If you love those who love you, what credit is that to you? Even sinners love those who love them. **33** And if you do good to those who are good to you, what credit is that to you? Even sinners do that. **34** And if you lend to those from whom you expect repayment, what credit is that to you? Even sinners lend to sinners, expecting to be repaid in full. **35** But love your enemies, do good to them, and lend to them without expecting to get anything back. Then your reward will be great, and you will be children of the Most High, because he is kind to the ungrateful and wicked. (like me) **36** Be merciful, just as your Father is merciful.

If that doesn't piss you off, I don't know what will. I've shared this teaching of Jesus with other "Christians" before and you could tell immediately they were trying to justify this away. They immediately jump on the defense. "Yeah, BUT he didn't really mean all of our enemies." We come up with a lot of logical excuses as to why we shouldn't have to love those who have hurt us. We feel pretty justified. We are the victims. This is a concept in the teachings of Jesus I have never understood. It is also a concept that is rarely talked about among Christians, probably because we simply don't know what to do with it. Especially considering how our Christian nation has a posture of hatred towards our enemies. Why in the world would God command us to love our enemies?!? Talk about unfair and senseless. When we take a hit on the cheek, we are supposed to offer our other cheek? What?!? I certainly don't want to love my enemies, so it is much easier for me to focus on something else Jesus talked about. Although, a lot of the things that Jesus taught are tough to swallow. I have pondered this idea for years.

If this doesn't sound crazy, then I don't know what does. Does this sound like a God who is fair? Not to me! So, I asked God why. Why in the world would Jesus command us to love our enemies? Because we serve a God who embraces US even though we are His enemies. One can draw the conclusion that we are to love our enemies for their sake, so that maybe our kindness might one day soften their hearts towards God and us. And I think that this is partially true, but I would like to offer an alternate perspective. What if God wants us to love our enemies for OUR sake? What if in our efforts to love our enemies, we get a tiny glimpse of what God experiences with US? What if in our efforts in extending mercy to those who do not deserve it, we begin to see the countless times when God has extended mercy to us when it made absolutely no sense. What if in loving people who take it for granted, we begin to see how often we take for granted the love of

God. What if we have all been, and still from time to time behave like enemies of God? The scriptures tell us that we have ALL been enemies of God. That while we were ALL murdering Jesus on a cross, He was pleading with his Father to "forgive us, for we know not what we do."

You see, Jesus called us to love one another as He has loved us. Does God love us because we deserve it? Does God love us only when we love Him? Does God forgive us only when we appreciate it? Or, in spite of the fact that at times I trample all over the love of God, He remains faithful to me when I am completely faithless? So, could it be that maybe Jesus called us to love our enemies so that for a brief moment we would have a little bit deeper understanding of His love for US? In my enemies, I catch a glimpse of the absolutely scandalous, and unconditional love of God for me.

Jesus told us to love one another as He has loved us. And, He said that the world would know that we are His disciples based on one thing: the way we love one another. It seems like this is a pretty significant point Jesus is trying to make. It is very easy to gloss over the statement "love one another as I have loved you." But this tiny statement is loaded with gigantic implications. Jesus is essentially saying, "When I was hanging on a cross being humiliated and brutally murdered by YOU, spit on and mocked by YOU, I was pleading with my Father at that very moment for Him to 'forgive you for you know not what you are doing.'" And Jesus is essentially telling us to love one another like that. Seriously?!? You mean we aren't talking about a touchy-feely, happy-go-lucky love where everything is peachy keen and everyone loves each other? We are talking about extending mercy in the very moment of the greatest betrayal possible! Another picture of this would be Jesus washing the disciple's feet and the scriptures specifically tell us before Jesus performs this scandalous act of love that He KNEW for certain Judas was going to betray him (John 13:11). What?!? Are you kidding me?!? After I read this, I was waiting for the part where Jesus struck him dead with a bolt of lightning! This, of course, can only be found in the JIV (Jordan International Version).

There is a reason we murdered God. As much as the Gospel is really, really Good News, there is a part of us waging war against the Gospel. The Gospel is the most offensive love story ever told. Isn't it funny how Love can offend us? We aren't offended that God would love us; we are offended that He loves our neighbor. We naturally have a ton of grace for those who struggle in ways we have, but we have no empathy for others who have struggled with things we don't understand and have never experienced. We demand a measure of grace for ourselves that we are completely unwilling to extend to others. This is what I find ironic about human beings. We love the Good News for us, but not for gays. Not for those in prison. They deserve the death penalty. The murderers, hookers, and thieves deserve death, but I deserve grace and mercy. I'm not like "those" people. Sorry to break it to you, but you ARE those people. I am thou.

This is the offensive Gospel. The Gospel is a paradox. It is both Good News, and bad news. Your soul longs for the Good News, but your flesh hates it. I would say "don't shoot the messenger," but I think it might be a little late for that. We already did that once.

SH*T HITS THE FAN

Chapter 3

WHEN THE SH*T HITS THE FAN

Allow me to explain. We accept grace in theory, but deny it in practice. If you say you love God but hate your brother, you are a liar (1 John 4:20). We can theoretically tolerate that God forgives certain people. However, when the shit really hits the fan, we reject the grace of God. When life happens and we are called to be instruments of mercy, we bring a weight of judgment. When a young woman on the worship team at our church gets pregnant and isn't married, how do we respond? In my experience, the overwhelming response has been a silent or not-so-silent judgment. We quietly remove her from the worship team and sweep her under the rug. We speak about grace with our words, but our actions communicate shame and rejection. This fragile young woman is left feeling like a disgusting piece of garbage that must be hidden. She is too filthy to be in the public eye, unworthy, and unfit to lead. It's as if what qualified her for ministry was how well-behaved of a Christian she was. We can't allow our youth to see her! If they do, then the whole youth group would be pregnant next! When we discover that a young man struggles with pornography in a culture that bombards him with sexual images all day long on television, movies, and the internet, how do we react? What about when a follower of Jesus struggles with addiction? What do we do with those in our church communities who struggle with substance abuse? We subtly dismiss them and let them meet in a back alley on a weeknight when nobody else is around. Silently ostracizing and distancing ourselves from those whom God is drawing near to. What do we do when a man or woman in our church is caught in adultery? Better yet, what did Jesus do when he was confronted with this very issue?

When a woman was brought to Jesus that was caught in adultery, what did He do? Man, how could he let her off the hook?!? She deserved punishment! I mean, come on Jesus, at least give her a guilt trip. Smack her over the head with the Bible a few times at least! This is standard procedure for repentance, right? To make matters even worse, this woman was not just committing adultery with one person; she had multiple partners! This is the Scandalous Lover of My Soul! Jesus broke every social, economic, geographical, racial, and religious barrier that existed to touch this woman! In the words of Brennan Manning: "Something is fundamentally wrong when the church rejects those who are embraced by Jesus." If the perfect creator of the universe came to earth and lived among us and said that He did not come to condemn but to bring life, how the hell do we think we have the right to condemn another human being?

An old friend of mine committed adultery and his marriage ended before they had even been married a year. I remember sitting down with him and listening to his story. Most of his family were Christians and his father had been involved in full-time ministry his whole life. He looked at me emotionless, wounded so deeply that he self-medicated himself in order to feel no pain. He told me how his family had reacted to finding out what had happened with his marriage. He spoke of how his family said things to him such as: "I always knew this would happen with you" and "I'm not very surprised."

This makes me sick. Sick for my friend. Putting myself in his shoes and absorbing the overwhelming guilt, shame, and self-hatred he must feel. I wanted to punch his dad in the face! This is what brings out the righteous anger of God towards us. Not righteous anger towards the adulterer, righteous anger towards the ones who are slamming the door shut to the kingdom in the face of those whom Jesus is relentlessly pursuing. This angers God. Not because He hates those people, but because He loves those who are being alienated from Him so much that He would endure death to be reconciled to them.

A friend of mine named Lisa shared with me a vulnerable story about her past. She and her ex-husband were very involved in a small church. Her husband was very religious and also very abusive. As it turns out, he had mental health issues. Lisa finally found the courage to get out of this destructive relationship for the sake of her children and herself. She told me, with tears in her eyes, when she was going through this very difficult divorce, her pastor denied her communion. I just about lost my mind! A PASTOR representing JESUS denied this woman the blood of Jesus?!? Are you freaking serious??? I wanted to cry and scream all at once.

It is in moments exactly like this that we have the opportunity to partner with God and what He is doing on earth. We can be a shoulder to cry on, a beacon of hope, or an instrument of reconciliation. Here was an opportunity for this church to rally around the broken family, and to show them what God looks like. Instead, they partnered with the enemy and became a wrecking ball to wreak havoc on this family and kick her while she was down. Denying her communion of all things. This is exactly what communion represents: The body and blood of Jesus that was poured out for us in the moment we least deserved it. To deny Lisa communion in that season of her life is to miss the entire purpose of the Gospel. It is in this exact moment when she is being denied communion that we should be pouring the blood of Jesus over her head, drenching her in love, mercy, and forgiveness. Jesus said that the world would know Him by the way we love one another. Well, this is precisely the problem. When we respond to the messy realities of life with judgment and condemnation, the world takes notice and thinks this is what God looks like. When this could not be further from the truth.

I own a real estate brokerage called Glass House Realty. One day, a business professional walked into my office and we got to chatting. She knows me a bit and knew I was writing this book and asked me to tell her about it. I try to be transparent, hence the name Glass House Realty, so I shared a little bit about my journey with God and my experience and why I was writing the book. I talked to her about my experience with the unconditional love of God even when life got really messy. I told her about this chapter called *When the Shit Hits the Fan*. It's a great conversation starter. I didn't know very much about her personal life. After I opened up to her a little bit she broke down and got pretty vulnerable with me for a minute. She went on to explain that she is a PK. For those who aren't familiar with that term, she is a "pastor's kid." Sadly, the running joke among PK's is you either end up in jail or on drugs. Being raised as a PK can really mess with a person's psyche. She and I actually grew up in very similar households. I am very grateful for my upbringing, and I am simply acknowledging the environment I was raised in. We both grew up in very devout religious homes. She told me her parents were very strict and "proper." Everything had to appear to be perfect on the outside. They had to maintain a perfect image to present the congregation and the rest of the world. Her family didn't know how to handle actual life when the shit hit the fan. Which it inevitably does. It's not a matter of if, but when.

She said her family didn't know how to respond with love and grace when the kids began to "color outside the lines." Years ago, when she was getting a divorce from her first husband, she said her own family told her they would not break bread with her. They always had family meals together. Yet when their own daughter was struggling and going through the most difficult time of her life, they responded with shame and judgment. Not mercy. Not grace. Not kindness. Not support. Not love. They ostracized their own child. These people are pastors for God's sake! They should be a living representation of what Jesus looks like on the earth, yet they couldn't have been further from showing the world what Jesus looks like. How they responded is exactly the opposite from who I believe Jesus revealed Himself to be in scripture. Unbelievable.

I'll never understand how a perfect God came to earth and said "I have not come to condemn," yet somehow we feel comfortable slipping into that judgment seat so easily. Let's throw out the fact that her parents were pastors for a minute. I believe every human, atheist or not, can agree on the fact that one of our greatest needs as human beings is unconditional love and belonging. We are desperately seeking this much of our lives. Our parents are one of the most significant human relationships we have on earth where we seek this unconditional love and belonging from. To have your own parents, your flesh and blood, look you in the face and tell you that because of your circumstances in life you disgust them so much that they are unwilling to break bread with you has got to be one of the most psychologically damaging experiences a human being can endure. I believe that this can do irreparable harm to a person. This breaks my heart and I am confident that this breaks God's heart as well. Throwing in the fact that these individuals claim to represent God just magnifies the potential damage that can be done to this woman. Not only did she experience severe rejection from her own parents, she experienced a perceived rejection from God as well. Some people never recover from this kind of experience or trauma.

I would like to quickly point out that all of these conversations and experiences were happening in real, everyday life. This wasn't a conversation I had at church, or a conference, or a home group. Nope. This was God showing up in everyday life. We have got to break this dualistic mindset in religious communities. So many of us think God is in a building, or retreat, or conference, or gathering. Yes, to be sure, He will show up in those moments. But we are missing out on the bulk of our life with God that is meant to be lived out in our actual daily lives. Many times we pack up our bags and leave our "everyday life" to attend a church service or gathering of some sort in order to "encounter God." We show up to a church service for an hour and attempt to interact with God in a crowded room with strangers, and once that experience is over, we get back to our "real life." Unfortunately, many times these two spheres don't intersect. We attend a conference, and our "real life" remains the same. Unchanged. Our actual daily life and reality remains untouched. We are inspired at best, but not transformed. Meanwhile, God is knee-deep in the mundane, messy, broken, trivial, difficult, rhythms of everyday life. He longs for us to invite Him into our marriages, our work, our homes, our parenting, our education, and yes, even our ministries.

I long to see the church partner with God and what He is doing on earth today. You know what I think He's up to? The same thing He was up to 2,000 years ago. I don't think Jesus all of a sudden changed who He is. I think He is roaming the earth, performing scandalous acts of mercy. Touching those whom society deemed untouchable. Forgiving those whom we have written off as unforgivable. Lifting up those who society is holding down. Whoever we have decided is unworthy. The burnt out. The addicted. The felons. The homeless. The prostitutes. The criminals. You do realize this is what Jesus did when He walked the earth in flesh, right? Does it make you uncomfortable to think America's most wanted might be the Kingdom's most wanted? Are you sure that you want to be a part of this Kingdom? Or, are you comfortable with the kingdoms we have created in the name of God that look nothing like the Kingdom Jesus demonstrated?

Someone challenged me once with a very difficult and controversial question: "Do homosexuals believe that the Gospel is good news?" My immediate response was an emphatic no, of course not. Why in the world would they think the gospel is good news? Many homosexuals are likely to think God hates them and wants to punish them for all of eternity. How could that be perceived as good news? He then proceeded to say, "Something is wrong when the very foundation of the Gospel is that it is good news for all of humanity, yet there are people who think the Gospel is very bad news for them." The Gospel is good news for all! Not just some, and not just for the religious elite.

I met up with a good friend a while ago and I could tell something was wrong. She looked completely dejected. Sadness and turmoil were written all over her face. This is a friend whom I care for deeply, so I couldn't help but ask, "Are you okay?" She tried to dismiss the question, but I could sense a flood of emotions beneath the surface just waiting to explode. I assured her I was there for her if she needed to talk. I could see that she was on the verge of breaking down. As tears began pouring out of her, she muttered, "I've done something that I don't think I could ever forgive myself for." One of the gifts of being an alcoholic in recovery is someone could literally tell me anything and it wouldn't shock or offend me. Been there, done that, seen it all, heard it all. If I haven't said or done it myself, I've heard it in recovery circles. I told her she didn't have to tell me anything, but there was literally nothing she could tell me that would change how I feel about her as a friend and as a person. I am a safe place if you are struggling.

She could hardly speak, as tears were breaking through her dam of emotions. A well of pain so deep it could no longer be contained. My friend began to share with me that she recently had an abortion. She barely uttered the words before she began to sob. I cried with her and reminded her that she is loved. I told her there is nothing she could do to escape the love of God. His love for her had nothing to do with how well behaved she was, and nothing is beyond redemption. It was too good to be true. She hated herself. I could see it. There is no such thing as unconditional love. It's a fantasy. She began to punish herself. Unworthy of love. She clearly believed she deserved to be punished. So, like myself, she tried to drink herself to death. Been there. Done that. I understand that on such a deep level because I have been there myself. She began drinking until she blacked out. Driving drunk. Intoxicated, she ran into a mailbox with her car and had no idea how it happened. No regard for her life. Shame and self-hatred had taken over. Religion can lead us to a dark place where we believe God's love is reserved for the healthy when Jesus said that he came for the sick.

One of her best friends has no idea she had an abortion. Probably, still to this day. She and her friend, who happens to be a conservative right wing Christian Republican, are no longer close. Her friend has boldly and openly made a public stance as anti-abortion. She is very passionate about it. I get it. There is absolutely nothing wrong with this. Now, I'm not looking to have a debate about abortion, and I am not making a statement either way about whether abortion is right or wrong. We'll save that for another book. But I will say the way her friend has publicly spoken out about abortion has everything to do with why one of her closest friends doesn't feel safe to share that she had an abortion herself. How could she? Why would she feel safe? When a close friend publicly paints a picture of those who choose to have an abortion as murderers, I think it is safe to say those who have had an abortion might not want to open up about that to you. But a murderer? So you think that person should be in prison for murder? Put them on death row. Execute them. Guilty! Hang them! Its one thing to take a stance against abortion, but accusing someone of murder is taking it a step further. Is there any room for grace for those who have experienced abortion for one reason or another? You can see why this woman, who is struggling deeply, would never trust one of those people to seek help? This unintentionally creates a culture of fear and condemnation. No wonder this woman is struggling with self-hatred. No wonder she doesn't believe she can be forgiven and made whole. No wonder she feels shame. No wonder she is overcome with guilt. No wonder she is lashing out with self-destructive behavior. Christians don't mean for this to happen, but sometimes I don't think we slow down to wonder how our words and actions affect others.

What kind of narrative are we creating here? A narrative of fear and shame. Is this the gospel? Is this the message that Jesus would tell this woman after she had an abortion? Think about those lame bracelets for a moment. WWJD. What would Jesus do? Seriously. What would Jesus do? Why not partner with Jesus and do what He would do in this moment? Why not say what Jesus would say in this moment? Jesus, who is perfect and blameless, said He did not come to condemn, but to seek and save the lost. She is lost. I think He would tell her that there is nothing she has done, or could ever do to change His love for her. He would remind her that He gave everything for her. Every regret in her life has been covered. He bore her shame.

Unconditional love and belonging is what we are all seeking. So while we are preaching inspiring sermons about grace, we are writing a narrative that looks much different than the gospel. We preach grace. Yet we live in such a way when the shit hits the fan that we create an environment of fear and shame. We are not safe. We are the ones with the pitchforks out when the woman caught in adultery is dragged out in the middle of town before Jesus. He is loving and forgiving and redeeming. We are shouting at Him to stone her.

Another friend I knew from church got married in his early 20's. I attended his bachelor party. Nothing "Christian" about that, haha, but we had fun. Fast forward a few years, and Jerry Springer came out in full force. Turns out he had been having an ongoing affair with the wife of his best friend and business partner. I'm talking about a long time best friend, best man, roommate, business partner, who lived across the street from each other kind of stuff. As you can imagine, this got pretty ugly in a hurry. Scandalous stuff. So much so that God must be absent, right? No. He is knee deep in the mud with us when things get ugly, just like how we discover in the Bible. Unfortunately for my friend, his family was full of well-known pastors in the community. His father was in full time ministry his whole life and had been the pastor of a very large, well-known church in town. And now, his brother was a pastor of a very large church in town as well, which happened to be growing rapidly and filled with the friends and family he had known his entire life. This was a public embarrassment; a black eye on his family. I can imagine the weight of humiliation he must have felt. Rumors quickly spread of this scandalous sex story. Christians spread gossip better than anyone, so it spread like wildfire. It felt as if someone had broadcast all of the gory details on the local news. Everyone knew. I mean EVERYONE. This scandal was the talk of the town for years.

Conflicted as to how to handle such a public spectacle, like any good Christian family, they encouraged both couples to reconcile and attempt to repair their broken marriages. Nope. It wasn't going to happen. No matter how much this family would try to will this into existence and save face, the affair had gone on for too long at this point.They were in love and did not want to separate. This wasn't an "oops, my bad, won't happen again" kind of thing. They claimed they really loved and cared for each other and wanted to be together. The family was so embarrassed, and all of them were in turmoil.The proverbial shit had officially hit the fan for this Christian family. With a family heritage of showing others how to follow Jesus, how would they respond when real life happens? Most likely, in an attempt to silence the Christian tabloids they decided it would be best for the son, who had just committed adultery, to not be at church. Since he was not "repenting" of his sin and reconciling with his wife, there was no positive spin to manufacture in the story, so the family thought it best to sweep the scandal under the rug. To sweep their son under the rug. I remember one year around the holidays they requested their son not come to Thanksgiving dinner with the family. Don't get me wrong, what he did was awful, but damn, that is rough. He is no victim, but I couldn't help but feel heartbroken for this family. They are a wonderful family navigating some very murky waters the best they could. But moments like these don't change what we believe, they EXPOSE what we actually believe.

This is psychologically, spiritually, and emotionally damaging for the individual being "swept" under the rug. It unintentionally communicates, "You are so ugly, we can't allow you to be seen," and "we are so ashamed of you that we can't be seen near you," and "you are such a mess that we need you to go away." Typically, this is my family's M.O. I, too, grew up with a family with pastors and leaders in ministry, so when things got a little bit "colorful" we had to preserve the family image and sweep whatever, or whoever, was out of line under the rug. We could not jeopardize our image as the perfect, Hallmark card Christian family.

The collateral damage of this is pretty deep. The shameful thoughts and feelings about yourself sink deep in your heart. So deep it could take years to remove the shrapnel from your heart. The lies of shame and self-hatred become so deeply intertwined with your identity, that it may take years of counseling and the Holy Spirit to remove and replace with words of truth, affirmation, and unconditional love in order to heal your heart. Some never recover. I can't speak for my friend, but just knowing my long journey of healing from my own self-hatred and shame, I would venture to say he is still recovering from these events. Years later, shame can still creep up from time to time. Today, I'm able to identify the root of shame and self-hatred as a seed planted years ago deep in my heart. I am still uprooting those lies in my own heart and soul. Healing is not a moment, it's a journey.

Years later, and this man is now married to the woman with whom he had the affair. He is married to his ex-best friend's ex-wife. They have a blended family. Children from prior marriages, and children from their current marriage. He is a wildly successful businessperson and still well-known in the community. And still, years later I hear Christian people slandering him and talking shit about him because of what he did. Were his actions okay? No, of course not. He would not deny that. Did he make poor choices? Yes, of course he did. Nobody would debate that, not even him. But how in God's name can we, as broken and screwed-up individuals, so easily slip into the judgement seat and slander another human being? Ironically, Christians are the best at passing judgement. We accept grace in theory but deny it in practice. When life happens, as it inevitably does, what message are we sending? I'm not talking about the messages we give when we are on a stage with a microphone. I'm talking about when we are in the trenches of life, and the shit hits the fan, what message are we preaching then? "Preach the gospel at all times and use words when necessary" - St. Francis of Assisi

The world is watching our sermons, not listening to them. So when we say the Love of God is unconditional, why then do we have so many conditions? Why do we, as broken sinners, create conditions to God's love, when the perfect Son of God who has the right to create conditions chooses not to? Are these conditions established by God, or created by us to feel superior to others? Who do we think we are??? Why have we created certain unforgivable sins? Why is YOUR sin forgivable, but your neighbor's is not? You are broken just the same as they are.

I've heard it said "there are two kinds of people in this world." I call bullshit! There are only PEOPLE in this world, and there is only one kind of people in this world: BROKEN people! We are all in the same boat, whether we know it or not. Of that one group of people, there are two subgroups; those who are aware of their brokenness and those who are not. That is all. You are individually unique and not unique all at the same time. There is no one like you. And because of your unique quality, your brokenness is expressed differently, but you are broken all the same. Your brokenness might be expressed with an addiction to alcohol, or with an addiction to the approval of others, or you might be addicted to yourself (AKA pride). Consumed by yourself and living in a world where you are all that matters; YOU are YOUR god. We are all sick and in need of a healer. Even if you are a follower of Jesus, you still need the healing and transformation of

Jesus on a daily basis. Those who are unaware of their sick condition are dangerous on two different levels. First, because the very fact they are unaware of their sickness hinders them from seeking healing, more specifically, a HEALER! And second, those who are unaware of their sickness spread their disease. I have a really difficult time being around people who have no self-awareness. The irony of these individuals is they are unable to see their own reflection right in front of their face, and instead fixate on the brokenness in others. Such people love watching the news and condemning the broken individuals exploited on TV for everyone else's entertainment. Yes, they are criminals and you tell yourself you are obsessed with watching because you need to be "informed." But the truth is, deep down there is a deep-rooted insecurity inside of you that it makes you feel better and more secure about your own life to know "those people" are more screwed up than you. This helps you sleep at night. They fill their days and conversations with everyone else's "junk" yet never face their own. They are never vulnerable and show their true selves. The person they present to the rest of the world is not who they are at all. They present a polished and shallow version of their true self, spending a substantial amount of time making sure to hide every blemish.

It probably looks rather silly to God looking down at his children, who all have the same disease but somehow find a way to judge and condemn one another. Can you imagine two cancer patients judging each other as if one kind of cancer is better than the other? "Well, you have breast cancer and I only have melanoma!" Do we see how ridiculous that sounds? Well, that is how ridiculous we sound! They are both sick and need help! Who cares who is sicker than who?!? Here is a story told by Jesus that illustrates this idea perfectly.

"Two men went up to the temple to pray, one a Pharisee and the other a tax collector. The Pharisee stood up and prayed about himself: 'God I thank you that I am not like other men-robbers, evildoers, adulterers-or even like this tax collector. I fast twice a week and give a tenth of all I get.'

"But the tax collector stood at a distance. He would not even look up to Heaven, but beat his breast and said, 'God, have mercy on me, a sinner'
"I tell you that this man, rather than the other, went home justified before God. For everyone who exalts himself will be humbled, and he who humbles himself will be exalted"

Luke 18:9-14

Awareness creates desperation. Desperation for healing. Desperation for the One who can heal. Not just heal my body, but the only One who can heal my soul. Jesus gravitated to those who had a deep awareness of their sickness, and in turn had a profound desperation for Jesus. They were in the perfect place to encounter Jesus. I want to stay in a place where I am ripe for an encounter for Jesus. And the only way to stay in that place is to live with a deep awareness of my brokenness, reminding me of my desperate need for Jesus everyday. So, you are unique, but you are not unique at all. There are not two kinds of people in this world. There are broken people in this world, and you are one of them. The only difference is those who choose to live with an awareness of their condition and those who live blind. Where do you land?

SCANDAL OF DAVID

Chapter 4

THE SCANDAL OF DAVID

Poor David. I feel bad even writing these words. This chapter is going to seem like I am "bashing" the life of David. So I want to apologize to David in advance for exposing him. However, it is necessary to expose the scandalous but miraculous life that he lived. We must tear down the fairy tale of David in order to discover the truth about the scandalous love of God. I am certain that if David were alive today, he would give me his blessing for writing this in order for God to receive the glory, and not him.

One of the lies from Hell that we have believed is this: "Your life is probably a mess, but when you meet Jesus, He is going to make everything peachy keen!" As if following Jesus is a perfect upward trajectory to heaven; a "straight and narrow" path with no pit stops or detours. What a load of crap! I absolutely believe this idea is a lie straight from the pit of hell to keep God's kids from following Him. Why would I say this? Well, because if you believe that your journey with God is going to be some glamorous pathway in which you are always victorious, you will be devastated when you come to realize it will never be. The journey with God is not a straight line in the correct obedient direction 100% of the time. A journey with God is not void of pain, suffering, sin, shame, guilt, or poor choices. Endless victories and unwavering faith will not be your only experience. You will experience deep failures and most likely lose faith many times along the way. If you believe a false narrative about what your life with God is supposed to look like, you will never be able to reconcile your screwed up journey with God. You hear stories all the time, "I was addicted to drugs, or I was in prison and then I met Jesus…" Those are amazing stories and I don't want to discredit them at all, but they feed into the false narrative that once you meet Jesus, He is going to make everything okay. Quite simply, that is not true. That has not been my story. And it surely is not the story that we find in the Bible. We can accept most people's brokenness as long as it was BC (before Christ). But when someone professes to be a follower of Jesus and share they are currently struggling deeply, we don't really know how to handle it. The reason I bring this up in the context of the life of David is because David had his greatest failures in life AFTER he met Jesus. He grew up as a young man tending his father's sheep alone on a mountain. Spending time with God day and night, he had amazing encounters with God in the secret place. Experiencing victories with God while tending his father's sheep against lions and tigers and bears, oh my! David was anointed by God as a young man to be King over all of Israel. And that was just the beginning of a slew of catastrophic failure and poor choices throughout David's life.

Yes, it is true that David slew a giant that was probably 100 feet tall and could kill a man blindfolded with one hand behind his back (I'm sure we haven't exaggerated the story at all). But, did you know that not long after he went to war with the Philistine Army, he was sleeping with the enemy in the same camp? Yup, that's right, he was sleeping in the same camp with the Philistine Army that he swore his allegiance against! Funny, they must have left out that part in Sunday school. It's complicated, I guess.

However, David did have an epic encounter with a giant. He did kill Goliath with just a sling and a stone. As a young boy, David had such a rich history with God that he had the faith to confront what seemed to be impossible. Why would God choose a boy to kill a giant? Because if God chose a giant to kill a giant, we would be in awe of how great the giant is, not in awe of how great God is! You see, this is where we get it twisted. We manufacture a narrative where WE are the hero, not God. We don't do this maliciously. We are deeply insecure. We feel that if we are the hero in the story, then we are worthy of love. Do NOT get this backwards. You are NOT the hero of your story. And I assure you, David was NOT the hero of this story. Why did God use David to kill Goliath? So there would be zero question as to WHO the hero was in this story. David wasn't big enough to defeat Goliath. He wasn't strong enough. God chooses the foolish things of the world to confound the wise. He uses a young boy to demonstrate how strong HE is, how powerful HE is, and how great HE is! The fact that we celebrate David so much for this victory only reveals how we have been telling the wrong story. Humans continue to miss the whole point of the story. Do you know what the people did after David killed Goliath? They wrote songs about how great David was! What the heck is wrong with us?!? 1 Samuel 18:6-7 says after the Israelite army had victory and was returning home after David killed Goliath, they began to celebrate and cheer for King Saul. They danced and sang "Saul has killed his thousands, and David his ten thousands!" Seriously. Dead serious. What the heck is wrong with us? How in the world could you watch this story unfold and end up dancing and singing about how amazing David is? Even David himself said in 1 Samuel 17:45-46 that he was coming in the name of the LORD and that today the LORD would conquer Goliath. Yet, when Goliath is actually defeated, we sing songs about David instead of the LORD? God help us!

And the funny part is, we are still doing this today. We have altered the narrative of our own stories in order to be the hero, so that people will sing and dance and tell of OUR goodness. You can witness this all over our culture. We are all familiar with the age of the "celebrity pastor." Do you think this is a coincidence? Do you think people accidentally start worshipping other humans? Nope. No accident. We allow it. We create it. We soak up their praises like a sponge. If people are saying how great YOU are rather than how great God is, you are telling the wrong story. You are not the hero. We have all been rescued on the cross. We are all, and have been enemies of God. He came to save the day, not you. When we project a shallow version of ourselves for the world to see, we censor our stories to preserve our image. We throw out the ugly parts and only show people what we want them to see. We hope they will love and admire the projection of ourselves they see. Some have even convinced others that they are the hero. I know I am guilty of this. They stand perched on the stages they have built for themselves. Physically elevated above the other common folk in the crowd. Many have bought into this bullshit. Buying into the false narrative that person is projecting to the world that they have it all together and their relationship with God is a perfectly straight upward trajectory to Jesus. The rest of us just have our crooked paths, but not them; their road is paved with gold. The thing is, just like David, when we begin to puff ourselves up and drink our own kool-aid, life has a way of bringing us back down to earth. The thorns in our flesh keep us from elevating ourselves so high that our heads are stuck in the clouds with no oxygen. This is exactly what happened to David.

AFTER David encountered God. AFTER he was anointed by God. AFTER he was already the leader of the entire nation of Israel. AFTER he asked Jesus in his heart. Not really, but you are tracking with me. This is AFTER David already had a long history and life with God. AFTER all of that, the Jerry Springer episodes began. Again, I think this really messes with our theology. So here David is. On top of the world. Unlimited wealth. Anything he wants at his fingertips, even someone else's wife. Every part of this story tells me just how messed up David was at this point in time. At the beginning of 2 Samuel 11:1-27, it says that during the time of year when Kings went off to war David stayed home. One late afternoon he woke up from a nap and noticed a beautiful naked woman taking a bath. Now, what healthy man in his 30's is staying home from his job napping during the middle of the day??? Sounds like a guy who lives in his parents' basement. David was lazy. He had become comfortable in his palace. I would venture to say David had lost his way at this point. His desperation and urgency for the LORD's presence is probably not his main focus lately. I'd venture to say it's not a great season of life for David. Perhaps he had lost his purpose and passion for life. I envision David struggling with depression, laying around in the palace, eating and drinking all day, sleeping at all hours of the day and night, unfulfilled, unsatisfied, and feeling distant from the God he had once been so close to. Unsettled. I too find myself in these places from time to time. I think we all do, whether we are willing to admit it or not.

In this condition, David wakes from his slumber and notices something from his balcony. Maybe that something will satisfy his aching soul. Settle the unrest he can't seem to shake. Well, that 'something' was actually a 'someone.' Someone he treats like an object that was meant for his pleasure. Talk about dehumanizing and objectifying women. Women should boycott the book of Psalms! You know you're powerful when you can simply "call" for another human being to be brought to you immediately to serve your every need or request. I can't even imagine. Totally nuts. Not too sure David was the King that God created him to be at this point. The story says that David noticed Bathsheba and sent someone to get the scoop on her. As it turns out, that girl is "Bathsheba, the daughter of Eliam and the wife of Uriah the Hittite." Bad news. David is confronted with the fact that this woman is married. More to the point, she is married to someone who happens to be in David's own army. An affair of this magnitude is no accident. Doesn't David know "bro code?" He can't have sex with the wife of one of his own army members! While these guys are off at war for HIM, he is lounging around in the palace being lazy and has the nerve to bang one of their wives? Honestly, what a dirtbag! What the hell bro! If you think that is screwed up, just wait, it gets better. Can you hear the chanting? "Jerry, Jerry, Jerry."

While David is told straight away Bathsheba is married to Uriah, it doesn't dissuade him one bit. David's immediate response is to "send for her." Which is fancy talk for summoning someone, whether they like it or not, because you are the king. One part of this story that doesn't get any air time is the real possibility all of this could have been against Bathsheba's will. She doesn't have a choice in this scenario. The entire scene could have been of rape. Nowhere in the story does it say Bathsheba sees David and wants him. The story says that David sees her, wants her, and sends for her like an object for his pleasure. As soon as he sent for her the decision had already been made. No objections from Bathsheba would have mattered at that point. She had no authority to refuse a king. What if she was happily married? What if she missed her husband Uriah deeply? And this perverted king sent for her like a piece of steak to satisfy his hunger? I don't know if you've thought about that, but I have. I think it is entirely possible. Could Bathsheba have been deeply distraught and scared when David summoned her? What if she didn't want to have sex with him? What if David is a rapist? Would that change how you read the Bible? Would that shatter your Sunday school image of David? Interestingly enough, later in the story one of David's daughters, Tamar, ends up being raped by her half brother Amnon. The Bible is full of some pretty jacked-up stuff, huh? Does that crush the action figure David we have created, who slayed Goliath in the name of the LORD? The hero that doesn't exist. David is not part of the Avengers. Even if Bathsheba was a willing participant, it gets better. When it comes to undealt with sin, we tend to up the ante. Evidenced by how David goes all in with his mistake. He shoves all his chips in the middle on this one. He can't take responsibility for his mistake at this point.

The Jerry Springer type episode is taken up another notch. Bathsheba discovers she is pregnant! Jerry, Jerry, Jerry. When she finds out, she sends a message to David. Again, I get the impression she doesn't love him and was possibly a victim. When she finds out she is pregnant she doesn't even want to talk to David. Instead she sends him the equivalent of a text message! She must not want to even see David. Doesn't want to look him in the face. Too much shame to bear. So she stays home, scared and alone, and shoots him a text. Once David learns about her pregnancy, he has a choice. Like all of us, not always willing to own our mistakes, he has to double down on his lie to cover it up. He comes up with a plan. Pretty smart plan if you think about it. David, in the back of his mind, thinks nothing could go wrong and he'll be able to wiggle his way out of this. Nobody will ever know! I can't count how many times I have found myself contemplating the coverup to my own questionable choices. We get swallowed up by the darkness of our own choices and believe concealing it is the only answer so that nobody will ever know. I've told myself that certain mistakes I have made are going with me to my grave. Yet, it's more like our secrets take us to the grave, rather than the other way around. We don't take our secrets to the grave, they take us to the grave. So, like me or anyone else, David begins an elaborate cover up.

David thinks if he can get Bathsheba's husband, Uriah, to come home and sleep with her then everyone will assume the baby is his, not David's. The perfect cover! Unfortunately, sin usually manages to find its way out. David sets his plan in motion, but it doesn't quite unfold the way he expected it to. Apparently, Uriah is some sort of saint. One variable David was not anticipating. David was banking on Uriah to give in to his natural human sexual desires and nothing else. Well, Uriah was a man of deep conviction to his brothers in arms. This makes it even worse that David screwed his wife. This guy is as noble as they come! Lets just say he is a much better man than me! So David sends Joab to bring Uriah home from war. David sets the table for Uriah and Bathsheba to get it on. He puts on the slow jams, lights the candles, puts them in the VIP suite of the castle, basically pulling out all the stops. Scripture says that David even sent Uriah a gift. No condoms though, David needed to seal the deal with this lie. No condoms in Israel. Unfortunately, Uriah doesn't take the bait. He doesn't fall for the slow jams and candles. It says Uriah refused to go home and slept outside the entrance of the palace. David wakes in the morning thinking, "I did it! I am free! I pulled it off! The perfect heist. I took someone's wife and I'm going to get away with it!"

To his surprise when David wakes up in the morning, he gets word that Uriah refused to go home. David responds by sending for Uriah and asks him, "What the heck is wrong with you?" Why wouldn't you go home and eat, drink, and sex up your wife after being at war for so long?!? Uriah, who must be a saint, basically states how all of his brothers are out at war sleeping in tents. How could he possibly go home to wine, dine, and sleep with his wife when his comrades are out there suffering? Good lord! Who is this guy? Is he even human? Wouldn't human nature lead all of us to go live it up for a night after being at war? I might have justified it a million ways and would likely have felt no shame or guilt over it. But not this guy. He takes the high road far less traveled. He pledges that surely he will "never be guilty of acting like that." David looks at this guy and says to himself "we'll see about that." If there is one thing no man can resist when it comes to having a good time, it's booze! David brings Uriah over and gets him drunk! Genius! Get this guy drunk and sit back and watch the magic happen! It's like fishing with dynamite, it's not even fair. David is convinced HE can figure this out. But David strikes out again. Uriah still would not go home and sleep with his wife. He slept at the palace entrance again. WTF? Maybe Uriah is a eunuch or something. He doesn't seem human! He's definitely not a man! We are much more stupid than this! Unfortunately, here's where the story takes a turn for the worse. A mistake that cannot be undone. David will soon take a human life. A husband. A son. One of God's children.

As mentioned earlier, when we try and cover up sin it has a way of becoming progressively more severe. This is a very sad turn of events. David does not cave in and own his mistake at this point. No personal responsibility. No confession. No remorse. He doesn't ask God to help him. He continues to take matters into his own hands. David's back is against a wall. Here he has a pregnant, married woman and no reasonable explanation as to how she became pregnant. His cover up failed, feeling helpless, he would rather harm another human than own his own choices. Pretty messed up, huh? His shame and guilt were so overwhelming that David would rather end a human life than face his own junk. If there is one thing I know about human nature, it is that we will go to great lengths in order to continue living in denial. You try and force us to look in a mirror and we will lose it! We lash out at anyone and everyone who tries to tear down our false realities because we can't bear to face the truth of our own choices. Well, at least that's true of me. So, back to David. He takes it to the next level. David does the only other thing he can think of to make this all go away. He must make Uriah go away. So, David sends another message to Joab, telling him to send Uriah to the front of a fierce battle and to pull back all the troops so Uriah would be killed. This was murder. No way around it. No sugar coating. No excusing it. This is cold-blooded murder. Murder to cover up sin.

In light of all of this, how in the world could God refer to David as "a man after his own heart?" Didn't David write the book of Psalms? Wait a minute. Are you telling me the man who wrote a portion of the Bible which we refer to as the perfect infallible Word of God, was a twisted, perverted, murderer? In short, yes. Don't we have thousands of worship songs that have been written based on the book of Psalms? Yes. How can this be? I can't accept this. I have difficulty reconciling the reality that somehow David wrote the infallible Word of God that would be read for thousands of years to come, and yet who is guilty of a crime today that would lock him up for life? One of the many problems with religion is that it is predicated on control. When something is predicated on control, it creates an "either/or" mentality. Black or white. It can't be both. We cannot embrace mystery because where mystery exists, we are no longer in control. The gospel is a paradox. The definition of a paradox is this: "A seemingly absurd or self-contradictory statement or proposition that when investigated or explained may prove to be well founded or true." The gospel is a paradox because it is not the black and white, "either/or" religion that you might think it to be. Most Biblical truth is a paradox. It is a "both and" reality. Is David a disgusting, perverted, lying, adulterous, murderer? Yes. Is he a man after God's own heart? Yes. But wait, those are seemingly absurd self-contradictory statements. Yes. Do you find the religious person inside of you getting frustrated? Losing control. Finding yourself in a bit of mystery? It's uncomfortable, isn't it? You aren't in control. You see, David is absolutely, unequivocally a man after God's own heart. God used David in very powerful ways. He did use David to write down part of the perfect Word of God. God does not need perfect people to do a perfect work in them. David's life is both scandalous and beautiful. Full of redemption and confession. Faith and doubt. Fear and courage. Love and lust. Sin and forgiveness. The truth is, David is not who makes his story beautiful. The story of David's life is so powerful and beautiful because of how great God was to David through it all. The story of David is not about how great David is. It is never about how great WE are. It is always about how Good He is! The headline of our stories is not that we avoided sin, failure, and doubt. The headline of my story is that in the midst of struggle, pain, sorrow, doubt, sin, and shame God is with me and He is GOOD! He has never abandoned me even when things got ugly. He was faithful when I had zero faith. He was strong when I was weak. He was merciful when I deserved death. This is a story about a perfect Father who has loved us every moment. The story of David is that even though he knocked up someone else's wife and had the husband murdered, he could not be separated from the Love of God. David encountered this love I am describing first hand. He described it in Psalm 139:7 when he said, "Where can I escape your spirit? Where could I flee your presence? When I go up to the heavens you are there, even when I make my bed in Hell YOU ARE THERE!" This is the story of the life of David! Even when he made his bed in Hell, God was with him. His whole life. Every moment. Not just David and Goliath. David and Uriah. David and Bathsheba. Every second of his life, the presence of God was with Him. Loving him. Forgiving him. Anointing him. Picking him up when he fell down. Encountering David when he was afraid. When he was hopeless. When he was on a hill alone tending sheep. Every. Single. Moment. David was a perverted murder who was deeply and unconditionally loved by the creator of the universe. I will end this chapter with the words of David in Psalm 139 because I believe that he describes his life better than I ever could. So I will let him have the last word over his life. Or should I say, here are the words of David that describe a God who has the final word over David's life.

Psalm 139

For the director of music. Of David. A psalm.

¹ You have searched me, Lord,

   and you know me.

² You know when I sit and when I rise;

   you perceive my thoughts from afar.

³ You discern my going out and my lying down;

   you are familiar with all my ways.

⁴ Before a word is on my tongue

   you, Lord, know it completely.

⁵ You hem me in behind and before,

   and you lay your hand upon me.

⁶ Such knowledge is too wonderful for me,

   too lofty for me to attain.

⁷ Where can I go from your Spirit?

   Where can I flee from your presence?

⁸ If I go up to the heavens, you are there;

   if I make my bed in the depths, you are there.

⁹ If I rise on the wings of the dawn,

   if I settle on the far side of the sea,

¹⁰ even there your hand will guide me,

   your right hand will hold me fast.

¹¹ If I say, "Surely the darkness will hide me

   and the light become night around me,"

¹² even the darkness will not be dark to you;

the night will shine like the day,

for darkness is as light to you.

13 For you created my inmost being;

you knit me together in my mother's womb.

14 I praise you because I am fearfully and wonderfully made;

your works are wonderful,

I know that full well.

15 My frame was not hidden from you

when I was made in the secret place,

when I was woven together in the depths of the earth.

16 Your eyes saw my unformed body;

all the days ordained for me were written in your book

before one of them came to be.

17 How precious to me are your thoughts,[a] God!

How vast is the sum of them!

18 Were I to count them,

they would outnumber the grains of sand—

when I awake, I am still with you.

19 If only you, God, would slay the wicked!

Away from me, you who are bloodthirsty!

20 They speak of you with evil intent;

your adversaries misuse your name.

21 Do I not hate those who hate you, Lord,

and abhor those who are in rebellion against you?

²² I have nothing but hatred for them;

  I count them my enemies.

²³ Search me, God, and know my heart;

  test me and know my anxious thoughts.

²⁴ See if there is any offensive way in me,

  and lead me in the way everlasting.

SCANDAL
OF
SAUL

Chapter 5

THE SCANDAL OF SAUL

On the other side of the world in Western Asia, in the country of Syria, is a young boy named Talut. He appears to be a normal boy being raised by a Muslim family, living a normal life in the Middle East. His parents are devout Muslims who have devoted their lives to following Islam. Not very shocking in this part of the world that is predominantly Muslim. Talut lived a pretty normal life, but that began to change dramatically in 2011. In 2011, a civil war broke out in the country of Syria that he called home. Syria's government, led by President Bashar al-Assad began to face unprecedented challenges to its authoritarian rule by protesters in favor of a democracy. These protestors demanded an end to these authoritarian practices put in place by Assad's father in 1971. The Syrian government began to use violence to suppress these demonstrations. What is the age old saying, "violence only begets more violence"? This response from the Syrian government only served to radicalize these protestors even more, which poured gasoline on an already hostile situation.

This rallied the opposition and they began to form militias, which led Syria into a full-fledged civil war.

By this time in 2012 Talut had grown into a young teenage boy about the age of 16 years old. Talut and his family were terrified. This was home. They felt trapped. Violence and death swirled all around them. They couldn't go to the grocery store without seeing death. They began to fear for their own lives. They did not take any side in this war; they simply wanted their country to be unified, and bring an end to the pain and suffering all around them. They longed for democracy and freedom, but knew this was not the way to see change. Murdering their fellow Syrian brothers and sisters was not the solution. Meanwhile, all across the globe it seemed like business as usual. It felt as if Syria was this bubble of pain and suffering and the whole world had turned a blind eye. Nobody wanted to face what was happening in Syria. They couldn't let the suffering of another human being disrupt their comfortable lives. The suffering went on for years. And when I say years, I mean YEARS! The suffering continued. Violence and death had become the norm. Talut had moved through the stages of processing trauma. Shock and night terrors were all he knew as a young boy. Waking up in a cold sweat, in the middle of the night, to the sound of gunshots. Explosions would rock the foundation of the home his family was living in. In California, we deal with the occasional earthquake caused by Mother Earth. For Talut, it was earthquakes manufactured by men. Earth-shaking explosions day and night. Most of the time, when these explosions came, he would crawl under his bed and cover his head with his hands. Once the deadly commotion ceased, he would crawl out from under his bed and poke his head out the front door to see if one of the blasts claimed the lives of his family or friends. Never knowing if the next explosion would claim his life or the life of his family. Talut moved beyond shock. He began to repress his fear and shove it way down deep. This is human nature. This was his survival mechanism. Talut had to grow up way too fast, robbed of any normal childhood. Unable to go out and play in the streets with his friends for fear of being struck by a stray bullet.

Fear. Anxiety. Terror. Death. Violence. Rage. Hatred. Hunger. These became Talut's reality. About 4-5 years had gone by, and his parents began to lose any hope of this civil war ever coming to an end. And if it did, they began to fear their family might not be alive to see it. Explosions too close to home. Too many stray bullets. Too many close calls. Many of their community members began to feel the same way. They had two options. Stay or flee. Stay and play Russian Roulette with the life of your family, or pack up everything you have ever known and flee the country. Where? Anywhere. Anywhere but here. Desperation. They had very little money or resources. They only had enough money to be on the run for a couple weeks. They would need to find refuge. At this point, 6-7 years after the civil war began, other parts of the world could no longer ignore what was happening. Reporters and TV cameras began to capture the horror of what was happening in Syria. I guess half a million people need to die before the world takes notice. Children. Mothers. Fathers. Meanwhile, it was business as usual in the U.S. Head down, chasing after that American Dream. News outlets all over the world began to cover this story. Just like Talut's family, Syrians all over the country began to pack up and flee the country. The world began to notice a Syrian Refugee crisis. These events sparked heated debates all over the world. Particularly in the United States. If there is one thing American's don't like, it's when something or someone comes along to disrupt the comfortable, little kingdoms we have created for ourselves. The global conversations about how to handle this refugee crisis began. It's not as simple as millions of people relocating to another geographic location. There are practical challenges to this. Where would these people find food and shelter? And more importantly, who was going to pay for that? So we watched as a huge game of hot potato ensued around the globe. The refugees being the hot potato. One nation passes the hot potato to the next, and that nation passes it to the next, and on and on. "I don't want to deal with it, you deal with it. I care, but it's not my problem. We have our own problems. We can't afford to deal with that." The hot potato got passed to the United States because we are one of the wealthiest nations in the history of the universe. And the debate began. Once the hot potato was in our lap, you saw a variety of different responses. "We can't afford to deal with those people. We have our own people to take care of. America first. How do we know we can trust those people? Most of them are Muslim, if we let them in our country who is to say that one of them isn't a terrorist. We have our own problems." The responses were all over the spectrum, from "let them in with no questions asked" to "don't let those animals in our country." The conversations were seen and heard on news programs for the world to see. A war of words broke out on social media as well. From compassion, to venom, to hatred. We saw it all. Threaten someone's comfortable bubble and you will see what is really inside.

Meanwhile in Syria, Talut was about 20 years old at this point. Thanks to the internet, Talut has access to watch and listen to this global conversation. Essentially, he is the "hot potato" that nobody cares about or wants to deal with. For Talut, this isn't a debate about refugee political policy. This is life and death. This is his family. These are his friends. The ones he grew up and went to school with. Many of whom he had watched die up until this point. Talut would jump onto chat rooms late at night and soak up the conversation. He would watch the debates on CNN and Facebook. He would hear Americans referring to his Syrian family as "dogs" and "terrorists". Something happened to him during this time. He knew he shouldn't keep watching and listening, feeling the anger and rage boiling deep within him, yet he couldn't seem to look away. Talut became obsessed with listening to the debate over the Syrian Refugee crisis. He'd tuck away each comment of hatred and venom spewed online, saving it as if keeping score. Each dehumanizing comment became a seed of bitterness and resentment in his heart. His heart began the slow process of turning to stone. He became so accustomed to pain that he no longer felt pain. Rage had hardened his heart.

As rage began defining Talut's life, he started to form friendships with others who were drunk with rage. Bonded by the same hatred for the western world sitting in their comfortable living rooms, referring to them as "dogs." Making their family and friends seem like a cancer that would infect their perfect culture if allowed inside their borders. They had enough. They created a formal gathering of extremists that were fed up. Rallied around the common denominator of hate. The hatred for western civilization. Hatred begets hatred and violence begets violence. Hence, we go round and round in a cycle of hatred and violence. Taking for granted all that they had. Americans appeared to care for nothing but themselves. Under a banner of Islam, they quickly progressed to an entire network of radical Islamic terrorists. Blinded by their shared hatred, they came to believe that this is what Allah wanted them to do. Believing so deeply that western civilization was evil, they felt compelled by their god to do something about it. This is what religion does. Black and white. Right or wrong. Us against them. Our team is right, and they are wrong. We cannot co-exist. If what western Christians believed was true, then it discredited everything they had ever known so they must eradicate it from the earth. One day Talut would cross a line from which he could never return.

Talut had crossed over into Turkey at this point. Now in his early 20's, radicalized, drunk with anger and rage, found himself as a leader in a radical Islamic terrorist group. His group abducted a young Christian family that had been trying to spread the gospel in Turkey. They could not accept this. They believed these missionaries were trying to poison the minds of their Muslim community with the lies of western Christianity. They could not be tolerated. They decided to send a message. Talut ordered the execution of this family. He did not pull the trigger, but he gave the order to pull the trigger. To make matters worse, they saw to it that the execution was filmed and posted on YouTube. The video went viral and the entire world knew who Talut was now. Now he was drunk with power and rage, a lethal combination. All the while, completely convinced that he was doing the work of Allah. All of Heaven mourning the loss of this family. Mourning a son who was so lost that he had given in to his rage. Talut allowed seeds of bitterness and anger to grow for years. Watered over and over again, the seeds reached full maturity in the form of murder. The seeds we plant today become the crops we eat for tomorrow.

Over the course of the next year or so, Talut would order the kidnapping and execution of about 30 Christians from the United States. Famous among radicals, his name was known around the world. Feared among those living in the suburbs in the United States. Everyone knew his name. These murders were not enough to quench Talut's thirst for revenge. Allah wanted justice. At least, that's what he believed. They conspired a plan to take this mission to the next level. Talut would sneak into the United States disguised as a Syrian refugee seeking asylum. Once safely inside the U.S. borders, he would plot a terrorist attack against one of the largest churches in the country. This was his plan, and he was actually blind enough to think this was god's plan for his life.

Under an alias name, he made it safely to the United States disguised as a Syrian refugee seeking asylum. It actually worked. His entire attack planned out. This was the end of the road for Talut. One last act of violence to satisfy this bloodthirsty god he came to believe in. A god that coerced obedience through fear and violence. Talut was drunk with his religion, not seeing clearly. His plan was to strap explosives to himself and fill his vehicle with enough explosives to level an entire block. He would wait for a Sunday morning to create as much devastation as possible. Talut didn't really want to live any longer at this point. He had nothing left to live for. His hatred was never satisfied no matter how many people he watched die. It just fed his appetite for more violence, more rage, more anger, and more revenge.

That dark day had finally arrived: the day he planned to take the life of thousands of innocent people. He went about his morning routine, getting dressed, putting on his vest of explosives, and loading his car. His heart raced. Fear and anxiety were sinking in. Was he really going to do this? Yes. He was resolute. His fate was already determined. Heaven had another plan. While Talut had his plans, so did Jesus. While Talut was drunk with rage, Jesus was mad with passion for him. He had seen every tear Talut cried. Every moment of terror he experienced as a boy that led him to this point. Jesus had not given up on Talut, and this would not be the final word over Talut's life. Jesus had another plan. Where Talut had a plan of hatred and murder, Jesus had a plan for redemption and mercy. The devil had a plan to steal, kill, and destroy. The Father had a plan to forgive, to love, and to redeem.

Talut jumped in his car around 9:30 a.m. to make it on time for the church service that was beginning at 10:00 a.m. He loaded up, and headed down that dark road of revenge having no idea what was about to happen to him. Not knowing that Jesus went before him, Talut headed down a major freeway, eager to destroy the Lord's followers. He was completely lost. As he was on his way to murder thousands of Christians, a brilliant light from Heaven suddenly beamed down and blinded him; he lost control of his vehicle, and his car flipped over and rolled a handful of times in the middle of the freeway. There were no other cars in sight. In the middle of that freeway, outside of the wreckage of Talut's car, stood the resurrected Jesus. He stood unshaken by the accident and what had just happened. He was resolute.

Talut's car rolled during the accident and he was trapped upside down at this point. Talut could be heard wincing in pain from outside the vehicle. Jesus slowly walked straight towards the vehicle. As Talut regained consciousness, he began to cry out for help. Scared and in pain, fearful the accident could trigger any one of the explosives, he began to cry out in desperation. Right then, a hand reached inside the vehicle to pull him out. As Talut reached out to grab it, he immediately noticed large circular scars on the wrist, almost as if something had pierced the area in the wrist. He was too desperate to care at this point. The hand reached out and grabbed him. He immediately noticed something different as he touched This hand. Talut felt peace. He felt a calming sensation wash over him, almost like the feeling a baby gets wrapped in the arms of their Father. Fear exited his body quicker than it came. The hand was strong and reassuring. Jesus pulled him out of the wreckage as if he were weightless.

Talut was bloody and bruised. He stood before the risen Christ, alone. There was not a soul in sight. He felt exposed. Naked. He felt seen. Almost as if this man could see right through him. Jesus said, "Why are you persecuting me?" Talut did not know what to say. In that moment one thing became clear. He was face to face with his Maker. One would assume that at this point he would fall on his face, singing "Holy, Holy, Holy." But that is not how the story goes. Talut began to feel a lifetime of bitterness, resentment, and rage boil to the surface as if it were about to explode, kind of like what happens if you drop an Alka-Seltzer in a two-liter bottle of soda. Explosive. He couldn't contain what was boiling over inside of him, and he erupted with a lifetime of anger all at once. Talut began to scream and curse at Jesus, physically assaulting him in a fit of anger. Drunk with rage again. Taking it all in, Jesus remained calm and wrapped his arms around Talut, embracing him with the strength that holds the world in his hands. Like a Father physically restraining a toddler having a temper tantrum, Talut could no longer move.

Talut kept fighting, sobbing, and screaming at this point. He screamed his resentment in a fit of desperation. "Where were you when I was 7 and I had to watch my best friend die in front of my eyes? Where were you when I was crawling under my bed in the fetal position desperately trying to avoid stray bullets? Where were you when night terrors and explosions went off in the middle of the night kept me from sleeping for years? I hate you! I hate you! Curse you!"

Jesus has the strength of a thousand armies wrapped around him. Holding him close. Jesus begins to repeat over and over again, "I was there the whole time." Jesus repeats this over and over like a mantra. Talut slowly stops fighting and his body calms down. No longer screaming, he continues to weep. He melts in the arms of Jesus. Jesus keeps repeating, "I was there the whole time." It is as if these words begin to melt the hard exterior that Talut has built up over the years. These words break him down. Jesus begins to explain, "I saw every tear. Every moment you were afraid, I was right next to you, holding you. When you felt alone, I was weeping over you. I sent an army of angels to protect you. I never left you. Not even for a moment. I am well acquainted with suffering. I know more than you could ever imagine. I am with you. I have always been with you. I am with you now. And I will always be with you. No matter how far you run, my presence will run further. No matter how fast you run, my grace can run faster. I would chase you to the ends of the earth. Even when you hate me, I love you. There is nothing you could ever do to make me love you less."

The unconditional love of Jesus has absolutely wrecked this man. Talut was undone. This man who was literally on his way to murder thousands of Christians in the name of his god just had a radical encounter with Jesus of Nazareth. The creator of the heavens and the earth has sought out this man, terrorist and all. Never abandoned. The Father's love never quit. Never gave up on him. There is no place he went, nor anything he did that disqualified him from the Kingdom of God. Our kingdoms, sure. But, to hell with our kingdoms. In that moment, Talut had an encounter with Unconditional Love, and he would never be the same. Before Jesus left, his final words to Talut were this: "With every breath you have left in your lungs, I want you to tell the world of my goodness. I am giving you a new name. You will no longer be called Talut. Your new name is Paul."

And just like that, Talut is forgiven, given a new name, and commissioned by God to be a voice for Him. Paul is a new man. Forgiven. Free. New heart. New mind. God removed his heart of stone and gave him a heart of flesh. He replaced the hate with love. Traded the rage for redemption. Resentment for mercy. He is full of the Holy Spirit and called by God to preach the Good News in the United States. Sent to preach the Gospel to the very people he intended to kill. Talk about irony. Jesus is pretty freaking scandalous! Paul is captivated by this risen Christ. So much so that he doesn't question the scandalous nature of this calling, he just responds because he was lost and now he is found. He was blind but now he sees! He doesn't think about how people are going to receive him.

Paul dusted himself off and headed to the same sanctuary where he was going before his encounter with Jesus, but this time for a much different reason. As I mentioned earlier, Talut was infamous across the entire globe. There were YouTube videos of him executing Christians that had gone viral on the internet. His face had been all over ABC, CNN, Fox, etc. He was America's most wanted. He had a reputation as large as Osama Bin Laden. He removed any disguise he had on and headed to church to tell the world the Good News that Jesus is much better than we think. The Good News is actually much "Good-er" than we think! He wanted to tell the world about this Jesus who could forgive any sin, no matter how big or small. God didn't just love good boys and girls. He doesn't just love us when we deserve it. He doesn't just love us when we love Him. He loves us when we hate Him. He loves us no matter what we have done, no matter how far we go. There is nothing we could ever do to make Him love us MORE or LESS. There is nothing in all of heaven or earth that can separate us from the Love of God in Jesus. No angels, nor demons, nor the power of hell itself could ever separate us from the Love of God. No matter how far we run, His love runs deeper.

Paul walked into the sanctuary of the church he sought to destroy and he stuck out like a sore thumb. Here is this Middle Eastern man who fits the profile of the most notorious terrorist on the planet. The moment he walks in the building, you could hear the audible gasps across the building. People started whispering, "Is that who I think it is?" Whispers turned into voices beginning to express fear. Once it was obvious who this man was, terror spread through the room like a hurricane. People jumped out of their seats and ran for their lives. Those who were frozen with fear began to murmur, "Is this some sort of a trick? He's going to try and kill us all." Paul tried to reassure those running for their lives that he came in peace and meant no harm. Nobody believed him. The guy who made it his life's work to murder Christians was standing before them. What the heck were they supposed to think? I don't blame them for being terrified. Paul began to preach and tell of his encounter with Jesus for all to hear. He shared with them how he had been on his way to destroy the very church building they were all standing in, but miraculously met Jesus of Nazareth on his way. A flash of light blinded him and stopped his car in its tracks. Jesus had rescued him. Jesus had forgiven him! Jesus opened his eyes! He was blinded by hate, but the unconditional love of God had opened his eyes and sent him to be a witness to western Christianity. He was sent to preach the Gospel. To tell of His great love! To open the floodgates of Heaven for ALL to enter in! Not just a select few. Not just the dignified. Not just the ones we are comfortable with. Swing wide the gates to the Kingdom of Heaven and welcome in the murderers, the drunks, the gays, the burnt out, the addicted, the afflicted, the perverts, the whores, the prideful, the greedy, the poor, the uneducated, the unwanted, the unlovable, the adulterers, the scholars and the skanks, and yes, even the religious self-righteous narcissists. Stop creating conditions to the love of God that He himself has not created. Just because you have limits to YOUR mercy doesn't mean HE has limits to His mercy. This is the Good News! The unconditional love of God is not an excuse to keep on sinning; it is the very reason for obedience. We are fueled and motivated by the Love of God that surpasses all human understanding. I am compelled by God to offer my life up for the one who gave it all for me. This is not only a love worth dying for, it is a love worth living for.

You can only imagine the intensity of this moment: a world-renowned terrorist preaching a Sunday sermon in the very place he set out to destroy. Needless to say, the audience wasn't very receptive. This was simply too scandalous for us to accept. No altar call today. Once the congregation realized that Paul was not armed with any weapons, fear turned to hostility. The crowd quickly turned into a mob. They rushed Paul and took him to the ground. They dragged him out of the building and decided to take matters into their own hands. When you are in any of the Southern states, there is a pretty good chance that a handful of people, if not ¾ people in the audience, carry a concealed weapon. Unfortunately for Paul, that was the case this Sunday morning. The angry mob dragged him out in the streets, having formulated their own execution scene. Hundreds of cell phones were out filming the entire thing. In a matter of minutes, Paul was executed, on camera, in the same fashion he was once guilty of. An angry mob, well over 1,000 people, were all cheering on the execution. Paul was executed that morning while the mob chanted, "God wills it!" Heaven mourned the loss of a Saint that morning. History has a way of repeating itself.

This is the life of Paul. Or should I say Saul. Does this make you feel uncomfortable? It should. It was not meant to appease your sensibilities. It makes me uncomfortable and I'm the one writing it! Are we all comfortable with the fact that one of the fathers of our faith was a serial killer? I don't know about you, but this story hasn't received many headlines in the history of Christianity. Gee, I wonder why? In order to preserve the face of a religion, we have lost our true identity. In fact, Saul (Paul) was the only one who wasn't covering up the scandal of his life. Paul would be the first one to rejoice in his identity as a scandalous sinner covered by the blood of Jesus. "Oh what a wretched man I am!" Hmmm… "I am the chief of all sinners."

Saul is leading the charge in the murder of many Christians. Saul might not always be the person physically killing the Christians with his bare hands, but Saul is the guy giving the orders to pull the trigger. Try really hard to imagine this scenario playing out today. Saul is well known all over the world as the "guy who kills Christians." Imagine your perspective of Saul through the eyes of a Christian.

Saul is out to kill you. His particular religious beliefs have led him to believe very strongly (strongly enough to kill people for it) that you are a threat to everything he has stood for and believed in. The things that you are preaching are compromising everything he has ever known to be true. He simply cannot tolerate this any longer. So he and his religious extremist buddies have decided the way to handle this little discrepancy is to kill those who are preaching the gospel of Jesus. In Acts 9:1 before Saul was converted, it says Saul was "eager to destroy the Lord's followers."

Saul is so infamous for his acts of terrorism that every Christian knows his name. They fear him. When Paul began to preach the Gospel, the whole town responded in Acts 9:21, "Isn't this the same man who persecuted Jesus' followers with such devastation in Jerusalem." The language here is so intentional. Not only was he "persecuting" followers of Jesus, but with such great "devastation." Sounds pretty severe. Christians around the region were terrified of Paul. In Acts 9:26, Paul tried to join the Christians in Jerusalem and scripture tells us they were all afraid of him. They were terrified at the sound of his name. He was notorious for his actions of violence against followers of Jesus. So much so, that when he began his ministry some of the believers thought he was pretending to be a follower of Jesus just so he could infiltrate their community and kill them. Crazy!

Jesus proceeded to press Saul as to why he was persecuting Him and told him he was going to be used to deliver a special message to Christians all over the world. Yes, you read correctly; God is going to use Saul to bring a special message to the very people he was murdering. Not only that, but God would use Paul to write down almost half of the New Testament, which would be read for thousands of years to come. That's right. The Perfect Word of God written by a religious extremist who actually took delight and was eager to murder followers of Jesus. What in the world is wrong with this guy named Jesus? Does he not understand the situation here? Of all people for God to choose for this task, He chooses the very person that is feared among Christians more than anyone. Wow! If you don't think that this is a scandalous situation here, I don't know what is!

I shared this story of Saul murdering Christians with a very well educated Christian and his response was: "Was it murder or legally sanctioned killing?" What?!? I almost passed out when he said this! Are you kidding me? So Hitler didn't murder anyone either?!? He just legally sanctioned the death of millions of people--totally different! World leaders throughout history have killed innocent people hidden behind corrupt laws of man. Does this excuse blatant evil because we created an evil system that allows heinous acts against humanity? Were the crusades of the early church against the Muslims justified? Do the laws and systems WE created reflect the laws given to us by God himself in Jesus that said to love our enemies? To turn the other cheek, to bless those who curse you, and pray for those who persecute you? Just because we create our own laws and our own kingdoms that look nothing like the Kingdom of God does not mean we are free to do as we please and hide behind the laws of a corrupt society. It is mind-boggling to me the lengths we will go to, and the logic we will throw out the window in an effort to protect what we think is the "holiness" of the Bible. I have news for you; the Holiness of Scripture does not lie in the perfection of the biblical characters. The Holiness of Scripture lies deep within the brokenness of humanity where you will find a Perfect, Holy, and unconditionally loving God. This is the Good News. This is Jesus coming to a broken world and submitting himself to death at the hands of those He loves in order to bring redemption and resurrection. This is the heartbeat of the Bible from Genesis to Revelation.

If you cannot accept the reality that God redeems religious terrorists, then I invite you to take your Holy Bible and rip out about half of the New Testament. We cannot in the same breath say that we believe in the Bible, yet if biblical events were to unfold today right in front of our face we would reject it wholeheartedly. Can't you see the obvious contradiction? God has not changed.

The Gospel has not changed. I believe with all of my heart He is still calling the broken, the drunks, the addicted, the murderers, the liars, the greedy, and even the self-righteous. God's Word is not finished. His Word is past, present, and future. His Story is still unfolding today. Right now. He is redeeming the broken. He is pursuing the hopeless. He is performing scandalous acts of Mercy. Can you handle that? Or does that offend your sensibilities a bit too much? Maybe you don't like Jesus very much after all. You do realize we murdered Jesus because he didn't always say and do things that made us feel good, right? God chose Paul as a vessel to deliver the Good News of God's great love for us. He used Paul's life to demonstrate the reality of the Gospel, to show there is nothing we could ever do that could separate us from the Love of God in Jesus. The only question is whether or not we actually believe that. I will end this chapter with a word from Paul and what he has to say about the love of God:

31 What, then, shall we say in response to these things? If God is for us, who can be against us? 32 He who did not spare his own Son, but gave him up for us all—how will he not also, along with him, graciously give us all things? 33 Who will bring any charge against those whom God has chosen? It is God who justifies. 34 Who, then, is the one who condemns? No one. Christ Jesus who died—more than that, who was raised to life—is at the

right hand of God and is also interceding for us.[35] Who shall
separate us from the love of Christ? Shall trouble or hardship or
persecution or famine or nakedness or danger or sword? [36] As it is
written:

"For your sake we face death all day long;

  we are considered as sheep to be slaughtered."

[37] No, in all these things we are more than conquerors through him
who loved us.[38] For I am convinced that neither death nor life,
neither angels nor demons, neither the present nor the future, nor
any powers, [39] neither height nor depth, nor anything else in all
creation, will be able to separate us from the love of God that is in
Christ Jesus our Lord.

Romans 8:31-39

SCANDAL OF ABRAHAM

Chapter 6

THE SCANDAL OF ABRAHAM

Let's take a look at the story of Abraham. What does the regular "church going" individual know about this story? I remember singing songs in Sunday school as a child that went like this: "Father Abraham had many sons, had many sons had father Abraham, I am one of them and so are you, so let's just praise the Lord!" In my experience, the two notable events in the life of Abraham that people are most aware of are the promise/covenant God made with Abraham to make his descendants number more than the stars in the sky (i.e., be the father of generations and nations to come). The second, more publicized event is the epic story where Abraham has SO much faith in God that he offers up his son Isaac to be sacrificed because of his unwavering faith in God. In fact, Abraham made the "hall of fame for faith" in the book of Hebrews. In Hebrews 11:17, Abraham is praised for his faith to offer up his only son Isaac as a sacrifice when God was testing him. He had faith that "even if Isaac died, God was able to bring him back to life again." Don't get me wrong, that is some legit, hardcore faith. Abraham should get some credit for this ruthless act of trust. But, just like all of the other biblical characters that we are taking a look at, these brief moments in their life do not tell the whole story. Just like we can't pull one bad moment out of someone's life to completely define who they are as a person. In the same way, we cannot pull out one moment of victory in a story to get the full picture of that individual's life. You need to look at the entirety of a story to see the whole picture. Otherwise, it's like standing 1 millimeter away from a 10-foot wide masterpiece and dissecting one speck of paint on the canvas. Sometimes you have to take a step back to see the entire landscape of a masterpiece. We need to do that with the Bible. Instead, we stick our face to a page and fixate on one moment or one sentence in the tapestry of Scripture only to end up confused and missing the larger, much more beautiful picture we see all throughout Scripture. If only we would step back and take it ALL in. So let's take an honest look at the full landscape of the life of Abraham, shall we?

Abraham's actual name, given at birth, was Abram. From the very beginning, we see a common thread throughout scripture. Abram married Sarai, and Sarai was not able to have children. Time and time again we see God intentionally choosing barren wombs to birth the Kingdom of God. Does this appear to be a giant coincidence, or do you see something we should be paying attention to here? God is calling the barren ones to birth His

Kingdom so that no one can boast. God routinely calls the foolish things of this world to do his most miraculous work so that no one can take credit for what He is about to do. When barren women have children, people stop to take notice. Here we are at the very beginning of Abram's story and God is already painting a prophetic picture of what He is about to do. In spite of our barrenness, He is going to birth nations. When God shows up in spite of our barrenness, all we can do is stand in awe of the goodness of God.

In Genesis 12:1, God instructs Abram to leave his country, his relatives, and his father's house, and go to the land that God will show him. That sounds pretty vague, which would make it very difficult to follow. Leave everything you know and I will show you where to go, but I won't tell you the exact destination yet. Complete faith. For the first time we see God give Abram a promise. In Genesis 12:2-3, God says to Abram, "I will cause you to become the father of a great nation. I will bless you and make you famous, and I will make you a blessing to others. I will bless those who bless you and curse those who curse you. All the families of the earth will be blessed through you." Dang, that is quite the promise! Again, Abram's wife Sarai was unable to have children, so you could imagine this promise might have been a little difficult for him and Sarai to believe at this particular moment in time. Especially since Abram was already 75 years old at this point in the story.

Here is our first glimpse into the cracks in Abram's armor. This mighty man of unshakeable faith tucked his tail between his legs and cowered in the moment. They found themselves retreating to Egypt to escape a famine across the land. Abram became scared that when the Egyptians saw his wife, they would kill him and try to take her for themselves. Sarai must have been pretty dang "hot.". If she was so good-looking that he was scared to take her out in public for fear of his own life, that tells you all you need to know. Abram was so terrified if they found out that Sarai was his wife that they would kill him, so he came up with a genius, cowardly idea. Why not pretend Sarai was his sister, so that way when other men approached his wife they wouldn't kill him? Wow, Abram, way to man up and throw your wife to the wolves! Save yourself, but who cares about your wife? Abram thought to himself: "They will treat me well if they think you are my sister because of their interest in you."

Sure enough, when they arrived in Egypt, everyone spoke of Sarai's beauty. When they saw her, palace officials sang her praises to Pharaoh. It didn't take long for Pharaoh to send for Sarai and bring her to his palace and take her as his wife. Pharaoh gave Abram many gifts because of Sarai. Sheep, cattle, donkeys, male and female servants, and camels. Abram's pathetic plan worked. They treated him great and took his wife. This was working out exactly as he planned. Fear had gripped Abram. I am sure that none of us have ever experienced fear that had a grip on us, causing us to do stupid things. On second thought, I think we can all relate to this.

Because Pharaoh took Sarai to be his wife and she was already married to Abram, God infected Pharaoh and his family with a disease. Pharaoh sent for Abram, and even he was shocked at the stupidity of Abram. He essentially told him, "What the hell, bro? Why would you tell me Sarai is your sister if she is your wife? What the heck is wrong with you?" He sends for Sarai, and tells Abram "take her and get out of here!" I guess even pagans marvel at the stupidity of these rag-tag followers of Jesus sometimes.

Abram, Sarai, and Lot headed out from Egypt because they were obviously not welcome there anymore. Lot was Abram's nephew. Abram and Lot had become very wealthy and were rich in livestock, silver, and gold. Abram was "ballin." They were so rich that when they came to a place to settle, there was not enough land to support both of them, so they decided to part ways to prevent any quarreling. After Lot and Abram went their separate ways, Abram settled in the land of Canaan. The Lord said to Abram, "Look as far as you can see in every direction. I am going to give all this land to you and your offspring as a permanent possession. And I am going to give you so many descendants that, like dust, they cannot be counted!" Dang. Again we have God promising the world to Abram. He promises to give Abram so many descendants they cannot be counted! That is quite the promise.

Later on we begin to see Abram become discouraged, doubting what God had promised. Isn't it comforting to know that even the hero's of our faith experienced discouragement and doubted God? It is medicine for my soul to know that doubt is a normal thing, even for those who do great things for God. In Genesis 15:2, Abram says to God: "what good are all of your blessings when I don't even have a son?" Abram is questioning God. This does not make God mad. He is not intimidated by our doubts or our questions, in fact, He welcomes them. Religion hates this reality. Abram continues, "Since I do not have a son, a servant in my household will inherit all my wealth. You have given me no children, so one of my servants will have to be my heir." He is calling out God. He is calling out the almighty, all-powerful, creator of the heavens and the earth. He is calling God out on the promises he made to Abram and his wife Sarai. Again, this does not make God angry. Abram specifically tells God, "YOU have given me NO children." Wow. That is real talk right there. Getting real with God. God loves when we strip the facades and come to Him as we are. Even when we are angry and frustrated. He knows our hearts, so what good does it do to try and pretend with a God who knows every thought, every word we speak before it's on our tongue? God's response is strong and steady. He does not rebuke

Abram for questioning Him. He reminds Abram of what he promised. He reassures Abram and says: "No, your servant will not be your heir, for you will have a son of your own to inherit everything I am giving you" (Gen. 15:4). Then God doubles down on His promise. He brings Abram outside beneath the night sky. In vs. 5 He tells Abram, "Look up into the heavens and count the stars if you can. Your descendants will be like that--too many to count." It says that Abram believed the Lord and the Lord declared him righteous because of his faith.

Genesis 16 is where we really begin to see things going "off the rails." Here we go again! Let the reality TV show begin! Jerry, Jerry, Jerry! At this point, Abram was about 86 years old. Can't really blame Abram for being a little skeptical about this whole "father of many generations" thing. I will avoid my urge to insert a Viagra joke at this point. You're welcome. Believe it or not, I did censor this book. It could have been much worse. My unfiltered thoughts are a scary place! He was an old man at this point and had ZERO children. How in the world is he supposed to have as many descendants as there are stars in the sky if he doesn't even have one descendant? In Genesis 16:1, we are reminded that Abram's wife Sarai still has no children. Ouch. I can imagine how awful she must feel. The weight of the world on her shoulders. Knowing the promises God had been filling her husband's head with. He was going to be the father of many nations, blah blah

blah. More kids than there are stars in the sky or like the dust that cannot be counted?!? And here she is, with no children. She must have felt so ashamed. In Biblical times, the self-worth and value of a woman was intimately connected to their ability to bear children. The pressure is still evident in our culture today, although nothing like it was in those days. If you couldn't bear children you would be viewed as useless. And here Sarai was, married to this man who God said would be the father of many generations, and yet she couldn't give him a child. She was crushed. Frustrated. Discouraged. Angry. Depressed. Hopeless. She became desperate.

She became so hopeless that God may never be able to deliver on his promise for her to have children that she contrived her own plan. Our plans are never as good as God's plans. She took her servant Hagar and gave her to Abram so she could bear his children. Sarai told Abram "The LORD has kept me from having children." This provides a lot of insight as to where Sarai is at emotionally. She is angry and blaming God. It's not that she is just unable to have children, but she is specifically blaming God for keeping her from having children. She is naming God as the source of her pain and suffering. HE has been the one that has kept her from having children. Pain and suffering have a way of clouding our judgment. They distort reality. They become a lens through which we see the world around us. We begin to shape and mold the character of God around our experiences. God easily becomes mean and evil in our mind. He is the source of my suffering and clearly he is not "good," otherwise I would not be enduring these trials. You can sense the bitterness and resentment that has been welling up inside of her, as it begins to spill over in her words and accusations towards God. She continues to tell Abram "Go and sleep with her, perhaps I can have children through her." Sarcasm and resentment in her voice. So Abram, being the brilliant man that he was, agreed. We men are not always the sharpest tools in the shed. Every man who has been married for an extended period of time can tell you with confidence that you cannot always listen to what your wife is saying and take it at face value. Sometimes women will give us non-verbal cues that we need to pay attention to. This was an obvious set-up. Don't take the bait, dummy. Sarai was wrong for proposing this idea. She was in a bad place and acting out of bitterness and resentment. But make no mistake; Abram should not have been dumb enough to agree. Sarai needed a man who was strong in this moment to object to her moment of vulnerability. She needed a husband to reassure her that God would fulfill his promise. She needed Abram to step up, and affirm her and remind her that she was loved and cared for. Unfortunately, Abram, like most men, responded instinctively with the wrong head. He quickly agreed. Insert "slapping head emoji." Idiot. He walked right into this trap! She didn't really want him to go along with this stupid plan! She wanted him to man up! Instead,

Abram agrees to sleep with another woman with his wife's blessing. Go figure. He took the hall pass. Big mistake. Is there any doubt this would blow up in everyone's face? I'm no rocket scientist and I don't have a PhD in human psychology, but I could see this coming a mile away. This is X-rated material we would never allow our children to watch if it were a movie! Yet, this is the Divine, Inspired, Word of God, right?!?

So, Abram quickly agrees. He sleeps with Hagar and she becomes pregnant. Unfortunately, it doesn't work out so well for Abram. As it turns out, bringing another woman into a struggling marriage, and a baby from another woman, created a bit of drama. Now we have a full blown biblical "cat fight." Hagar becomes pregnant and is probably scared, uncomfortable, emotional, hormonal, etc, so she begins to treat Sarai with "contempt." No way! You're kidding me! I thought they would all live under the same roof and be one big happy family! Nope. That's not what happened. Hagar starts being rude to Sarai. I'm sure there was a snide remark here and there. Guess what Sarai does? She goes to Abram to chew his head off. This helps me feel normal about my marriage. A legitimate knock-down, drag-out fight. Blaming, yelling, accusing. The foundation of any healthy marriage. If you haven't fought like this, you probably don't have a real relationship that has moved beyond the surface. Sarai went full "biblical" on Abram, and yelled at him, "This is all your fault! Now this servant of mine is pregnant, and she despises me, though I myself gave her the privilege of sleeping with you. The LORD will make you pay for doing this to me!" Daaaannnng, Gina! I fear the day my wife threatens me with "The Lord will make you pay for this!" That is some righteous anger right there! This is a biblical marital blow-up! I love it. I like to envision Sarai throwing dishes at Abram as she yells at him that the LORD will punish him for what he has done.

Abram tries to conveniently stay out of it now that he got what he wanted. He tells Sarai to do with Hagar as she wants; it's not his problem anymore. Sarai turns around and starts treating Hagar horribly. It's pretty messed up to treat a pregnant woman terrible. Aren't pregnant women going through enough? Not only is that messed up to treat a pregnant woman badly, it's pretty brave too! I wouldn't mess with a pregnant lady! I'm not that stupid! They will kick my butt. Pregnant women tend to lose their "give a crap" filter. If you poke the bear, you might not like the result. Not to mention, this was Sarai's idea to begin with! Hagar didn't approach Sarai and propose the idea of sleeping with Abram so they could have a child. This was all Sarai's idea. But now that her plan is unfolding, she's not happy about it? Tough. You made your bed, sleep in it. Sarai was so terrible to Hagar that Hagar ran away.

Put yourself in Hagar's shoes. Here she is a young servant, and her boss tells her to have sex with her husband so that Abram can have children. That's pretty screwed up. Hagar didn't really have a choice. She didn't have the authority to say "no." She was essentially forced into this mess. I can't imagine how uncomfortable and scared Hagar must have felt. She must have been worried about what was going to happen after the child was born. How was this actually going to work out? Giving birth and having a child is scary enough without having to deal with all of this drama. She was so overwhelmed that she fled. She ran, as fast as she could and as far as she could. Guess what? God found her. He always finds us. No matter the mess we find ourselves in, HE never bails on us. He never abandons us. No matter if we are the one to blame for our mess or we are the victims of someone else's poor choices like Hagar. When we find ourselves running from Him, He is chasing us. His love is faster than our sin. His love is greater than our mistake. We cannot escape his love. David said in Psalms 139:

> 7 Where can I go from your Spirit?
> Where can I flee from your presence?
> 8 If I go up to the heavens, you are there;
> if I make my bed in the depths, you are there.
> 9 If I rise on the wings of the dawn,
> if I settle on the far side of the sea,
> 10 even there your hand will guide me,
> your right hand will hold me fast.

> [11] If I say, "Surely the darkness will hide me
> and the light become night around me,"
> [12] even the darkness will not be dark to you;
> the night will shine like the day,
> for darkness is as light to you.

Verse 8 literally translates "even if I make my bed in hell, you are there." What a profound statement. Even when I make my bed in hell, He is still with me. My poor choices do not remove the presence of God in my life. There is no depth that He will not go to find us. His love is always in front of us, it is always behind us, and it is always with us here and now. It is covering whatever we have done, whatever we do, and whatever we will do. His love is greater. This is such a beautiful, prophetic picture of who God is. What an incredible exchange we see here between an angel of the LORD and this young woman, caught up in a sex scandal and pregnant by the wrong person.

The angel of the LORD found Hagar and told her that she would have a son and "the LORD has heard about your misery." It would be so easy to just gloss over that short statement and miss a profound truth. God KNOWS what you are going through and he CARES. He is not a distant God, sitting in the clouds watching from afar. He sees you. He knows you. He knows your pain. He has seen every tear you have shed. He sees Hagar and He cares.

His love for this woman compels Him to do something. He cares about her misery and pain so much that he sends an angel to find her. God is desperate for Hagar to know that He is with her. In this intimate moment, Hagar encounters the LORD who will pursue her and find her no matter the circumstance. He sees us and knows us and loves us. He is constant. Through this angel the LORD sent, Hagar has such a powerful encounter with God that she gives Him the name "El Roi." This translates: "the God who sees me." Hagar says in Genesis 16:13, "for I have now seen the One who sees me." Wow. What a powerful and life-changing moment with God. God finds Hagar and pursues her even in the midst of the Jerry Springer episode she found herself in.

Fast-forward a few more years and Abram is 99 years old. He's got 99 problems but a kid ain't one. Bad joke. Couldn't help myself. In Genesis 17:1, the LORD appeared to Abram again and said, "I will make a covenant with you, by which I will guarantee to make you into a mighty nation." Abram fell on his face before God. The LORD continued, "This is my covenant with you: I will make you the father of not just one nation, but a multitude of nations! What's more, I am changing your name. It will no longer be Abram; now you will be known as Abraham, for you will be the father of many nations. I will give you millions of descendants who will represent many nations. Kings will be among them!" Dang. God doubles down on his promise. He continues to build up this promise for Abram in spite of the fact that he was now an old man. Not only this, but God changes his name from Abram to "Abraham" which means "father of many." God wants his very name and identity to be wrapped up in His promises. How disappointing would that be, to be named "father of many" without any children born from your wife? His only son, Ishmael, was basically a bastard son born from a giant sex scandal gone wrong. I can imagine the jokes around the water cooler at the office. He had one of those ironic names. I once had a friend named Caleb "Little," and he was huge! He had an ironic last name that we would tease him about. We would say that he should have been named Caleb "Huge" instead of Caleb "Little." And here Abraham is, given the name "father of many," and guess how many legitimate kids he has at this point as a 99 year old man? A giant goose egg. Zero. Zilch. Nada. God names Abraham "the father of many" when he is quite literally the "father of none." The only child he has is one born from terrible decision making, and serves as a constant reminder about the time they had so LITTLE faith in God they tried to knock up a servant to make God's promises happen. Not the best idea by any stretch of the imagination.

God goes on to say that Abraham's wife Sarai will no longer be called Sarai, but her name will be Sarah. The LORD says again, "I will bless her and give you a son FROM HER!" Not your way, Abraham. Not you fulfilling God's promise. God promises that He will fulfill HIS promise the way he originally planned. His plans, not ours. God goes on to say in chapter 17:16, "Yes, I will bless her richly, and she will become the mother of many nations. Kings will be among her descendants." How does Abraham, the hero of faith, respond to God's resolute promises? With unwavering faith??? Nope. He had so LITTLE faith that his immediate response to God was to laugh. Yup. Hero of faith. He doubts God so strongly that he literally laughs to himself when God tells him that he and Sarah would be the father and mother of many nations. In vs. 17:17, it says, "Then Abraham bowed down to the ground, but he LAUGHED to himself in disbelief. 'How could I become a father at the age of one hundred?' he wondered. 'Besides, Sarah is ninety; how could she have a baby?' And Abraham said to God, 'Yes, may Ishmael enjoy your special blessing!'" Wow, stop right there. Abraham laughed in God's face. Granted, I don't blame him for his doubt. I mean, he was right to wonder how in the world he would be a father at 100 years old and Sarah was 90; so how in the world was she supposed to have a baby? That is a legitimate question. But let's not pretend like this guy was some superhero of faith that never doubted God and he was unwavering. It is quite the opposite. Abraham sarcastically tells God that maybe his bastard son will enjoy the blessings that God is talking about. What he is really saying is this: "Well God, since YOU didn't give me any kids, I had to take matters into my own hands because you couldn't be trusted to make good on your word. And since you have still not delivered on your promise, maybe the kid that I had on my own without your help will make this work out somehow. Since clearly God can't give me a kid, I had to go and figure it out myself. I made the promise happen." God responds to Abrahams's doubt, sarcasm, and chuckling to Himself by remaining steadfast, "Sarah, your wife, will bear you a son. You will name him Isaac, and I will confirm my everlasting covenant with him and his descendants. As for Ishmael, I will bless him also, just as you have asked. I will cause him to multiply and become a great nation. But my covenant is with Isaac, who will be born to you and Sarah about this time next year." Now, Abraham has probably given up on this promise ever coming true. God tells him specifically that Sarah will have a son in about a year. I think God knew Abraham needed this encounter to jolt his fleeting faith. I find it fascinating how many times God shows up to remind Abraham of the same thing over and over again. But this time, even more specifically, God unveils more details to boost Abraham's faith.

Later, three men come by the place where Abraham and Sarah are staying. Abraham welcomes them in and offers to feed them and replenish them so they can rest on their journey. One of the men gave a prophetic word to Abraham. He tells Abraham the same exact thing God just told Abraham a short time ago. He tells

Abraham that one year from now Sarah will have a son. How wild is that? Right after God tells you something, He sends someone along the way to remind you of what He has promised. He sends someone to affirm the word of the LORD. I love how God does this in our own lives. He will send someone to encourage us along the way. Who knows, this could have been an angel of the LORD or maybe God in disguise himself. You never think about whether or not you are interacting with the Divine. Have you ever been struggling and someone came around at just the right place, and just the right time, to say the exact thing you needed to hear to lift you up and help you get through a hard time? I have. Have you ever wondered if that was a complete coincidence? Or maybe it wasn't. Maybe it is the love of the Father pursuing us and meeting us right where we are at. Anyway, Sarah overhears this man tell Abraham that she would have a son a year from now. Sarah has a familiar response. She laughs. Again. These heroes of faith laugh at the promises of God. In Genesis 18:11-12, it says: "And since Abraham and Sarah were both very old, and Sarah was long past the age of having children, she laughed silently to herself. 'How could a worn-out woman like me have a baby?' she thought. 'And when my husband is also so old?'" Again, a completely legitimate question. I don't blame her for having her doubts at this point. I would too. But again, we have painted a perfect picture of faith with these two and it could not be further from the truth. Again, we see them have such LITTLE faith in God at this point that they laugh at Him and His promises. Wow. I mean if you just look at the circumstances here on the surface, it would seem impossible at this point for God's promises to come to pass. God seems to enjoy showing up at exactly the time when it seems impossible so that no one can boast or take credit for what He is doing. If Abraham and Sarah had a bunch of kids when they were in their 30's, nobody would step back in awe and wonder at the works of God. But when He births nations from barren wombs, we have no choice but to fall facedown and worship Him for how great He is.

When Sarah laughed at God, He asked Abraham, "Why did she laugh? Why did she say, 'Can an old woman like me have a baby?' Is there anything too hard for the LORD? About a year from now, just as I told you, I will return, and Sarah will have a son." The only person in this story who has unwavering faith is God. He is constant. Steadfast. Resolute. Determined. Here is a funny footnote in the Bible. At this point Sarah is getting called out on laughing in God's face. She was scared and tried to deny that she laughed. Not gonna fly. She is busted. He tells her that is not true, she did laugh. Can't squirm your way out of this one. He knows our thoughts, no point in trying to deny them. He knows us better than we know ourselves.

In Genesis 21, God delivers on his promise! Right on time! Not our time, but right on His time! Vs. 1 says "The LORD did

EXACTLY what He had promised." Abraham and Sarah had a son and named him Isaac, just as the Lord told them to. Abraham was the ripe young age of 100 years old! Dang! Talk about a miracle. Nobody can take credit for that. No 100 year old sperm has made any babies! No one can boast in what the Lord has done! No barren 90+ year old womb has carried any children. We have no choice but to stand in awe and wonder at the goodness of God. Mission accomplished. Guess what happened to Sarah's laugh? She was originally laughing in doubt, but now we find her laughing in sheer awe and wonder at how good God truly is. She could not contain her joy and elation. She was so overcome with emotion in that moment. Imagine being her for a moment. Decades of disappointment. Countless years of depression and hopelessness. And now, almost 100 years old, she is holding the promise of God in her hands. A son. A baby boy, finally in her arms. Sarah declared in Genesis 21:6-7, "God has brought me laughter! All who hear about this will laugh with me. For who would have dreamed that I would ever have a baby? Yet I have given Abraham a son in his old age!" This is a beautiful moment in Scripture. I can see the smile on her face. I can picture her holding Isaac in her arms, laughing in pure joy with tears running down her face. Like I said before, when God shows up, you have no choice but to worship. I bet they were singing songs to God in that moment. He is far better than we think.

Let's move on to the famous story of Abraham and Isaac. This is when Abraham's faith was tested. God comes to Abraham and says in Genesis 22:2, "Take your son, your only son-yes Isaac, who you love so much-and go to the land of Moriah. Sacrifice him there as a burnt offering on one of the mountains, which I will point out to you." I would like to mention something at this point of the story. Sometimes Christians believe that idolatry is okay as long as the object of our worship is a "good Christian idol." God was pretty direct when He commanded that we shall have "no other Gods before Him." That pretty much includes everything else but Him. Good or bad. Just because we worship something that is "good" does not mean it is acceptable to God. God wants our faith and trust in Him, not in others, because ultimately everything else will let us down. I will go out on a limb to say at this point in the story Abraham may have put some of his hope and faith in becoming the "father of many nations" in Isaac. After all, he is the son that will literally give Abraham more descendants. Without Isaac, how was Abraham supposed to become a father of many nations? Maybe Abraham and Sarah treated Isaac like "bubble boy." Maybe they smothered and protected him so much because they believed their hope was in HIM and no longer in God. Is that so hard to imagine? Man, if I waited 100 years to have a child and finally, at the age of 100 I miraculously had a son, I think I might be a little overprotective of him. Don't let him travel too far from home alone. What if something were to happen to him??? Then all of our hopes and dreams would be crushed. We slowly, subconsciously begin to misplace our hope and trust in others. We gradually move our faith in God and place our faith in people. We begin to worship the "creation" instead of the Creator. This is nothing new to God.

In Romans 1, God rebuked some negative things that had crept in to the Church. One of those things was idolatry. Romans 1:23 says, "Instead of worshiping the glorious, ever-living God, they worshiped idols made to look like mere people." Vs. 25 goes on to say: "So they worshiped the things God made but not the Creator himself, who is to be praised forever: Amen." Sound familiar? The hang-up for many Christians today is that we have deceived ourselves to believe that so long as we worship "noble" idols, it is somehow acceptable to God. You think this doesn't apply to you because I use the word "worship." You think to yourself, "I don't get on my hands and knees and sing worship songs about anything else. I'm good. Not my problem." Think again. What I mean here is ANYTHING else we subtly and subconsciously place our love, affection, trust, faith, fulfillment, joy, and hope in things other than God. Our hope, our joy, and our faith is meant to be in Him alone. Every other "object" that you place your faith and trust in will fail you. EVERYTHING. PERIOD. When we look to anything other than God to be our source of life, joy, fulfillment, and peace, we are setting ourselves up to be crushed. Nothing was meant to fill that place in our lives like only God can.

I would say that marriage has become one of the greatest "acceptable" objects of idolatry in Christian culture today. I also believe this is the single reason as to why divorce has been skyrocketing among Christian communities as well. For this very reason. If you are looking to a spouse to fulfill you, good luck with that. Marriage was not meant to "complete you," even though these are messages we see and hear all over romantic books and movies. Marriage was not designed to "complete you." If anything, marriage exposes you. God is the only one who can make us feel whole. Marriage is not meant to be a picture of two desperately "incomplete" individuals coming together to feel whole. Quite the opposite. Our culture has allowed codependency to masquerade around as "love." Codependency is narcissism. Marriage is meant to be two individuals who are being made whole by God, coming together full and overflowing from God, who in turn are not looking to have their own needs met, but looking to bless the other person. Isn't that the foundation of love? Love and concern for someone else. Selflessness. When you are constantly looking to others to fulfill YOURSELF, isn't that at its core completely selfish? All you are thinking about, subconsciously or not, is yourself. Your needs. Your desires. Your wants. And the other person exists to serve your needs. Wow. That is love? Really? It doesn't sound very loving. In fact, it sounds pretty self-serving to me. True love puts someone else's needs above their own.

My point here is simple. No matter what the object of your affection is besides God, it can easily become idolatry. Maybe Isaac had slowly become the object of Abraham and Sarah's hope. Maybe they started putting a little bit too much of their faith in Isaac, instead of the One who made Isaac. Is that too hard to imagine? I don't think so. I believe we do this all of the time. And I don't think Abraham and Sarah are any different than the rest of us. How ironic that we can begin to worship a gift rather than the One who gave us the gift. Don't we all do this from time to time? I know I do. How silly this must look to God. We begin to worship His good gifts instead of worshipping Him. He is the very source of every good and perfect gift. The One who deserves all of the glory and all of the praise, and yet here we are worshiping His creation instead of the One who spoke creation into being. We aren't always the brightest lights in the room.

Maybe this story was meant to be a reminder for Abraham and Sarah. Maybe God was reminding them WHO their faith and trust should be in. Not in Isaac. He was simply the object through which God was going to fulfill His promises. Isaac was just the creation, he was not the Creator. Abraham passed this test of faith with flying colors. He woke up early the next morning, saddled up his donkey, took two of his servants and Isaac, and headed up the mountain. Once they made it up the mountain, Abraham chopped some wood to build a fire for a burnt offering, just as God told him to. Dang. What had to be going through his mind at this point? If I were him I would probably be thinking, "You gotta be kidding me." I waited 100 years to have Isaac and now that I have a son, God asks me to kill him. What the heck is wrong with God?!? So, Abraham and Isaac headed up to the place where he was instructed to sacrifice Isaac. Isaac had no idea what was going on at this point in the story. Once they got close to the place where they would sacrifice their burnt offering, Isaac began to question what was happening. He asked his father in Gen. 22:7, "Father, we have the wood and the fire, but where is the lamb for the sacrifice?" Abraham responded, "God will provide a lamb, my son." When they arrived at the place that God had instructed him, Abraham built an altar and placed the wood on it. Then he tied up Isaac and laid him on the altar over the wood. Abraham took the knife and lifted it up to kill his son as a sacrifice to the LORD. At that exact moment, the angel of the LORD shouted to him from heaven: "Abraham! Abraham! Lay down the knife. Do not hurt the boy in any way, for now I know that you truly fear God. You have not withheld even your beloved son from me." Then Abraham saw a ram caught in some bushes, and took the ram and sacrificed it as a burnt offering on the altar in place of Isaac. Abraham named the place "Yĕhovah ra'ah" which means "the LORD will provide."

What a story! This is a beautiful story of trust and faith. Abraham, now well over 100 years old, finally trusts this God he has gotten to know. The God who has consistently shown up for him time and time again. Abraham displays a ruthless act of trust that God is indeed Good. Yes, Abraham trusted THIS time. But he did not trust ALL of the time. None of us do. Yet the only versions I have heard about the life of Abraham have been incomplete at best. I grew up in church. I've heard the story of Abraham preached 1,000 times. I've heard amazing sermons about Abraham's unwavering faith in the story of Abraham sacrificing Isaac. I sat through Bible lessons a million times that taught us about Abraham's faith. I was told that I need to have faith like Abraham. We set the bar at an impossible standard. Abraham wouldn't even hit that benchmark of faith. None of us would. Now that we dove into the life of Abraham, we have seen firsthand how he doubted far more often than he trusted. He was afraid. He was all over the map in his journey of "faith." Yet we paint a picture of his life of faith that is not true to his journey.

I need to accept the fact that I am a jumble of paradoxes. The definition of paradox is: "a seemingly absurd or self-contradictory statement or proposition that when investigated or explained may prove to be well founded or true." I trust and I don't trust. I'm courageous and afraid. I doubt and I'm full of faith. I love and I hate. I bless and I curse. Sometimes I believe and sometimes I don't. It is not one or the other, it is "both/and." Abraham's faith was unwavering in this moment, but this is not the whole story. Abraham had faith and he doubted. He was victorious, and he failed miserably. He was obedient and disobedient. He was courageous and a coward. He had faith, but he was also faithless at times. He trusted God, and he didn't trust God at all. He and Sarah laughed at God in disbelief. It is so important for us to paint the whole picture. It is critical that we hold both sides of this paradox in reverence. If we approach biblical characters or ourselves with this "either/or" mentality instead of "both/and," we are sliding down a slippery slope. One side of the coin leaves us ashamed, and the other side of the coin leaves us prideful and arrogant. Both are toxic and dangerous. When we only tell the side of the story that makes us and Abraham look like superheroes, we end up alienating those whom God is calling. When I was told I needed to have faith like Abraham as a child, I quickly realized as I grew up that I could not measure up to that standard, so I quit trying. I sat on the sidelines, feeling ashamed and unfit to participate in the Kingdom of God. I quickly realized my journey did not align with the story of Abraham sacrificing Isaac on an altar, so I gave up. What was the point in trying? I knew I could never measure up to that kind of faith. When I experienced the very real side of my broken humanity, I had no capacity to reconcile my brokenness with the story of God. Not knowing the full story. I had no context to help me see the larger narrative of being human, which is to be both broken and beautiful simultaneously. Had I known the full story of the life of Abraham, I would have felt welcomed into the dysfunctional family of God. I would have seen my own journey align perfectly with the roller coaster journey of faith that Abraham and Sarah had. Up and down, faith and no faith, trust and no trust, doubt and fear, mistakes and all. When we finally lay down the false narratives about ourselves and Scripture, we will begin to invite others into the Story of God. We fit right in. Our mess fits right in.

My point here is this. In my experience, when I have shared these stories in the life of Abraham in a room filled with average "church-going folk," about 8 out of 10 people have never heard most of these stories in their entire lives. I'm not talking about Bible scholars here. I'm talking about people that have gone to church off and on, here and there, for most of their life. This is the majority of people sitting in church two weeks a month, not the church leadership team. I believe the Bible is filled with scandalous stories just like this all over the place. These stories never make it on the felt boards in Sunday school. They rarely make it to the pulpit (so to speak). I grew up in church and have heard probably a million sermons. I have heard probably 1,000 sermons on the story where Abraham sacrificed Isaac and heard inspiring messages about how amazing Abraham was and how much faith he had in God. I have literally, in 35 years, never heard anyone give a message about the story of Abraham and Hagar. Why? How does this happen? I think that we don't know how to "marry" the mess of scripture and real life with the redemption of God. We don't know how to explain the Jerry Springer season of Abraham's life, so we just sweep it under the rug. My main point here is this: in our subconscious censoring of these stories, we have robbed the story of redemption of its beauty. If we read about the life of Abraham and at the end of the story we say, "Wow, Abraham was such an amazing man of God with a faith that never quit!" We have completely missed the entire point of the life of Abraham. The life of Abraham was meant to put the faithfulness of GOD on display, not the faithfulness of Abraham on display. His life was meant to put the goodness of GOD on display, not the greatness of Abraham on display. When we censor the stories in Scripture and the story of our own life, we conceal the Face of God that we were meant to put on display.

SCANDAL OF THOR

Chapter 7

THE SCANDAL OF THOR

This is actually about the scandal of Samson, but I picture Samson looking identical to Thor, so I decided to title the chapter after the Avengers character Thor. This is my book, so I can do what I want! In a time when Israel (God's children) had become so evil that the Lord allowed them to be handed over to the Philistines and live under the rule of their enemy for 40 years, God raised up a man that He would use to rescue Israel for the Philistines. Samson was chosen by God before he was even born, just like all of us. But Samson was chosen in a very special way. Samson's mother was barren and had been unable to have children. But God had other plans. He sent an angel to speak to Samson's mother. The angel of the Lord came to her and said: "Even though you have been unable to have children, you will soon become pregnant and give birth to a son." Sound familiar? God seems to be in the habit of choosing barren women to birth the Kingdom of God so that no one could take credit for the miraculous work He was going to do. This angel went on to give Samson's mother insight and instruction on how to raise this child. She was instructed to dedicate him to the Lord as a Nazirite from birth, and he was going to rescue Israel from the Philistines. A Nazirite in the Bible is simply one who has been "set apart." Those who were chosen to live this life were consecrated, or made holy and dedicated for a higher purpose. Nazarites would take a vow to never cut their hair, abstain from alcohol, and to avoid contact with the dead (that shouldn't be a tough one, but the other two are a different story). Wow, what a calling to have on your life. You have been chosen to rescue a nation from captivity. This is the making of an epic story of redemption.

In Judges 13:24-25, it says God blessed Samson as he grew older, and in verse 25 it says that as he grew older, the "Spirit of the Lord began to take hold of him." Just to clarify, the rest of Samson's story was AFTER he had already been chosen by God and AFTER the Spirit of the Lord took hold of him. He makes some questionable choices at best AFTER he invites Jesus in his heart, so to speak. I can say pretty confidently that Samson has a lust problem. In Judges 14:1, Samson "noticed" a certain Philistine woman. Everyone out there knows EXACTLY what "noticed" means in this context! I hate to see you go, but I love to watch you leave kind of moment. Bow-chicka-bow-wow. Samson falls for the wrong woman. Keep in mind, Samson was the chosen one who was supposed to rescue Israel from the Philistines, not seduce their women. Men don't always think with the right head, if you know what I mean. This was scandalous. His family objected and pleaded with him to find another woman in his own tribe and not this pagan Philistine woman. There was no talking sense into Samson after he "noticed" this Philistine woman. His mind was made up. So he instructed his parents to fetch her for him as if she were a piece of meat. Turns out, even when we fall for the wrong person, God continues to work through our broken journey. God was still at work. When we begin to "color outside the lines," this does not restrict God working in us and through us. He is so much bigger than our junk.

In true Thor fashion, in Judges 14:5, Samson was attacked by a lion and ripped the lion's jaws apart with his bare hands. Crazy! Notice what the Scriptures say right before that: "The Spirit of the Lord powerfully took control of him" and THEN he ripped the lion's jaws apart with his bare hands. So Samson did not rip the lion's jaws apart with his own strength. This was the power of the Spirit of the Lord that gave him the strength to rip a lion to pieces. Subtle part of the story that if you miss, you would become enamored with the strength of Samson without realizing, it wasn't his strength, it was the power of the Spirit of the Lord in him.

Can you hear that? Jerry, Jerry, Jerry. Here it comes. Let the scandals continue! Samson had one conversation with the Philistine woman and realized she was "the one." He must have been really captivated by her "personality." You can learn a lot about a person in one conversation. No. No you can't. Let's not kid ourselves. Samson liked what he SAW. Their conversation probably went something like this: "Hey girl, I was reading the book of numbers last night and I just realized I don't have yours! Now I know why Solomon had 700 wives…because he never met you!" That doesn't really make sense since Solomon hadn't been born yet, but you get what I'm saying. I don't think they had this deep intimate conversation. I think Samson saw something he liked and he was determined to have her. So he took her.

In this culture, it was tradition to throw a huge party for a week to celebrate a marriage ceremony. So Samson invited 30 of his best friends to party for a week. Samson has a thing for riddles. Strange, I know. Samson makes a bet with his buddies that they can't solve his riddle in seven days during the party. He wagered 30 plain linen robes and 30 fancy robes. I've never heard of a high stakes bet of robes, but these were different times. Robes were actually a pretty significant form of currency back then. There was a lot on the line. So Samson gives these men the riddle. "From the one who eats came something to eat; out of the strong came something sweet." Three days went by and they still couldn't figure out this riddle, so they approached Samson's wife. These guys were pissed off at this point. They don't want to have to pay up on their bet. They threaten Samson's wife and tell her that if she doesn't get the answer from Samson they will burn her father's house down with her in it! Dang! Those must be some expensive robes!

Samson's wife must have been terrified, so she approached Samson in tears telling him that he didn't really love her because he didn't tell her the answer to the riddle. She was manipulating him. She wanted him to give her the answer so in turn, she could tell these men. Samson refused, so his wife persisted to nag him and cry for the duration of the celebration for the next 3-4 days. That sounds terrible. Samson finally broke down on the 7th day and gave her the answer to the riddle. Once she knew the answer, she immediately told the men. The men of the town came to Samson and told him the answer to the riddle. Samson was furious! His response is pretty graphic but speaks to his anger. He said; "If you hadn't plowed with my heifer, you wouldn't have found the answer to my riddle!" Geez, they had been married a few days and she had already manipulated and betrayed his trust and he was calling her a fat cow. Sounds like a pretty accurate depiction of marriage!

Have I mentioned that I think Samson has anger problems? He could definitely benefit from some anger management counseling. Samson is so furious that he goes to a neighboring town and murders 30 random, innocent men. He takes their belongings, and gives them to the men who had answered his riddle to pay up on his bet. Geez. Where was God when this crap goes down? That's messed up. He throws a temper tantrum and kills 30 innocent people, and steals their belongings. How many of the 10 commandments did he just break? Crazy. So Samson goes home to live with his parents instead of facing his wife, reconciling, and finding healing and forgiveness. Meanwhile, his wife married the best man at the wedding! What? Jerry, Jerry, Jerry. Betrayal, lies, murder, theft, and now the best man at Samson's wedding marries his wife! This is messed up! You think your life or marriage has had some Jerry Springer moments? Well, welcome to the dysfunctional family of God.

Meanwhile, Samson literally had no idea that his wife had left him and married his best man. Dang, he was going to be pissed. As I mentioned earlier, Samson needs to go to anger management, so this news probably wasn't going to go over well. Later on, Samson headed back to see his wife and did what any reasonable man would do. He brought her a young goat. Nothing says, "Baby, come back," like a goat. Pure romance. In Judges 15:1, it says that he brought her a young goat and he "intended to sleep with her." Not reconcile. Not work through their issues. He was horny and wanted to get laid. Cheap love. But his wife's father refused to let Samson sleep with her because she was married to someone else now. Her father explained that he thought Samson hated her and wouldn't want to be married to her anymore, so he married her to his best man. Oh, but there is a consolation prize. Look, her sister over there is more beautiful than she is. Marry her instead. Let's just say Samson wasn't thrilled with this proposition. His rage was boiling over. Samson went out and caught three hundred foxes. He tied their tails together in pairs, and he fastened a torch to each pair of tails. Then he lit the torches and let the foxes run through the fields of the Philistines. He burned all of their grain to the ground, including the grain that had already been bundled in piles. He also destroyed their grapevines and olive trees. Talk about anger problems. Samson went on a rampage.

The Philistines saw the damage that had been done and demanded to know who had done this terrible thing. "Samson," they replied. They told the Philistines he had done this because his father-in-law had given his wife to be married to his best man. So the Philistines went and took this woman and her father and burned them to death. Holy cow. That's pretty graphic. They burned them alive to punish them for pissing off Samson. Now, do you see why I said in the opening chapter of this book that the Bible is filled with stories that are like Jerry Springer episodes with a lot more violence?

After all of this drama had transpired, the Philistines set out to kill Samson for what he had done. Not really a plot twist here. You figure even Samson had to see this coming. You can't destroy an entire people group's food supply and think they are going to just lay down and accept it. So Samson went to a cave to hide. Not very brave or Thor-like. I'm very disappointed. So the Philistines went to the Israelites in Judah and demanded they hand over Samson. 3,000 men from Judah went to find Samson in his cave and told him they came to hand him over to the Philistines. The Israelites were afraid that the Philistines were going to harm them for what Samson had done, so this was purely motivated out of self-preservation. They confronted Samson and told him: "Don't you know what you have done to us?" They were scared. Samson's reply is similar to that of a 3-year-old; "They started it! I just did to them what they did to me!" Really mature, Samson. Samson made them swear not to kill him, but to turn him over to the Philistines. So they tied him up with two new ropes and led him to the Philistines. The Philistines saw him coming from a distance and were chomping at the bit to torture this man. They came at him shouting, and right then "The Spirit of the Lord came powerfully upon him." The ropes that bound him became weak and he snapped them off as if they were merely straw. He found the jawbone of a recently killed donkey and killed 1,000 Philistines with it! That is badass! That is what I am talking about! Definitely bringing down the hammer of Thor on this one! Once again, God showed up in a powerful and mighty way for Samson.

Samson was appointed as a judge over Israel for 20 years while they were ruled by the Philistines. God shows up for Samson in a miraculous way and Samson responds like any man of God. He goes out to find a hooker. What?!? Seriously. Stop. What the hell is going on? God delivers you from the mess you created. From one bonehead move to another, and you think it's a great idea to go find a prostitute? This guy is an idiot. Think about that. The Spirit of the Lord takes control of Samson and gives him supernatural strength to kill 1,000 men with the jawbone of a donkey. THEN he is appointed as a judge and leader over the entire nation of Israel. And after all of that, THEN Samson goes to the enemy's camp again and spends the night with a prostitute? It's easy to gloss over this because it makes us uncomfortable. We don't know how to reconcile the crap that actually happens in life, with a God who is actively engaging with us and showing up, even in the messes that we find ourselves in. It's much easier to censor this story to make it suitable for children. Get your sharpie and start crossing out all of the parts that make us uncomfortable. We don't know what to do with this. I certainly don't want my kids to read this and think its okay to have sex with prostitutes. So let's just leave that part out of the story. Lets smooth out the rough edges of scripture so that it makes us feel comfortable. We like our religion to be polished and proper. Hookers are not proper. We need a dignified religion. This is what Jesus would want. Don't mind us, we just think your Word needs to be polished up a bit to fit our religious sensibilities. Nope. Can't do it. You cannot manipulate scripture to suit yourself. The minute you tweak the gospel to accommodate yourself, you are removing the life giving power that is found in the Good News. YOUR gospel is void of life. You cannot remove the hookers from the Bible. Believe it or not, the hookers, thieves, murderers, and adulterers unlock the mystery hidden in the pages of Scripture. They are the key. They are preaching the Gospel. Do you see it? Can you hear it? Can you hear the Gospel? That no matter what you have done, no matter where you have been, there is nothing in all of creation that can separate you from the Love of God in Christ Jesus. "Neither death nor life neither angels nor demons, neither the present nor the future, nor any powers, neither height nor depth, nor anything else in all of creation, will be able to separate us from the love of God in Christ Jesus," Romans 8:28-29. Even when the shit hits the fan, HE is faithful, HE is forgiving, HE is full of mercy, HE is compassionate, HE is loving, HE does not condemn, HE is pursuing us, & HE is kind to the ungrateful and wicked (Luke 6:35). This is the Gospel 101. How did we miss the very foundation of the Gospel that is so plain to see? "Yet when we were still sinners Christ died for us," "For all have sinned and fallen short of the glory of God," Romans 3:11. "There is no one righteous, not even one; there is no one who understands; there is no one who seeks God. All have turned away, they have together become worthless; there is no one who does good, not even one," "It is by GRACE, through faith that we have been saved, and this is not from yourselves, it is a GIFT of God-not by works, so that no one can boast," Ephesians 2:8-9. How did we turn the gospel into a love story about how great WE are? We have completely turned the gospel upside down.

Samson's weak spot for women ensued. He fell in love with a woman named Delilah. The Philistines approached Delilah and offered to make her rich if she tricked Samson into telling her the secret to his strength. Samson and Delilah must have had a very meaningful relationship built on trust, because she immediately agreed to the Philistine's request. Sarcasm is my second language. Obviously, Samson's spiritual gift was creating dysfunctional relationships. So Delilah approached Samson and begged him to tell her what makes him so strong and what it would take to securely tie him up. Samson must not really trust this woman, because he lies to her. He tells her that if he were tied up with 7 new bow strings that have not yet been dried, he would become as weak as anyone else. Delilah told the Philistines and they brought her the 7 new bowstrings. Delilah tied up Samson with the 7 bowstrings. She hid some Philistine men in one of her rooms, and once she had him bound up she shouted, "Samson! The Philistines have come to capture you!" This was the cue for the Philistines to come out of hiding and take Samson captive. Luckily for Samson, he lied to his trustworthy wife Delilah and broke the bowstrings immediately. Delilah was very upset that Samson had lied to her, so she came to him at once, saying, "You've been making fun of me and telling me lies! Now please tell me how you can be tied up securely." Hmmm. Fool me once, shame on you; fool me twice, shame on me. So Samson lies to Delilah again, and the exact same scenario unfolded. Samson lied, Delilah set him up, and when the Philistines came for Samson he broke through whatever Delilah used to tie him up. This happened three separate times until Delilah nagged him, day after day, and he was finally "sick to death of it." Samson let down his guard and confided in his wife, even though she set him up to be captured three separate times. Lets just say that Samson isn't the sharpest tool in the shed. I picture him like a buff Neanderthal with long hair. Not exactly a rocket scientist. It seems pretty obvious at this point that he shouldn't trust his wife. But again, it appears that women are his "Achilles heel." They are his blind spot. Samson tells his wife that his weakness is his hair. So he's basically a male version of Rapunzel. Really macho, Samson. My power is in my golden locks. His wife tricked Samson again, lulled him to sleep, and had a man shave his head. It says that his strength had left him immediately. Samson woke up and tried to free himself, but had not realized his strength was gone. So the Philistines captured him and gouged out his eyes and threw him in prison. Brutal punishment for anyone.

The Philistines celebrated this great victory. They held a festival and offered sacrifices to their god, Dagon. They proclaimed their god had given them victory over Samson. Everyone was drunk and they decided to bring Samson out for their amusement. In epic fashion, Samson had one last feat of strength. They brought him between the pillars that were supporting the roof of the temple. There were about 3,000 men and women on the roof of the temple who were watching as Samson amused them. The temple was completely filled, including the Philistine leaders. It was then Samson prayed to the Lord. He asked the Lord to remember him again and strengthen him just one more time. Again, notice a subtle yet vital part of the story here. Samson did not crush the temple on his own strength. He cried out to the Lord to strengthen him. This story was never about how strong Samson was. It was always about how strong the LORD was IN Samson. In the final moment of Samson's life, he put his hands on the two center pillars that held up the temple. Pushing against them with both hands, the temple crashed down on the Philistine rulers and all of the people. In that last battle scene of Samson's life, he killed more people than he had killed during his entire lifetime.

So there we have it: the scandal of Thor. Lust, women, murder, anger, lies, manipulation, prostitutes, Rapunzel, brides leaving the groom for the best man, and everything in between. In it all and through it all, God continued to show up. HE continued to be faithful and strengthen Samson even after he had blown it time and time again. Even when he spent the night with prostitutes AFTER he had been appointed as a judge and leader over the nation of Israel. This should bring some comfort to all of the ragamuffins out there like me. What's your story? I will say it again. Welcome to the dysfunctional family of God; you fit right in.

MY SCANDAL

Chapter 8

MY SCANDAL

Let me tell you the story of how God found me. Hello, my name is Jordan and I'm an alcoholic. This is not my identity. In the same breath, my name is Jordan and I am a son of the creator of the heavens and the earth. I have been adopted by the One who spoke the universe into existence. This is a profound, life-changing reality. I am not a biological son that God is stuck with. Before He made the world, He saw the beginning of my life, He saw every moment, and He saw my life unfold from beginning to end. Every mistake, every failure, every scandal in the light. Nothing was hidden from Him. He knew me completely. Yet, He still chose me! How can this be?!? He was thinking of me when He was hanging on a bloody cross. Giving His own life so that I could live. This is my identity. I have been chosen.

I became an alcoholic after I met God and chose to follow Him. I've pretty much done everything backwards. Most people who give their testimony share stories of brokenness, addiction, prison, etc. But then they met Jesus and now everything is butterflies and rainbows. Well, my story is quite the opposite. I met

Jesus and then everything went to hell. Hahahahaha. How can this be??? Well, it's pretty simple, actually. Just because I decided to follow Jesus doesn't mean that my life would be immune to failure, sin, disappointment, addiction, and loss. I will shout this from the rooftops! Why? Aren't I ashamed? Well, in short, yes. It's humiliating to my ego. But I will boast in the things that show my weakness so that the goodness of God will be on full display in my life. Why don't we see prominent leaders in the church ever do this? Why is it that all we see are leaders boasting in the things that make them look strong? I'm always skeptical and guarded with people who lack vulnerability. Why is this you might ask? Because I know, whether they are willing to admit it or not, they are deeply flawed and broken just like the rest of us. And the fact they aren't aware or open about their flaws is much more concerning to me than someone who appears to be a complete mess but at least I know what I'm getting. How does that saying go? "Better the devil you know than the devil you don't know."

Why is it that the guy who wrote half of the New Testament that we uphold as the perfect Word of God refused to accept the praise and adulation of others? Why was he constantly deflecting praise away from himself? People would try to exalt the Apostle Paul and his response would be: "I'm the chief of all sinners."

I am convinced that every single human being should be forced to go through the 12 steps. Alcohol is not my problem. Wait, you must be saying to yourself, you just said you were an alcoholic. Yes, I did say that, but alcohol is not my problem. I am addicted to escaping. Alcohol is simply MY way of escaping. What's yours? Just because I drink to escape life when it becomes too much to bear doesn't make me any different from you. I'm convinced that we are all addicts. Different cultures create more socially acceptable coping mechanisms and look down on others who have a different vice than they do. This is silly. The goal of the 12 steps is to find wholeness with God and others. Do you think you could use any work in that department?? If you think you don't, then you need more work than the rest of us, because you are living in complete denial. Moving beyond denial is one of the first steps in AA, so if you haven't crossed that bridge yet, you better get with the program. If your answer is yes to the question of whether or not you could use some work in the wholeness with God and others, well, then welcome to the human race. We are all in the same boat, whether we like it or not. Some of us like to convince ourselves that we aren't as bad off as the rest of us and we are in a nicer boat. A more dignified, holy boat. Maybe a yacht or something. Again, complete denial. This is the most dangerous boat to be on. You are on a giant boat with all of humanity. You are on a boat with addicts, adulterers, porn addicts, prostitutes, pastors, and pedophiles. Sorry to be the one to break the bad news, but this is reality.

So here it goes: a bit of my scandal. I will not boast in these things because I am proud of them. I am incredibly ashamed of these stories. I have no confidence in what I have done to earn grace, I will boast in the One that saw it all before He knit me together in my mother's womb and still chose me. He is worthy of it all.

The pages of this book were written by the hands of a liar, alcoholic, narcissist, adulterer, insecure, and self-absorbed man. I am addicted to escaping. I am constantly escaping reality, pain, hurt, rejection, and loneliness. The way that I tend to escape is through alcohol. This is my drug of choice. I've been hungover more times than you could ever imagine. I really pushed the limits of the 77 times 7 forgiveness rule. I've relapsed too many times to count, even as I wrote this book. You have no idea how many times I almost threw in the towel and quit writing because of very deep, very real self-hatred and shame. I felt completely unworthy and unqualified to write this book for God. I never quit. Isn't this the whole message of The Divine Scandal? I am not qualified based on what I have done for God. I am qualified for one reason, and one reason only: The God of the universe did FOR me what I could never do for myself. I am worthy because HE has called me worthy.

For some, their means of escape might be work, shallow relationships, money, drugs, sex, or even religion. Some of these are more socially acceptable than others, but they are the same nonetheless. My drinking began around the age of 15 to deal with social anxiety. My family moved and uprooted our lives when I graduated middle school. My first day of high school was on the other side of California (the good part of California). It was a new town, a new school, and in a school of about 1,500 students, my brothers were the only people I knew. That was all. Two brothers, who are twins and a couple years older than I am. I knew two people that were also probably just trying to survive high school as well and probably didn't need a scrawny younger brother hurting their street cred. Terrified. I had not yet discovered who I was; it didn't help that my face was covered in acne for much of the time. I started to drink to fit in because I was desperate to fit in. Kill or be killed. I developed a sharp tongue to defend myself and hide my deep insecurity. I still have that sharp tongue that rears its ugly head occasionally. I was the class clown. Sometimes I still am, and if I'm honest, there might still be an insecure little kid hiding behind it. My drinking started out innocently enough, if that's a thing, but it created a very dangerous coping mechanism that would stick with me for years to come. When I became overwhelmed, uncomfortable, scared, insecure, felt unloved, and overwhelmed in life, I began to drink to temporarily escape life. My drinking had not become a full-blown addiction at that point. I drank occasionally at parties and social gatherings, but I never drank alone. Ever. Until I did. Then I never drank with others. Ever. My drinking progressed over the years as I grew older. My mistakes and failures began to pile up, so I drank more to wash away the guilt and shame. I'll get into more of those Jerry Springer episodes later.

If I am going to boast in anything, I am going to boast in the things that make me look weak. God deserves every bit of glory that emerges from the scandal of my life. I have no righteousness on my own accord to stand on. Thank God I do not stand on my righteousness. I am not a child of God because of anything I do; I am a child of God because of the senseless love that the Creator of the universe has for me. God doesn't love me because I am good; God loves me because God is good. A saint is not one who is good, but one who experiences the goodness of God. This is the firm foundation I stand on.

If there is any part of scripture that I identify with, it is Romans 6, where Paul lets down his guard and reveals to his audience that he is a fellow "struggler." Paul is aware of his human condition and the depth of his weakness. Until we reach this point, we will never discover God's strength. We will simply live our whole lives spinning our wheels, relying on our own depleted resources. We are so weak. I am so weak. I understand what it feels like to have your soul long to live completely surrendered to God, yet have every part of your flesh fighting you. I know what it means to do what I hate. Longing to just let go! As if it were that simple. I can't count how many times I have wept before God, begging Him to help me let go of certain things that keep holding me back, yet they still find their way into my life from time to time. I'm not saying at all that God wants those things in my life. I'm just acknowledging the limitations of Jordan, not God. I am learning how to live dependent on the Father. Everything I have ever known or been conditioned to do has been screaming at me to be independent. I don't need anyone! I will make my fortune! I will build my empire and create my own future! I am not a weakling that needs others to help me get what I want! Asking for help is weak. I will perfect myself! I was conditioned to believe that true strength is the absence of weakness. I will make myself righteous if it kills me! And it just might.

And here we have Jesus speaking to us in a way that is in glaring contrast to the picture I have just painted. In John 15, Jesus uses an analogy about vines and branches to illustrate what our relationship with him looks like. Let me tell you right off the bat that this illustration does not paint a picture of independence in any way, shape, or form. I refer to this verse as the "giant horse pill of life that I refuse to swallow." Jesus starts off this analogy by saying that "apart from me, you can do nothing!" Did you hear that? Nothing!?! But Jesus, you must be mistaken, look at the empire I have built. Look at my job, my house, my family, my retirement plan, my 401K, my car, my swimming pool, my church, and my endless good deeds. How is it possible that I can do nothing without you? This reality sums up a LOT of the root problem in trying to overcome addiction. I refused to accept this. My ego and pride have fought this reality kicking and screaming. And I promise you this one thing, LIFE has a way of teaching you that this reality is absolutely inescapable. You don't control shit. We create illusions of control to feel safe. But at the end of the day, when life happens and our illusions of control come crashing down, for a moment we see clearly what has been true all along. I don't control shit. Oh, how God longs for my will to live apart from him to be broken. That is all He has ever wanted. ME. He didn't create me because He needed slaves to work, He created us for his pleasure and at the root of the fall of humanity was a will that tried to assert his independence from God. We wanted to feel in control.

When our sin causes us to distance ourselves from God, it is revealing our tendency to assert our independence from the Father. This means we have not discovered the treasure of grace. When our sin fuels us to draw closer to him out of the revelation of our utter dependence and desperate need for Him, we begin to experience true freedom. This revelation of grace is the key to unlock our freedom.

Just like how I began this chapter. Let me tell you about a God that found me. Not the other way around. Don't get this twisted. This is not a story of how great my love for God is. This is a story of a son that was running as fast and as far as possible from the Father. But thank you Jesus, there is no depth that He would not go to find me. One of my favorite passages in all of scripture is when David poured out his heart to God and said, "Where can I go to escape you, where can I flee from your presence? If I go up to the heavens, you are there, even when I make my bed in HELL, you are there!" Man, am I a living testament to that truth. This story pretty much set the tone of our relationship. One of the most powerful encounters I have ever had with God was in a park in Antioch, California, in the middle of the night. This experience would set the stage for the rest of my life. God showed up at the wrong place, at the wrong time. After I had been kicked out of church, I began to run from God as fast as I could. My drinking and partying began to get more intense. I drank a lot and began smoking weed because a lot of my co-workers did. I went off the deep end pretty quickly. Beneath the rebellion was a deeply wounded young man.

I was out late one night, drinking with my friend/partner in crime, Nathan. I'm not sure where we had been partying that particular evening, but I remember for some reason we ended up at a bowling alley. We had two other girls with us that we had been drinking with and they were pretty drunk. When we went inside the bowling alley, we were soon approached by security and asked to leave because we were all so noticeably intoxicated and underage. So we left the bowling alley and headed to my friend Nathan's house. I really needed to go pee and there was a park in Nathan's neighborhood, so I pulled over, and Nathan and I got out and went into the park to go to the bathroom and left the two girls in the car. I had no idea that what was about to happen would alter the course of my life forever.

So here we were, in a park, in the middle of the night, and pretty drunk. I was in a bad place in my life. I was very lost. Very hurt. Very confused. Very angry. And the list goes on and on. At this particular moment in my life, God had absolutely no business showing up. I wasn't in a church service. I wasn't living for God. I was making poor choices on a daily basis. I was living in sin. I was not pursuing God. But apparently he was pursuing me. So after we relieved ourselves in this park, something shifted in the atmosphere. My friend Nathan was VERY drunk. Sorry to throw you under a bus, my friend, but it is an important piece of information to the story. He was so drunk that 30 minutes after this happened, he was vomiting on the side of a curb outside of his house. After he peed, he turned around and walked towards me and began to say, "Why are you running from God?" I was taken a little off guard that he would bring God up at this moment. A little out of place, don't you think? He did not hesitate and kept going as if he were possessed. "Why are you running from God?" he asked again. This time he had my attention. He kept walking towards me and began to cry as he got close to me and he began to plead with me, "Stop running from God, he has such big plans for your life! Stop running from him, he loves you so much." At this point, Nathan was sobbing, he grabbed me, hugged me, and kept repeating, "Stop running from him, he loves you so much, he has huge plans for your life." Something happened. I broke. Like a dam that had been holding back an ocean of tears. It was like a switch had flipped. I was 100% sober in an instant. And something in the atmosphere changed. I know exactly what it was. It was Him. He came. To Antioch, California. In a park. In the middle of that neighborhood. While we were drinking, smoking, and fooling around with girls all night. He showed up. Not later that night, so I had a chance to sober up. Not a few days later at a church service, when I had a chance to clean myself up. Not the next day. Right then. In that moment. In the exact moment when it made the least amount of sense for Him to show up. That is exactly when he decided to show up. When my rebellion had reached the pinnacle. He came. Kinda like when Jesus showed up and we murdered him? He came when humanity was so messed up that it murdered God. Something about Jesus showing up in the most inappropriate and offensive moments is too much for our sensibility. We were so offended by Jesus that we killed him. Don't be surprised when you see the same ole' Jesus showing up in the same ways, to the same sinners like me, offending the religious elite. Because if you aren't careful, you might just miss Him. And you might just find that not only did you miss Him, but you could be crucifying Him all over again because He doesn't look like YOUR messiah. Because, trust me the Jesus I encountered that night officially screwed up my theology for life. Try to fit that Jesus in a box.

In that moment, one thing became crystal clear. The God of the universe came to speak through my intoxicated friend just to tell me how much He loved me. While I was running from Him, He was chasing me down. He was pursuing me. He didn't wait until my rebellion ended to show up. In the midst of the mess of my life, He came. How could this be? This was not the God that I had come to know from church. This was not the God who loved good little boys and girls. I was certainly not behaving like a good little boy. This really screwed with my theology. Everything I thought I knew about God melted in that moment. It was like being introduced to someone for the very first time, yet I was already a Christian. This God that I met that night was relentless. He would stop at nothing to meet me. To speak with me. Just to let me know how much He loves me. It was like I had run to the corner of the globe to escape Him and He searched the whole world just to find me. And when He arrived, it felt like He had run through walls to get to me. Well, He did. David describes this God in Psalms 139, when he says: "Where can I go from your presence? If I go up to the heavens you are there, even when I make my bead in HELL you are still there." Pretty much describes my life. There was nothing that could stop God from rescuing us. Even hell. Jesus went to the depths of hell itself, inside the belly of the whale just to get to us.

That night I met the creator of the universe. And let me tell you from personal experience that He is very, very good. I experienced on a very personal level the goodness of God that the Apostle Paul said surpasses all understanding. That night I had nothing good to stand on. Not a single reason I could come up with as to why God should love me. I had been stripped of everything that made me feel loveable. Sometimes God needs to strip us of all of the filthy rags we are wearing to let us know that He doesn't love us because of anything we have done to deserve it. This seems simple but was revolutionary to me. God didn't love me because I went to church. He didn't love me because I read my Bible everyday. He didn't love me because I didn't drink. He didn't love me because I didn't have premarital sex. He didn't love me because I was "in ministry" (whatever the heck that means). He didn't love me because I wasn't looking at porn. Nope. His love for me had absolutely nothing to do with what I did or did not do for Him. As I said at the beginning of this chapter, God doesn't love me because I am good, God loves me because God is good. I experienced that reality firsthand. Stripped of my own righteousness, I realized that my righteousness was just filthy rags. His love for me is constant. He is not a fickle God who's affection for me ebbs and flows with how well I perform for Him. He doesn't love me because I love Him. He loves me when I hate Him. This blew my mind, but I began to realize that this was the God that was revealed in scripture. It just wasn't the God who was shown to me in religion. This is gospel 101: "Yet when we were sinners, Christ died for us." "Not that we love God, but he first loved us and sent his Son to die for us." How could I have missed this gospel message that was screaming from the pages of the Bible? This would not be the last scandalous encounter I would have with God. You figure I would have learned my lesson after God came down from heaven to meet me in a park in Antioch, but apparently I have a pretty thick skull.

After I met God, I slowly picked up the pieces of my broken life and moved to Redding, California, to go to Bible College. I wasn't sure what to do with what had just happened to me, but I figured the only way to truly give my life over to God now was to become a pastor. (If you could only see the expression on my face as I type those words, serious eye-rolling going on). I went to Simpson University and got serious with Jesus. Before I moved to Redding, I threw my last bag of weed out the window on the freeway. I stopped drinking for a long time after I moved up north to go to school. However, I had not dealt with some of the serious heart problems that were going on underneath the surface, so naturally my military devotion to God began to fade. I was still following Jesus the best that I could at the time, but still very much struggling with my faith. After I graduated college, my house of cards began to fall apart again. I was wrestling with some very deep issues and became isolated from healthy community. I began to drink regularly again. This time, I was drinking as a follower of Jesus. I was drinking while "flipping the bird" to religion and legalism that told me I had to behave. Kind of like a "middle finger" to the establishment. I was exercising my freedom in Christ in a very negative way. Now I drank with all of my Christian friends. But I began to drink more frequently and heavily. We started to go out to bars and drink till' the wee hours of the morning. I couldn't figure out who I was or how I fit in this world.

This next season of life I would characterize as the "Jerry Springer season of my life." One of my close friends and I were looking for a place to live and found another guy about our age with a 3 bedroom house who was looking for a couple other roommates. It was perfect for us. We moved in and things went downhill pretty quickly for me from that point. I was in a really dark place. Struggling at work. Struggling internally. Battling loneliness. Even though I was constantly surrounded by people, I felt deeply alone. I felt abandoned by God. Even when I tried to pray or spend time with God, it felt cold and lonely. I saw all of the holes in the church and became angry and resentful towards religion. Rage Against the Machine became my Sunday morning worship. Fight the power! I saw how much the church had lost its identity and become so hypocritical. It didn't look like Jesus, and I didn't know how to handle that.

So I began to rebel against God again. Not a good idea. My new roommate Josh was a great guy. He was a CDF firefighter, which was a career I was always incredibly jealous over. He basically worked 9 months out of the year during fire season and then he would get laid off from work, collect maximum unemployment (which was much more than I actually made working) for 3-4 months during winter, and then get hired back on in the spring. This was the cycle of his job every year. It was a dream job for a single guy in his 20's. A four-month paid vacation every year?!! Anyways, Josh was great. He was a really nice guy and probably one of the best roommates I've ever had. Well, I was about to screw that up big time.

Josh was new to living on his own and hadn't been out of the "nest" long, so he jumped right in to our drinking and partying. We would make family meals together and get drunk and have a good time together. Josh had a girlfriend named Shelby. Shelby came over to the house all the time when Josh was home. Josh would usually leave town for work for a few days at a time during fire season or sometimes longer. So he would be home for a few days and then be gone for a few days. After we had all become good friends and gotten acquainted with each other pretty well, something began happening. Shelby started showing up at the house even when Josh was out of town. At first it was very strange. While she didn't live with us technically, she did have keys to the house. In the beginning, she made it seem like she had a reason to come over. She would help clean up the house and stuff while Josh was gone. She would do nice stuff for him while he was out of town so when he got home his room would be clean, or have something nice for him when he got home. Eventually, this just became normal. She became our friend, and not just Josh's girlfriend. We had a relationship with her outside of her relationship with Josh. We spent time with her while he wasn't around. At first it was strange, but then it was kind of nice having a cute girl around the house, cleaning up and hanging out. She would come over and we would hang out and drink as if Josh were there, but he wasn't. I'm not exactly sure how or when this happened, but one night when we all were drinking and having a good time something happened between Shelby and I. In our drunken state, it became obvious chemistry had developed between us. We could both feel it. We went out dancing at a bar one night by ourselves. We invited other people, but they bailed. Which is exactly what we both wanted. That night I think we kissed. I'm not sure how or where, but something to that effect happened. I was pretty drunk, so the specific details of that night are a bit fuzzy. I do remember we had a discussion about it the next day. We both apologized for being out of line. We knew it was wrong and we both felt bad. Unfortunately, this was not the end of our relationship. It was just the beginning. It wasn't long after that night when Josh left town again, that Shelby and I had sex. I don't remember how, or the details of the first time it happened, because I always had to get myself drunk enough to make that kind of terrible decision. Not that she was bad, but what I was doing was so messed up that I had to drink to talk myself into it. It was the only way to silence my conscience long enough to do what I knew was wrong. Well, that led to an affair for the next few months. Late night rendezvous. We would get together behind everyone's back when Josh was home or out of town. My wife and I were dating on and off at the time, and the worst part was that Shelby was in the same circle of friends as my now wife. I was really asking for it with this one. This was a ticking time bomb ready to blow up in my face. And it was. And it did.

After sneaking around for months, our secret finally got out. Kaboom. Before the full weight of my poor choices could explode, I quickly found an apartment so I could move out. I pretty much figured I wouldn't be welcome to continue to live under the same roof with Josh anymore; and rightfully so. So I attempted to get ahead of the collateral damage before it got any worse. I lied to my other roommate as to why we were moving out and brought him with me. And just like that, I practically moved out of the house in the middle of the night. In our small circle of friends in Redding, California, it felt like the whole world knew. I would go out in public only when necessary with my head down. Not looking up at anyone. Hoping not to run into someone that I knew because if I did, they would most likely know what had happened. I mean, I worked at a church and local non-profit ministry, for God's sake. And here I am, the town whore sleeping with my roommate's girlfriend?!? What a scumbag. Some of you are thinking it, so I might as well say it. I remember interacting with people back then, and when I was talking to them I was wondering in the back of my mind if they knew about what I did or not. Major social anxiety. Fear. Shame. Guilt. You name it. My drinking really turned a corner at this point.

Like I said earlier, I used to drink socially with friends. We were all in our early 20's and it seemed harmless. Not anymore. Overwhelming sin and shame had entered my life. This was more than I could handle. I did not have the capacity to deal with the amount of shame and guilt that was crashing over me like waves in the Pacific Ocean. I reverted back to my old coping mechanisms because it is all I had known what to do when life became overwhelming. I drank to shut up the shame that was screaming in my head, "You are a piece of shit." I deserved to die. I drank to deal with the social anxiety that was overwhelming me at times. This is the same thing I did when I was 15. It was like cuddling up to an old, familiar friend. I was isolated and I just sank deeper into isolation. I went to my non-profit ministry job every morning hungover so bad I thought I would die. I would pray to God I could make it through the day, and as soon as I would get off work, I would buy a bottle of Bacardi Superior, crawl in my hole in my apartment and drink until I blacked out. Eat, drink, sleep, repeat. I didn't realize at the time, but I was very much a "functional alcoholic." At the time, all I knew was that I had a problem, but I did not stay sober long enough to identify what was really happening inside of me. This went on for years.

I would just like to say that my wife Morgan is a saint for not leaving me after all of these years. She eventually forgave me for sleeping with her friend, and it was obvious we were in love. I asked her to marry me on the beach in Cancun, Mexico. How could she say no to that? I was still a broken mess. Now that I was going to get married, I figured I better clean up my act. So I tried some shallow behavioral modification without ever submitting to any real process of transformation. I did what religion had always taught me to do. Clean the outside of the cup. Pick yourself up by your bootstraps and conquer your sin. Duh! Not a good idea for someone battling addiction. Actually, the worst thing you can do.

Go to war alone. Throw a shallow prayer at my brokenness instead

of dealing with my brokenness. Saying some shallow prayer or

jumping through religious hoops was much easier than dealing

with the actual shit that was going on inside of me. It's amazing to

see human beings sink deep into some sort of religion as a means

of staying in denial or escaping reality. True religion is meant to

draw us out of hiding and into real life transformation. But I have

found that many times we actually use religion to escape reality.

Escape our sin. Escape our shame. Escape our doubt. Escape our

brokenness. Some of us need to get in counseling and deal with the

deep brokenness that is causing our destructive behavior. But none

of us want to do it. I don't want to deal with my crap. I don't want

to face my junk. It's a whole lot easier to go to a church service

and pretend like everything is okay, which only sends me free-

falling into deeper denial, where I convince myself that "I'm

okay," "it's not that bad," "at least I'm not like so-and-so." I have

jumped through religious hoops like a circus animal to convince

myself that I am okay. I don't need help. I don't have to be

ruthlessly honest. I don't need to be in recovery. I don't need to

confess my sin. I don't need to make amends. I don't need to ask

for forgiveness. I'm good. The most dangerous place to be is

convinced that you are not sick. Jesus said, "I did not come for

those that think they are well, I came for the sick." This is the beginning of getting well. Admitting that I am sick and in need of a Healer.

This was killing me. I would stay sober here and there for a week or two; meanwhile, my poor wife had no idea how sick I was. I would be able to drink socially and pretend I was like everyone else. Everyone I knew drank, what's the big deal??? So when we were with friends, I could get drunk and it was "normal," yet I knew it wasn't the same for me. I could drink hard alcohol straight out of a bottle like it was water. Definitely not normal. A girl in high school taught me how to chug hard alcohol straight out of the bottle like it was no big deal. A dangerous skill I would use many times in my life. Like any addiction, my drinking progressively got worse as life continued.

As life went on, I got married, bought a house, had kids, but things became more difficult. All of those things are amazing, but it was like turning up the heat on a pressure cooker. Without a healthy release, it's going to explode. My wife was slowly starting to become aware that I had a serious problem. I knew it. But now I lived with someone else and she was beginning to see my toxic behavior. Now that we have a family, my drinking didn't just harm me. It harmed my wife and kids. Shoot. Thank God this story doesn't end with me killing someone driving drunk or something which could have easily happened. If not for the grace of God, there go I. No joke. I'm not special. I am lucky. I played Russian

Roulette one too many times, and it's a miracle I'm alive. It was in THIS wretchedness that I discovered my BELOVEDNESS! This was my unraveling. Unfortunately, my unraveling lasted for years. But I remember one thing consistently, throughout the entire journey. The absolute undying, never-ending, limitless, relentless love of God routinely showing up in my life. Just like He showed up at the park in Antioch, California, and revealed Himself to me, God would not stop there. He was relentless. No amount of alcohol I drank could keep Him from me.

Growing up, I heard over and over again that our "sin separates us from God." I don't believe this anymore. Why? Because that does not line up with my experience with God. It actually doesn't line up with scripture either, if you read it in context. Once we are "in Christ," there is nothing that can separate us from the love of God in Christ Jesus. Neither death, nor life, neither angels nor demons, neither our fears for today nor our worries about tomorrow--not even the powers of hell can separate us from God's love. Romans 8:35-39. Seems clear enough. I tried to drink God away. I drank to shut everyone and everything out of my life. He was the only thing I could not shut out. If my sin separates me from God, then "riddle me this."

One morning I woke up in a boozy fog. Incredibly sick and hungover, and probably still intoxicated from the night before, I tried to peel myself off of my mattress the next morning. No small task on this particular day. I practically drank myself to death the night before and was barely able to sit up in bed. I slowly and painfully sat up, trying to get my wits about me. But then something happened. Then HE happened. That same scandalous Savior showed up. I remember this like it was yesterday. I sat up, and instantly felt the comforting presence of God wash over me. I can't explain it. It wouldn't do justice to how powerful this was. As if something washed over my mind, and moved through my whole body. At once my mind became clear. Just like the experience I had in that park in Antioch, I knew exactly what was happening. No doubt. Here He was again. I remember resisting His presence at first. I objected. I was almost angry. "What the Hell are you doing here?!?" I'm not sure if I said this out loud or just shouted at Him in my spirit, but it felt like I audibly shouted at Him. His presence was too scandalous. The God of the universe showing up in my room where you could probably smell the booze on me from the night before. How could He co-exist with my disgusting sin? I thought He was a Holy God. Wasn't He dignified. Shame was the main reason I tried to push Him away. I felt too disgusting to be in His presence. Just like Adam and Even hid in the garden of Eden, we've been hiding ever since. My sin and drunkenness did NOT separate me from God. My sin and drunkenness lie to me and distort reality. My sin opens the door for shame to come in and lie to me about my true identity. They cannot CHANGE my identity.

The devil has no power over me. The only power he has is lies. Sin cracks the door open for the father of lies to come in. My sin does not separate me from the love of God. Nothing in the heavens or the earth could separate me from the love of God in Christ Jesus. I am IN Christ. My sin does not undo the cross. My sin does not go back in history and un-crucify Jesus. Jesus meant it when he said, "It is finished." There is nothing I could ever do to make God love me less OR more.

I couldn't wrap my mind around the reality that the God of the universe would show up while I am knee-deep in a pile of shit and shame. Try as I may, I could not convince Him to leave. He would not relent. He would not give up. He would not lose hope. His love never fails. As I felt the presence of God fill me from head to toe and flood my room with mercy, I began to hear Him speak. "Mercy triumphs over judgment. Love conquers all." He spoke directly to my heart and told me: "Jordan, I had to come and let you know THIS is how I love you! JUST LIKE THIS! Knee-deep in your sin and shame. I love you HERE and NOW. Not when you sober up. Not when you clean up your act. I don't love you because you love me. I love you when you hate me." When I couldn't scrape two pennies together of my own righteousness. Completely bankrupt. Broken. I had been stripped of all of my righteousness. There I was, completely exposed. Sick. Broken. Addicted. And there He was. He left His throne in Heaven to find me in my pile of shit to tell me that He loved me. Even in my pile of shit. Not because I deserve it. Not because I'm obedient. Not because I love him. The Bible says it plainly: "Yet when we were sinners Christ died for us." This is Bible trivia 101! How did I miss this simple yet liberating truth? How did I spend my whole life constructing a shallow facade of my own righteousness? This is not the gospel. That is the definition of self-righteousness. For those of us who are "in Christ," your sin does NOT separate you from God. That is a fear tactic that religion uses to control and manipulate people's behavior. We are all seeking Unconditional Love & Belonging, and his name is Jesus.

Ironically enough, religion is terrified of unconditional love. Religion fears the Good News, because if unconditional love is real, how are we supposed to manipulate people to behave the way we deem acceptable? There is no fear in love, but religion has used fear for thousands of years to get people to "fall in line." People will just throw caution to the wind and do whatever they want without fear of consequence. We can't allow this. It would be pure chaos. We can't allow this. I can tell you with confidence that unconditional love and belonging is not an excuse for me to keep on sinning, but it has become the very reason I wake up in the morning. I have encountered a love worth dying for. I used to try to stop drinking and try to be sober SO THAT God would love me. Now I choose to be sober NOT so that God will love me, but I am sober today BECAUSE God loves me! Seems like a subtle differentiation, but one leads to life and the other leads to death.

This is a theme in this book: "It was in my wretchedness I discovered my belovedness." This is not a fancy catchphrase. This is the reality of my story. He is much better than you think. I am SO grateful for the kindness of God. There is no amount of shame or self-hatred or fear that could change me. You couldn't beat me into submission. You couldn't threaten me with punishment enough to get me to change my behavior. Shame and self-hatred were THE reason I was trying to drink myself to death. More shame was not the answer. "His kindness leads us to repentance" -- Romans 2:4. Ain't that the truth. Unconditional love and belonging are healing my heart. He is picking up the pieces of my broken heart and loving me into wholeness. I have been in recovery for years now. Counseling, AA, Celebrate Recovery, my sponsors, accountability partners, and my family have loved me into recovery, and have truly saved my life. The unconditional love and belonging of God has wooed me out of denial and into the lifelong journey of healing.

I am a jumble of paradoxes. I am broken and I am whole. I am weak, but I am strong. I am wretched and I am beloved. I am wounded but I am healed. I am sick and I am getting well. Religion longs for control. We desperately want everything to be black and white. We want to box it up, package it, and control Him.

Unfortunately, this is not how God works. I embrace the mystery and wonder and reality that He is making ALL things new. Including me. He is restoring the whole earth. All of creation. I am "in process." I am being made whole. I wish God didn't work this way. I wish I could say some magic prayer and instantly be healed and no longer need God and others. But then I would probably just choose to live disconnected from God and others, and I think that is a pretty accurate description of hell. This is my story. As I type these words, for the first time in my life I feel no shame. Not that I don't feel bad for my mistakes and all the harm I have caused to others, but because I put no confidence in my works. I am embracing the fact that I am beautifully broken. I will celebrate my weakness, I will boast in my weakness so that the power of Christ may rest on me. I will sing of the goodness of God all the days of my life. This is my final arrow. My last breath. He is GOOD.

KICKED OUT OF CHURCH

Chapter 9

THE DAY I GOT KICKED OUT OF CHURCH

I was hoping I could leave this chapter out of the book. In fact, this is the chapter I wish I could leave out of my life. I never thought I would have the strength to write this down because of the shame attached to it. Thank God He has the power to heal my soul. Well, the title of this chapter pretty much says it all. Yes, that's right, I got kicked out of church. Actually, two churches, to be exact. It still makes my stomach turn as I type these words. The memory and pain of these experiences come rushing back like a flood in my soul. God, I just ask that You would grant me the grace to relive this experience for your glory, Amen.

I grew up going to church. It wasn't really something I chose to do; it was just the way things were. Growing up, our family just went to church every Sunday, and usually Wednesday as well. My parents are so wonderful and all they have ever wanted for my brothers and myself was nothing but the best and they knew that Jesus was the only thing in life that would fulfill us. I thank

God for my family and their love for God and me. That being said, going to church was just a part of life. However, intimacy with God was not something that had been developed in my life at this point. But, man, was I searching! Ever since I can remember, even as a young child, I have always been searching. It's as if my soul knew something was missing, and even though I didn't know how to communicate that and I had no idea what was missing, that feeling has always been with me. So, like any young kid, I looked for that missing part of my soul in all sorts of places. Acceptance, success, popularity, girls, competition, etc. When I was a teenager I went through a rebellious phase because I didn't know what else to do. I couldn't just accept "Christianity" as the missing part in my soul because that's what I was being told. I needed to find out for myself if that was true or not, I couldn't just accept it because I was being told to accept it. And I'm very glad that I didn't just adopt Christianity because my family thought I should. If I had done that, I would not have the relationship with God that I have now, which is more precious than life itself.

When I was a sophomore in high school, I experienced a few tragic deaths among my friends that became a huge wake-up call for me. In a very dramatic fashion I was confronted with that thing that was missing in my soul in circumstances where I could not ignore it any longer.

It all started years ago, when I was young, confused, and desperately searching. One day, my battered and fragile soul stumbled its way into a church, which will remain anonymous, in the east Bay Area in northern California, where I lived during my high school years. One day, my brothers and I went to a youth group at this church, and I remember right out of the gate this beautiful young girl approached me, which is a huge plus if you are looking to fill a youth group with troubled young teenage boys! This girl, who we will refer to as Mary, began to speak into my life. I don't remember much about what she actually said, because come on, I'm like 16 years old and a good-looking girl is talking to me! But I do remember her speaking passionately to me about God and how much I mattered to him. That was it. I was head over heels. I mean, not only was this girl good-looking, but there was something about her life and passion that I was drawn to beyond her looks. She was a couple years younger than I was, but that wasn't about to stop me.

I ended up having multiple encounters with God over the next year or so. I gave my life to God and was on the fast track to dedicating my life to serve God in whatever capacity He wanted. As my relationship and love for God grew, so did my relationship and love for Mary.

Mary had a VERY conservative Christian family. I believe her parents genuinely loved her and wanted the best for her, but holy cow, were they controlling. It felt like she was Rapunzel, locked away in a tower by her parents to protect her from the big bad world out there! Just to give you an example of how controlling this environment was, they told her that they wanted her first kiss to be on her wedding day at the altar! For real! Her family loved me at first. When we first met it seemed like they were encouraging us to be together. They were big into the idea of "courting" as opposed to "dating." Maybe because it sounded more holy to say you were courting someone instead of dating. We were not allowed to spend time alone together. The idea of courting is that we always spent time together in groups. It didn't matter to us. We could be in a room full of people and still feel like we were the only two people on the planet. So we were constantly getting our friends together so we could spend time with each other.

Simultaneously, I was becoming more and more involved in the church. I began to lead worship at our youth group and serve in various other ways. This was probably a good thing because I was so involved in our church that it kept me out of a lot of trouble as a high school kid. I was nearing my high school graduation with no real direction of what to do next. I knew that I wanted to give my whole life to God and serve him, and I was in love for the first time in my life, so I had no intention of leaving the area for college. With a genuine desire to serve God, I knew my only option was to become a pastor if I wanted to be fully committed to

Him (haha). The church that I was serving at had a ministry training school where you could get your education in Bible & Theology and get hands-on ministry training at the same time. This sounded like a perfect fit for me. I could get on the fast track to become a pastor, get training in ministry, and be as close to Mary as possible because she was currently attending the private Christian school at the same church. It was a perfect set-up. I would be attending a ministry training school at the same campus as Mary. It was perfect. I was addicted. I would get my fix multiple times throughout the day when I saw her. Life was great. I had just turned 18 and graduated high school, was young and in love, and was on a fast track to move my way up the ladder in ministry. Life was good, or so I thought.

One day, everything changed. Once you hear what happened next you might find it silly or insignificant. But a small, seemingly innocent kiss triggered a series of events that would alter the course of my life. That's right! Mary and I kissed! That sounds pretty anticlimactic now that I write it down, but allow me to elaborate. Some of you might be thinking, "Two teenagers who have been dating for almost two years kissed?" Big freaking deal, that's what teenagers do! Some of you are probably thinking, "You mean to tell me that you only kissed? Nothing more? Not even 2nd base? You deserve an award for sliding in at first base and not trying to steal 2nd and 3rd, or go for a home run!" Haha. I remember it like it was yesterday. We were in the living room at Mary's house and her parents were upstairs. And then it happened: a kiss. Everything was great, until I realized very quickly that when we kissed, her mother was outside spying on us through a window! She came running in the house as if she just caught us having sex! No joke. From that moment on, everything changed.

After being caught in the act, I was no longer allowed to see Mary. We were treated like two disgusting perverts that had just been caught doing something so heinous that we should feel nothing but shame and guilt for what we had done. Again, I want to reiterate that we had been dating for about two years at this point before we ever kissed. This sounds crazy as I write this, because if my teenage kids dated for two years before having a first kiss, they should get an award. That's virtually unheard of. Two teenagers with raging hormones head-over-heels for one another that have the discipline and integrity to try and have a godly relationship are made to feel like monsters because they kissed. This gets me fired up all over again, thinking back on how we were treated. Not only do I have empathy for myself, but I think back and have empathy for how Mary must have felt like a whore for how she was being treated by her parents and other Christian leaders in her life. At this point other pastors and leaders were informed of our sexual deviance. A great deal of guilt and shame followed. I was subtly, and not so subtly, warned to stay away from Mary. She was off-limits. I was directly and indirectly threatened. Despite the intense effort on the part of her family and others to keep us apart, it was all for naught. Nothing could keep us from seeing each other. I mean, come on, we went to school on the same campus five days a week. Walking by each other in the halls, seeing each other at youth group, and at every leadership meeting. So, naturally, since we were forbidden to see each other, it simply forced us to continue our relationship in secret. A little piece of advice for all parents: do not let your children think there is forbidden fruit, because inevitably they begin to obsess over it, and the forbidden fruit must be tasted! If we have learned anything from the Garden of Eden, it is this: if you tell us we can't have something, we won't be able to sleep until we have it! This happens with my toddlers! If they find out that I don't want them to have something, guess what? They will spend every waking moment trying to get the very thing I didn't want them to have. The trick is to not let your kids figure out the things we don't want them to have! Nevertheless, I digress.

Moral of the story: where there is a will, there is a way! We had secret text messages and phone calls. We would sneak around any chance we got! It almost created an added layer of thrill to the whole thing. Not only did we desperately want to see each other, now it was this thrill and danger of trying not to get caught. Like most things in life, we do things in the dark that we wouldn't necessarily do in the light. Meaning: it is never a good idea to live your life in the dark or in secret. That is a dangerous thing to do. So, our innocent kiss in the light became serious makeout sessions in the dark! Again, nothing too serious beyond that, but it definitely progressed from our innocent first kiss. Something I will take away from this experience is that I NEVER want to force my kids to feel like they have to live their life in the dark. I want them to feel loved and safe enough with me that they can come to me with whatever they are experiencing. That doesn't mean I will excuse their behavior if they are making very poor choices, or that they might not have consequences for their actions, but if my kids don't feel loved or safe with ME and I am their father, then who will they find to be vulnerable with? I would rather my kids be living in the light and honest with me even if they are struggling, rather than living in isolation and darkness. End of soapbox rant.

So, long story short, we got busted! I don't remember exactly how it all went down, but it blew up in our face. We were taking more and more risk of being caught, so it was just a matter of time. This is when the shit really hit the fan. Things escalated very quickly. In the blink of an eye, things went from "strong suggestions," to stay away from Mary, to legitimate threats if I did not stop seeing her. I was kicked out of the ministry school program. I was told by my youth pastors, mentors, and those I looked up to and trusted that not only was I kicked out of the program, but I was no longer welcome to attend church at all.

What? I was in shock. I was scared. I was confused. I was

embarrassed. Overnight I went from being loved by my church

community to being treated like a sexual predator. I was reminded

over and over that I was now "18 years of age" and Mary was a

minor, therefore, if I did not leave her alone there would be serious

consequences. I was crushed. I was told by pastors and leaders,

those who had been the only representation of God to me at such a

vulnerable stage in my life, to repent to the church board for my

sins and maybe I would be allowed to come back to church. Wow.

What kind of message does that send about who God is to a

vulnerable young man at the very beginning of his journey? God

must be ashamed of me as well. How could He not? I must be a

monster.

So, I limped into a church board meeting one night, broken

beyond repair. I remember there was a circle of men waiting for

me. You could hear a pin drop. Tension in the air so thick you

could cut it with a knife. You would think I was on trial for murder.

It was intense to say the least. I was terrified. Humiliated. All I

remember is sobbing uncontrollably. I was repeating over and over

again how sorry I was for what I had done. The shame and guilt

were like waves in an ocean swallowing me up. I think at the end

of that meeting, I was technically allowed to come back to church

on Sundays, but I'm not totally sure. I was in so much pain I couldn't see, think, or hear. I think they actually said they were going to talk about me when I left the room and decide what to do with me. You see, I forgot to mention that Mary's family was a part of the small group of families that had originally planted this church. They were one of the major financial contributors in the church. Her dad was on the church board and was one of the men in the circle that night as I groveled and begged to be allowed back in church. This was the first church I had ever been kicked out of, but little did I know it would not be the last.

This sent me into a downward spiral very quickly. Alienated from all of my friends, kicked out of church, no longer welcome at youth group which was my community, kicked out of the ministry school I was in, and left alone with nobody to turn to. My family knew about what had happened but didn't really know how to help, so they supported me the best they knew how. I immediately turned to old friends from high school and coworkers, and started to self-medicate with drugs and alcohol. I didn't know where else to turn, and the pain was too overwhelming for me to handle. I never did any hardcore drugs, but would drink and smoke pot at parties with my friends. This wasn't a gradual unraveling; this was an overnight drop off a cliff! Before I knew it, I was hanging with the wrong people, making terrible choices, partying, hooking up with other girls, etc. I was a very, very troubled young man. This was one of the darkest seasons of my life. One night, I was hanging out with a buddy of mine that I used to go to youth group with, and we were considering going to an event at a church in another town. This church was the same denomination as the church I had been kicked out of; they are all a part of the same network. The church was about 20 minutes away in the next town over. I remember thinking that night about how I knew I was making terrible choices and I didn't want to keep living this way. I began to feel a bit of a nudge to get out of the pit that I had found myself in, so I decided to take a step and go to this church event.

My friend and I decided to go to this church event instead of a party we were originally going to. We felt proud of the small step in the right direction we had taken, and headed up the hill on the freeway to church. This was a drama with music and theatrical components put on for the youth in the area. We walked into church; it was dark, lights flashing, loud music, and a huge crowd of young people. We were hanging out in the back of the room keeping to ourselves when we were approached by a tall man who was noticeably older than any of the young people there. I assumed this was an adult leader, or security of some kind. The man approached us and called me by name and proceeded to tell us that he thought it was best if we left. Turns out he was the youth pastor of the church and said that the event was only for youth; he knew I wasn't in high school anymore. I was incredibly embarrassed and sick to my stomach for being singled out in a crowd of people that large. We turned around and headed out the door. I think we were both in shock and didn't really know how to process what had just happened. I came to find out later that my old youth pastors and leaders had given this other youth pastor a heads-up about me in case I ever came around. As if I were a dangerous predator that they needed to beware of. So instead of taking a step out of the pit I found myself in, I got kicked out of another church, and I'm pretty sure we went to that party we originally planned on going to and got really drunk.

That was then, this is now. I needed to high-tail it out of town. The shame was too strong for me to bear. So I ran out of town for good, and I never came back. I moved to northern California to go to Bible College and get a fresh start. I cried a lot of tears during this season. I mean the weeping, ugly crying in the fetal position of my bedroom floor type of crying. This experience nearly broke me. But I found God in the midst of my scandalous circumstances. I hated every single person who was a part of this story that hurt me, including myself. My old youth pastors, mentors, friends, Mary, her parent's, church leaders, board members, and the list goes on and on. I can honestly say that I have forgiven every single person on that list. I only talked to Mary a handful of times after I moved. At first I was angry with her. But as I have walked through my own brokenness, my heart has softened towards her. I can only imagine how she must have felt through all of this. What she has struggled with, and how she may have wrestled with God over the same things that I have. We have moved on. Both of us married with families of our own. This is a chapter in the scandalous love story of my life that God has been writing since I was in my mother's womb. It is good. He is Good.

I'm reminded of a quote from Brennan Manning in The Ragamuffin Gospel where Brennan says, "Something is fundamentally wrong when the church rejects those who are embraced by Jesus." I couldn't agree more. As a young person who was vulnerable and just beginning my journey to follow Jesus, that experience crushed my spirit. These events wounded me in such a deep way that I still find slivers of shrapnel deep in my heart that I am still digging out to this day! My perception of God was shaped by these toxic experiences. My opinion of what God thought about me was perverted by the way I saw people respond to me. I projected other people's behaviors and thoughts about me onto God. It is very true that the world will know God by how we love one another. And my perception of who God was and what He was like was shaped around the behavior of those who claimed to represent Him. They were not forgiving, so my god was not forgiving. They were not merciful, so God must not be merciful. They treated me like I was a piece of garbage, so I assumed God must think of me that way. I know that seems silly to say now, but when you grew up in a very religious environment where God's affection towards me, or lack thereof, was totally dependent on how well I behaved, it opens you up for subtle lies to creep into your heart about the character and nature of God. That's the only power the enemy has. Deception. This is his only tool in his tool belt. His only power is to distort the truth. He cannot change God, but if he can distort my perception of who God is to the extent that I walk away from God, then he has won the battle.

It has taken me a long, long time to heal from these wounds. It has taken even longer for God to show me who He really is, and what He really thinks about me. I lived under the bondage of depression and self-hatred for a very long time. I believe one of the reasons I went through this experience was so that I would never become someone who slams the door to the kingdom in the face of those who Jesus gave everything for. I was probably on the fast track to becoming those very people who wounded me so deeply. I can also honestly say that I might not have written this book had I not gone through this particular experience. I am not grateful for what happened to me. The Bible does not say to be thankful for all things; it says to be grateful IN all things (1 Thessalonians 5:18). There is a very big difference between being grateful FOR something and being grateful IN something. I am grateful IN this chapter of my life where resentment and unforgiveness used to dwell. I am more compassionate and gentle towards others because I walked through this season. Thank you God for every chapter in my life. Help me to not shape who You are around my experiences, but give me the strength to allow who You are to shape my experience. I will close this chapter of my life with another quote by Brennan Manning from The Ragamuffin Gospel:

"The story goes that a public sinner was excommunicated and forbidden entry to the church. He took his woes to God. 'They won't let me in, Lord, because I am a sinner.'

'What are you complaining about?' said God. 'They won't let Me in either.'"

SEX
OFFENDER

Chapter 10

SEX OFFENDER

Before I type a word, I would just like to open this chapter and speak to victims of sexual abuse. My heart grieves with you, and I believe God weeps with all who have suffered sexual abuse. The damage cannot be quantified for those who have been forced to endure such terrible things. Nothing I say or write is condoning the behavior of those who have abused others. People need to be held accountable for their poor choices, and from the depths of my heart I want to let you know how sorry I am for what you have suffered. It is not okay. I pray that God will comfort you and restore you in a miraculous way. There is nothing beyond redemption.

I'm about to get burned at the stake, or maybe crucified for this one. According to the words of Jesus written in the book of Matthew, every man and woman alive is a "sex offender" when compared to the standard and law of God. According to the standard set by God himself, "anyone who looks at another person with lust has committed adultery." There is not a man OR woman alive, or who has ever lived (besides Jesus) who has not looked at another human being with lust. Pretty much every single man and woman in scripture, by our laws and regulations today, would be locked up for the heinous sexual deeds they committed. Many of you reading this might be in the same boat. Many individuals born in the 70's or earlier were having consensual sex before the age of 18, which was completely normal back then. People used to get married much younger. I remember when I was in high school, people had sex with each other all the time. We were all minors at the time. Upperclassmen having sex with freshmen, or even those who recently graduated that were over 18, having sex with students still in high school who were technically underage. Nobody thought a crime had been committed or thought we should call the police. It was a different cultural climate back then. I'm not saying that behavior was acceptable; I'm just saying that if we were to take our current laws and regulations today and force them on other cultures or times in history, many of our parents would be locked up. Yet now we could classify some of those behaviors a crime.

Scripture is filled with polygamy, rape, incest, minors having sex, prostitution, sexual assault, sex trafficking, thousands of concubines (sex slaves), and the list goes on and on. And I'm not just talking about one-time mistakes, I'm talking about lifestyle choices that are offensive to the intent God had when He designed sex. The self-righteous Christian will ignorantly and blindly jump to the defense of our "holy book," afraid that any blemish might tarnish the "perfect" reputation of the Bible, as if our salvation depends on it. God doesn't require a perfect delivery system to deliver a perfect word. Quite the contrary. I have already heard the lazy arguments that people so casually throw at very difficult and complex issues found in scripture.

Hoping to dismiss the argument and sweep it under the rug, we defend King David and Solomon (our Christian "Avengers") for having hundreds of "concubines," many wives and lovers, and even someone else's wife to put a little icing on the cake. We jump to his defense and pull the "it was cultural back then" card. What a convenient argument! Cut and dry, case closed. We shut down the conversation because we are too uncomfortable to sit in the mud of scripture and ask the difficult questions. How would that shallow intellectual defense hold up today? No critical thinking or open-mindedness. We need easy answers. We can't wrap our minds around the truth that some of the biblical characters did things we cannot accept. We would be calling for their execution if they were alive today. We love the Bible, right? We love David; he is our hero. But seriously, there is no way we would allow him to be a pastor of a church today. Let's be real! We would want him rotting in prison for the rest of his life. Quit fooling yourself. We would lock him up and throw away the key. So how do we preserve the face of our dignified religion? How do we reconcile "David and

Goliath," with David the murdering pervert? We "polish the turd," so to speak. We try to diminish the fact that shit is shit. Don't over-spiritualize or "contextualize" poop. Poop smells. It's messy. No way around it.

Could you imagine if I made a case to conservative Christians, that people living in homosexual relationships today were somehow "okay" and they could still be "heroes" of our faith, even though they were choosing to live a lifestyle that we would consider sinful? It's cool because it's "culturally acceptable," right? Those same conservative Christians who are defending biblical characters with shallow contextualization would lose their mind if I tried to use that same logic and reason to a different context. Also, I would like to make it clear that I am not making a statement on what I believe about homosexuality. This is a very complex topic involving flesh and blood people I care about that are created in the image of God. I don't rush to make judgments about these things. I have not formed my opinions in stone, I am still learning, growing, and listening to others on the topic of homosexuality. I am definitely not an expert in this category. And I am perfectly okay living in the tension of not fully understanding everything. I don't think this is a simple cut and dry conversation. I am merely pointing out the contradiction within many conservative evangelicals when it comes to how easily they dismiss sin in the Bible in order to preserve the face of their religion.

How about a leader of the Christian community having sex with another man's wife, impregnating her, and then killing her husband to cover up his sin? Or just simply a young Christian couple living together before marriage? Or polygamy? Let me get this straight: as long as these sins or lifestyle choices are "culturally acceptable," we can completely disregard them? I laugh at such a notion. Yet, all of these behaviors I pointed out ARE culturally acceptable, and we attack these "sinful" behaviors with such hatred and vitriol that the people behind these behaviors become a casualty of our "holy" war. We claim to only "hate the sin and not the sinner," but it sure sounds like you hate people. You attack people. You slander people. You shame people. You curse people. "If you say that you love God and you hate your brother you are a liar," 1 John 4:20. That's a quote from your Holy Book. No need to speak Greek or Hebrew to understand that. Plain English will suffice.

I am well aware that what I am going to address next is extremely controversial; however, I must be obedient to the things God has communicated to me. So here goes nothing. For those of you who don't know me, I have been a part of a non-profit organization called Living Hope Compassion Ministries that serves the poor and disenfranchised in Redding, California. I have been connected to this beautiful organization since January 2008, and it has changed my life forever. Our ministry started a culinary arts vocational rehabilitation program called The Shack. Our mission was to employ, equip, and empower the poor in our city with dignity and accountability. The program was designed to help provide employment opportunities and training to those living in poverty, to help give them a job and the skills to become self-sufficient. It was a beautiful experience.

When we first started the program, we were considering hiring our first employees. I had gotten to know a great guy that I thought would be a perfect fit to work with us at The Shack. He was hardworking, loved God, was incredibly motivated, and wanted to grow. I started sharing with a friend about the person I felt would be a great fit as one of our first employees at The Shack. When I brought up this person's name, my friend began to share some very valid concerns. My friend told me he had heard from valid sources that this person was a registered sex offender. He started asking me a lot of very tough questions I wasn't prepared to answer. These were valid concerns I hadn't spent any time thinking about before.

He asked me: "What if the press finds out?" and "Do we really want the first person to work at the Shack to be a sex offender?" and "Do we really want this person to be the face of the Shack?" My friend was coming from a very good place and simply exploring a different perspective to make sure we were making wise decisions. It is critical to have friends like this who will challenge your choices and give you perspective, to ensure you evaluate your decisions, both personally and professionally. As he was speaking, I remember running those questions through my mind and agreeing with him. These were all very logical concerns. As I processed this information with my human mind, I began to disqualify this person based on what he had done. I remember as I entertained this train of thought in my mind, I felt the Holy Spirit come over me, halting the thoughts going through my mind. I heard the Spirit of God speak to me and say, "If you are going to disqualify this man based on his mistakes and his past, then you have no place being where you are and you need to disqualify yourself as well." This was a major reality slap from the Holy Spirit.

We are not qualified based on how well we have "performed" for God. We are qualified solely on what Jesus has done for us, period! So my response was YES! Yes I want this person to be the face of the Shack! Yes, I want to lift him up and sing songs of mercy together! Yes, I want the first person we hire at the Shack to be a testament of the scandalous mercy and unconditional love of God! I say that we, the church, start lifting up those who have been redeemed for the whole world to see how GOOD GOD IS! Instead of holding down those whom Jesus is lifting up, I say that we partner with God in his scandalous acts of forgiveness and mercy. Instead of padlocking our kingdom for only the dignified, I say we return to the kingdom of God that Jesus came to establish and begin to open up the floodgates to the broken, oppressed, sinners, tax collectors, prostitutes, strippers, drug dealers, murderers, adulterers, and yes, even the redeemed Pharisees! It's as if we are the bouncers in Heaven and we think it is our civil duty to keep out the very people Jesus died to save. Do you want to know why Jesus showed so much righteous anger towards the Pharisees? Not because of their pride or arrogance. Jesus could not sit by idly and watch them shut the doors to the kingdom in the faces of those He came to welcome in! He loves us so much that He has a righteous anger towards those who run around in the name of God and slam the door shut on the Kingdom that He died to establish.

If the Gospel does not offend you, then I think you might have the wrong idea about what exactly the "Good News" is. If you think everyone gets what they deserve, that is not good news…for ANYONE! If God only loves good little boys and girls, we are all screwed. He took upon Himself what I deserve, so that I could receive what He deserves. This is offensive by nature. It offends our sensibilities, our sense of justice, and the older brother in the story of the prodigal son inside of us that thinks we deserve something different than our brother, because of what WE have done. The prodigal son AND the older brother receive the same reward. This makes no sense, this is not fair, where is the justice?

If you are an older brother, this reality of grace probably pisses you off. If that same Father walked down death row in a prison and uttered the words, "All that I have is yours" to an inmate, what kind of feeling would that evoke deep in your bones? If this reality evokes any feeling other than unspeakable joy, then maybe you believe in a different Gospel.

I am intentionally leading us to a very uncomfortable place. I have taken us on a journey to find the limits of our mercy. I am intentionally poking at them. Not to piss you off, but to expose something very simple, yet profound. Just because we have limits to OUR mercy doesn't mean God has limits to HIS mercy. Just because we created conditions to OUR love, does not mean Jesus has conditions to HIS love. Just because we might not have grace for someone does not mean He does not have grace for them. I would challenge you to search your leather-bound Bible for a sin that Jesus cannot forgive. Name one thing that the blood of Jesus can't cover. Interestingly enough, the only things that come up in the Bible that we see Jesus speaking about with harsh language are unforgiveness, not loving our neighbor, and stifling the Holy Spirit. That's it. So apparently, Jesus takes very seriously the things we don't take seriously, and the things we assume send people to hell, you can't find Jesus condemning people for. Seriously. It's crazy. Let's try a little experiment. I want you to write down the top "sins" you think are the most egregious to the less serious sins.

Rank them from top to bottom. One being the most terrible sin you can commit, and ten being the less horrible sin. This is fascinating. I'm guessing your list would look something like:

1. Murder
2. Rape
3. Adultery
4. Stealing
5. Lying
6. Greed
7. Anger

So, here is my list. You won't even find unforgiveness on my top ten. Yet Jesus said the most outlandish statement about unforgiveness. Jesus said in Matthew 6:15, "But if you do not forgive others their sins, your Father will not forgive your sins." What?!? The only thing Jesus said with his own mouth that he will not forgive you for! Not murder. Not rape. Not adultery. Not having sex before you're 18. Nope. Unforgiveness. Unforgiveness? Jesus, you have got to be kidding me. We don't even take unforgiveness seriously, yet Jesus clearly takes it VERY seriously. We feel so comfortable in our bitterness and resentment. We feel justified in our unforgiveness. Yet Jesus lays the smack down on our unforgiveness when He tells us that He can't forgive us unless we forgive others. Dang.

One of the only stories in all of Scripture in which Jesus speaks about hell is in Luke 16:19-31. Jesus tells a story of a wealthy religious man who walks by someone in need on his way to church everyday and never stops to care for or help the man he passed by. In this story, the well-to-do religious man ends up in hell. Meanwhile, the poor, broken man named Lazarus, he walked by everyday was in heaven. Absolutely crazy. We do this all day, everyday. We pass by people in need constantly. Not a thought or care about those suffering all around us. Yet THIS is the example we are given of why someone ends up in hell?!? Wouldn't you assume Jesus tells a story about a serial killer being in hell? Or a rapist? Definitely sex offenders. They are most certainly in hell. That supports our values. We would understand that, Jesus! Nope. Rejecting the second greatest commandment is apparently serious business. Love your neighbor. Apparently Jesus was not messing around when He said this was the second most important commandment. He doubled down on that statement right here.

Jesus told us that the world would know what He looked liked based on the way that we love one another. Well, let's just say we haven't done the best job showing the world what the unconditional love of God looks like. We have created so many conditions to God's love that we have people thinking they need to die on a cross for their own sins in order for God to love and accept them. Our mercy is very limited. Some more than others.

What is truly fascinating to me is that I have found many times (not always) religious people have more conditions to love, and a shorter leash of grace than those who do not claim to be religious at all. That makes no sense to me. We should be the most gracious, compassionate, and kind people on the planet! We have been forgiven! Even Jesus said "those who have been forgiven much, love much." Man! Shouldn't that be our mantra as followers of Jesus? How are people who don't even follow Jesus a better reflection to the world of the love of God than those who claim to know God? I don't understand how this is possible. This is a complete contradiction. As I said earlier, in 1 John 4:20, "If someone says they love God but hates his brother, he is a liar." The two cannot coexist. God is love. You cannot condone bitterness, resentment, unforgiveness, judgement, and condemnation. There is no excuse. No sin that someone could commit would justify our unforgiveness and hatred. Jesus said to love our enemies. Pretty clear. Bless those who curse us, pray for those who persecute us, and turn the other cheek.

Based on the standard set by God, I am a sex offender. So are you. We are all a bunch of perverts. As I quoted earlier in Matthew 5:27, "Anyone who looks at a woman lustfully has already committed adultery with her in his heart." Brutal. If you are a human being, good luck with that. There is not a person alive or who has ever lived who has been able to accomplish this except

Jesus. He did for me what I could never do for myself. He was blameless so that I would not have to be. Unless you plan to gouge your eyes out, you have no hope of living up to this expectation, and to be quite honest, even if you were to gouge your eyes out, you would probably have to gouge out your brain as well. Our sick, twisted minds are born corrupt. It is impossible to live a lifetime without a single lustful thought. The Bible doesn't say we won't have lustful or impure thoughts, it tells us to be transformed by the renewing of our mind and to take those thoughts captive. If impure thoughts didn't exist, then why would God instruct us to take those thoughts captive? That is part of being an imperfect human being. Welcome to the club, I am the president.

The main purpose of this chapter is to make one simple statement. Nothing, and no one, is beyond redemption. No one. Nothing. Period. End of story. In the words of Jesus, "It is finished." This is the most taboo sin that we won't say out loud, but we are all thinking to ourselves, "those people are going to rot in hell." These thoughts are exposing our true belief systems. What do we really believe? You can preach a sermon all you want about how forgiving God is, but this is where we find out what we truly believe. Is the love of God truly unconditional? Is He really powerful enough to redeem "those people?" Was the cross enough? Is the love of God really powerful enough to cover "this?" We have found the limits of OUR mercy. We have discovered the limits of OUR grace. You are probably squirming as you read this. I'll confess, this was intentional. Don't blame me. I didn't want to write this chapter. This was uncomfortable for me. This was His idea. I fought Him. The thing about God is that He always wins in the end. So here it is. A love that has conquered sin and death. A love that has no limits. No bounds. No conditions. No prejudice. There is nothing beyond redemption. There is no one that His love cannot heal. A love that welcomes in sex offenders and preachers. Prostitutes and drug addicts. Alcoholics and sex addicts. Prideful religious leaders and orphans. Greedy and generous. Rich and poor. Murderers and liars. Refugees and Republicans. Workaholics and egomaniacs. Women and men. Black and white. We are ALL under the blood of Jesus. Now you can see clearly why we murdered Jesus. Not everyone loves THIS kingdom. If you want to know what God is up to on the earth, here you go. Open the floodgates and welcome "them" in. Just like He opened up the floodgates and welcomed YOU in.

THE BRIDE AND THE WHORE

Chapter 11

THE BRIDE & THE WHORE

Once there was a young couple named Hosea and Gomer. Hosea was madly in love with Gomer. He would give anything for her. He was head over heels. Gomer was more beautiful than she realized. She had body dysmorphia. For those of you who don't know what this is, it is when a person does not see their own reflection clearly. Self-hatred and shame consumed Gomer so deeply that whenever she looked at herself in the mirror, she was disgusted. Even though she was stunning, she was incapable of seeing her own beauty. She literally distorted reality in such a significant way that she saw herself as overweight even though she was thin. She hated the way she looked. She hated her figure and wished she had the figure of every other woman she saw. She hated her features. She hated her complexion. Hosea however, loved everything about Gomer. He loved her just the way she was. He wouldn't have changed a single thing about Gomer. Nothing about her appearance. Not her personality. Not her funny quirks. Nothing. She was perfect in HIS sight.

As a young girl, Gomer was sexually abused. This wrecked her at such a vulnerable stage in life. Before she was able to create a positive self-image and become secure in her own skin she felt robbed. Robbed of her innocence. Robbed of her childhood. Robbed of her purity. Used and abused. She felt an overwhelming feeling of shame and guilt for what happened. Even though she was a victim and in no way responsible for what happened, she could not help but blame herself for what had happened. As if she did something wrong. She felt disgusting. She felt gross. She couldn't stand to look at herself in a mirror. Her confidence was crushed. Devastated. She felt dirty. Lies crept into her mind. It's her fault. She asked for it. She deserved what happened to her. She was unredeemable. Damaged goods. Nobody was going to ever want to be with her now. Not if they really knew what had happened to her. She was a whore. Nothing more. She would never become anything more than this. She could not escape the lies that kept getting louder in her mind.

Gomer's self-hatred ran deep. It moved way beyond physical appearance. She was so consumed with shame and guilt for mistakes she had made that she could not seem to forgive herself and love herself. So there was no way she was going to accept the love and affection of another person. She was incapable of receiving love. This broke Hosea's heart. He saw her and he knew her completely. He knew Gomer better than Gomer knew herself. He knew her deepest thoughts and fears and insecurities. Yet he still chose her. Gomer hated herself so much that she lashed out with destructive behavior. She sabotaged situations because she felt unworthy of love. She believed that she was a piece of shit, so she acted out and treated herself like she was a piece of shit. She slept around to find some sort of self worth. If she felt that someone wanted or desired her even for a moment, it would temporarily quench her thirst to be loved and cared for. She started using drugs to silence the voice in her mind that kept getting louder, telling her she was worthless. The voice was telling her that she was a slut and didn't deserve to live.

In spite of all of her brokenness, Hosea proposed to Gomer. He knew everyone she had been sleeping around with. He knew that she was sexually abused. He knew she was a drug addict. He knew that she hated herself. There was nothing that was hidden from him. Yet his love for Gomer was relentless. He would not give up on the apple of his eye. He knew everything she had done, everything she was doing, and everything she was going to do in the future, yet he still pursued her. He continued to woo her. To lavish love and kindness on her. So Hosea asks Gomer to be his bride. Gomer resists. No way. "Not me," she thought. "Marriage isn't for me," she told herself. Again, sabotaging the situation because she felt unworthy of love. Hosea would not give up. He was persistent. He was relentless. She told him there was no way that he could actually love her. He reassured her that he would give anything for her. He had already given everything for her. There was nothing she could ever do to change the love that he has for her. He loves her exactly as she is, not as she should be. Gomer finally conceded. She gave in. She caved in and finally agreed to marry Hosea. He was over the moon for this woman. He was filled with elation and joy that she would finally reciprocate the love that he had for her. This was just the beginning.

Not long after the wedding, reality sank in. She was still broken. She still resisted love. She was still overcome with self-hatred and shame. Just because she was married didn't mean she was transformed. Not long after they married, she was back to her old destructive ways. Punishing herself. It didn't take long before she began to sleep around again. Her drug addiction mellowed out during the honeymoon phase, but that didn't last more than a few months. Pretty soon she was "using" regularly again. Sex, drugs, and rock and roll. She showed little to no interest in Hosea at all, yet he had not changed one bit. His love for her had not changed one bit. His love was constant. Dependable. Unconditional. Steady. Patient. Kind. His love kept no record of wrongs. His love always protects, always trusts, never loses hope. His love never failed.

Gomer became so sick that she hardly ever made it home. On a good month she would come home once a week for an hour on Sundays. Most of the time, she was out binge-drinking, getting high, barely remembering who she ended up sleeping with the night before. Even when she came home, it was as if she weren't even there. She paid no attention to Hosea. She usually ignored him completely. She didn't hate him, but she was so ashamed of herself that she couldn't even make eye contact with him. She was now CONVINCED there was no possible way Hosea could actually love her and forgive her if he really knew everything she had been up to. Little did she know, not only did he know exactly what she had been up to, he still loved her to death.

Hosea was a faithful provider. He worked hard to provide for her, even when she was running to the arms of other men. Just because she was running around cheating on him wasn't going to keep him from remaining faithful to her and the promises he made. His love was not dependent on her behavior. It was much greater. He didn't chase her down when she was out on a bender and drag her back home. But he was ALWAYS at home waiting for her, hoping she would realize how much he loved her. If she could just know and trust that Hosea loved her as she was and not as she should be, it would change everything. His love wasn't forceful, abusive, or manipulative. He simply remained constant in his love for her. Whenever she came home on a Sunday morning to take a hot shower and grab some clean clothes, he would plead with her to stay a while. He would remind her of how much he loved her. Most of the time she would shut out his voice. Again, her self-hatred was so deep she could not receive love. She had to love herself in order to receive his love and affirmation. Most of the time, when he tried to affirm her and remind her that he loved her, she was glued to her cell phone. She was on social media posting provocative pictures of herself and planning her next rendezvous. This broke Hosea's heart but never made him angry. It grieved his heart to see the one he loved suffering so deeply. He desperately wishes he could fix her, but love doesn't force itself on anyone. Still, Hosea would not lose hope. He would not give up on Gomer. He would lay down his own life for her.

Hosea would leave little signs for Gomer everywhere as a reminder of his everlasting love. He would leave love notes in her car telling her how beautiful she was. Every sunset would be a reminder of Hosea's faithfulness. He would leave gifts and surprises for her constantly. Texting her poems and songs randomly even when she was on a bender. Voicemails professing his love and affection for her. Gomer would usually ignore the messages, not even giving Hosea the courtesy of a response. Gomer would wake up to flowers, and go to bed listening to the sound of his voice singing over her. Washing her mind with kindness and unconditional love.

One day, Gomer came home and Hosea thought to himself, "Could this be the moment?" Maybe she finally came to her senses. Maybe, just maybe, she was tired of punishing herself. Has she hit rock bottom? Was she ready to come home for good? He was so excited at the possibility of reconciliation. Gomer walked through the door with her head down and asked Hosea if he had a minute to talk. Hosea excitedly agreed and quickly replied, "Of course!" Gomer asked him to sit. She sat down on the couch across from Hosea. She pulled out a piece of paper that was folded in her coat pocket. Hosea's eyes lit up! What could this be?!? Was this the moment he had been waiting for? Was this a love not from Gomer professing her love for him? After all of the years he had been so faithful to her, was she finally going to reciprocate the love and affection he had consistently demonstrated to her? He was so eager for her to pour out her heart. As she unfolded the note, he snuck a peek at it. It looked like a list. What could be on this list? Could it be a list of all the things she was grateful for? Perhaps it was a list of all of the things she loved about Hosea? He was eagerly anticipating what she was about to share with him. Gomer sat up straight and cleared her throat as she began to read:

"Hosea, I have come to realize that I feel unhappy. I find myself feeling empty and unsatisfied. I see a lot of people who have much more than I do and seem to be much happier than I am. I have come up with a list of things that I think will help me to be more satisfied and fulfilled in life. If you could just provide me with better things, I think I would be much happier.

1. Nicer car - 2020 Range Rover

2. Bigger house - Larger home on the other side of town, with updated kitchen

3. Plastic surgery - Boob job, tummy tuck, and face-lift

4. Vacation house - Cabin in South Lake Tahoe

5. More money

6. Better job - more fulfilling job that pays better

7. Better physical health

8. Open relationship - I would like to see other people. The affection of other men will help boost my self-confidence

9. Boat for the summer - Nice ski boat to take to the lake in the summer

10. More followers on social media who love me. I would like to be an influencer. People who are interested in my life and follow me.

11. Hosea to improve his physical appearance.

This list is just the beginning of things I trust will bring me more fulfillment and satisfaction in life. There are more things that would make me happy, but this list is a good starting place. If you are not able to provide me with the things that I need, I will probably have to explore finding another spouse that can make me happy. If you are not able to provide the items on the list within the next couple weeks, I will pursue another spouse who will better serve me."

Hosea's jaw nearly hit the floor. After everything he'd done for her. After years of enduring her cheating on him, the drugs, the neglect and all of her brokenness, she didn't say a single "thank you." She didn't reciprocate any of the love and affection he constantly showered her with, and the only time she ever wanted to talk to him was to ask what he can give to her. No acknowledgment of all he has done for her. She just asked him for more. Gomer didn't actually want to spend time with Hosea. She simply wanted what Hosea could get for her. She didn't show an ounce of gratitude. No remorse. No love. No affection. Not a single word of something she is thankful for. He had been so faithful to her, in spite of her unfaithfulness. He was a faithful provider. Every good and perfect gift she had came from him. He had shown her nothing but grace and kindness, even when he knew she had just cheated on him. Hosea knew that she had just been in the arms of another man. Even when she was overcome with addiction, sin, and shame.

I could only imagine putting myself in Hosea's shoes. I would be furious. How dare she! Hosea wasn't angry. As Gomer began to read her list, tears began to run down his face. He knew the full extent of Gomer's torment and the depths of her pain. Hosea knew there wasn't a single thing on Gomer's list that would ever satisfy her. In fact, quite the opposite. He knew most of the things she was asking for would only bring her more pain. More depression. More anxiety. More emptiness. He knew the only place she would ever find peace was in Him. His everlasting love was the only thing that would ever satisfy her soul. He was filled with compassion for her. His heart was breaking for her because he knew her heart was broken. He wanted nothing more than for her to find joy and peace and love. Hosea knew that every drug she used was to silence the longing in her soul for unconditional love and belonging. Every man she slept with was a desperate attempt to feel loved. He knew that her soul was crushed. As much as Hosea loved Gomer, he knew that if he gave her everything she requested of him, it would probably kill her. The most loving thing he could do was not grant her request. She had no idea what she really needed. Her request could not mend her broken heart. It could not bring her inner peace. It could not satisfy the longing in her soul for unconditional love and belonging. With tears in his eyes, Hosea had to tell Gomer he wouldn't be able to grant her requests. Gomer became furious and lashed out. Like a toddler throwing a fit when they don't get their way, she quickly became hostile and abusive. She called Hosea every name in the book. She told Hosea that he was being selfish and only cared about himself. If he really loved her he would give her what she wanted. Gomer began to scream at the top of her lungs. She stood up and yelled

"You are a shitty husband! You have never made me happy. Everything that has gone wrong in my life is your fault! You are a selfish asshole! If you really loved me, you would care about making me happy! You have the ability to give me what I want, and you choose not to! How could you do this to me? You call yourself 'good,' that is a load of shit. You aren't good. If you are so good, you wouldn't let bad things happen to me! I'm leaving you and I'm never coming back. Fuck you!" Gomer spit in his face, stormed out of the house, and slammed the door behind her.

Hosea was devastated. Not because of what she said, but because he could see beneath her rage. He could see past the anger and see her pain. He saw the root of the pain. He saw deep into her soul. He saw that little girl that was abused, lost, hurting, afraid, and broken. Hurt people, hurt people. It broke Hosea's heart to see her pain. Hosea fell to his knees and began to weep. Hosea wept. He wept for his wife. He wept for the one he gave it all for. He was moved with compassion for his bride. He cried out to his Father in heaven. His soul was crushed to the point of death. He began to weep tears of blood. He cried out to God for his wife. He pleaded with God. He interceded on her behalf. He asked God to intervene with radical love and kindness. He prayed that God would use him to put His love on display. He asked that God would use him to show Gomer how much he loved her. Scandalous mercy. Unconditional love and belonging. Radical forgiveness and restoration. Pick up the pieces of her broken heart. Hosea was resolute on one thing. He was going to win Gomer back. His love would conquer all. Love wins. Mercy triumphs over judgement. His everlasting kindness would radically change Gomer's life. He would never give up. Never lose hope. Never fail. He kept no record of her wrongs. His love was patient. It was constant. He would love his bride into wholeness. It was finished.

Meanwhile, Gomer was in a tailspin. Her addiction and her poor choices had escalated quickly. Addiction progressively gets worse unless it is getting better. There is no neutral. Gomer went from cheating on Hosea occasionally, to sleeping with anyone who would show her some attention and help feed her addiction and poor choices. She routinely drove under the influence. She was a freight train going 100 mph off the tracks. She was literally playing Russian Roulette with her life. Her shame and self-hatred were securely in the driver's seat of the freight train. She was going to die. Or worse, she would take someone else's life.

One night, as if the universe was in mourning, it seemed exceptionally darker than usual. After Gomer had been drinking she hopped in her car to meet up at her next rendezvous. Little did she know this night would change her life forever. It started pouring down rain. The night sky was so dark, and the rain was so heavy, her windshield wipers couldn't keep up with the deluge. She could barely see. It didn't help that she drank a fifth of vodka before getting behind the wheel. As Gomer sped through a residential neighborhood, squinting just to see in front of her, a young woman was crossing the street in a crosswalk. By the time Gomer saw her, it was too late. Her reflexes were too slow. Between the vodka and low visibility, she was a couple seconds too late hitting her brakes. Her car slid on the slick, wet road and plowed into the young woman in the crosswalk.

Gomer was in shock, too scared to exit the car. She couldn't face what she had done. By this time she was shrieking and sobbing uncontrollably, at a loss for what to do. She was terrified. She froze. Her life was over. There was no way the woman in the crosswalk could have survived. Gomer knew her poor choices had caught up to her. She was likely going to spend the rest of her life in jail. She couldn't wiggle her way out of this one. Gomer had an alarming amount of heroin and alcohol in her system. No judge or jury would let her off easy for this. This was no manslaughter case. This was no accident. She was a loaded gun and pulled the trigger, and the bullet just happened to hit someone this time. Gomer had been a loose cannon for years at this point. She knew she would be convicted of murder for what had just transpired. Still frozen. Her mind began to race. What was she supposed to do? The only person who came to mind was Hosea. She grabbed her cell phone and called him. Hosea quickly answered her call. He always answered when she called.

Hosea answered, and could hear the terror in her voice. He knew exactly what had happened. He didn't jump in and immediately interject his opinion or advice, he simply listened to her cry. Gomer was frantic, crying and trying to speak at the same time. Hosea's voice was calm and reassuring. He knew it wouldn't help the situation by getting worked up as well, so he tried to calm Gomer down. "Take a deep breath," he said. "Count to 10, breathe, count backwards down from 10, and tell me what is happening." Even though he already knew what had happened, he wanted to give her a chance to tell him in her own words. He knew how important it was for her to speak the words. There is something about uttering the words ourselves that forces us to acknowledge reality. Gomer couldn't escape this. She had to face what she had done. Slowly, she uttered the words between deep breaths. She told Hosea she had been using drugs and drinking, and after choosing to drive, she hit a woman crossing the street. As she finished explaining what had happened, she felt as if she were going to die. She couldn't stop crying. Hosea told her to stay exactly where she was, and he was on his way. "Everything is going to be okay," he assured Gomer. Hosea hung up the phone and raced to meet Gomer.

It was still pouring down rain when Hosea showed up at the scene of the accident. The atmosphere felt as if heaven was grieving. The rain felt holy. As if God himself was mourning the loss of a loved one. Hosea showed up resolute. Unwavering. He was a man on a mission. He got out of his car and walked over to help Gomer. She was hunched over the steering wheel, her face in her hands, sobbing uncontrollably, Hosea helped lure her out of the vehicle. In a calm, reassuring voice, he told her it was going to be okay. When he finally got Gomer out of the car, Hosea wrapped his loving arms around her. He wept with her, as she let out an ocean of tears. It was as if a dam had broken inside of her, and a flood of emotions came spilling out that she could not control. This was the accumulation of a lifetime of pain. Hosea held her tightly and whispered repeatedly, "There is nothing you could ever do that would make me love you less." At first, Gomer fought his words. She could not accept what Hosea was saying to her. He kept repeating the same thing over and over like a mantra. Soon his words began to wash over her like rain, soaking her from head to toe with words of love and affirmation. In a moment, her mind became clear, as if she hadn't used any drugs or alcohol. After what felt like an eternity, Hosea said it was time to go. Hosea handed her the keys and pointed to his car, where his friend Sam was waiting. Where did he come from? He appeared like an angel out of thin air. He told Gomer that Sam was going to drive her home.

"What do you mean, Hosea? I can't just leave the scene of a crime, that will only make matters worse," she replied.

Hosea responded, "I will stay and take care of everything. I already called 911." Gomer was incredibly confused. She didn't understand what was happening.

"Hosea," she pleaded, "I am going to rot in jail for the rest of my life! My life is over!" she exclaimed. "I know I am going to die for this. I deserve to die for what I have done. This innocent woman is dead because of me! I know I will get the death penalty for this. No one will take it easy on me when they find out how much drugs and alcohol are in my system. I don't deserve to live. Let me stay. I'm not going to run from this. I'm tired of running." Hosea said he understood, but he was going to stay.

"I would rather they take my life," Hosea said.

"No!" she shouted. "I can't let you! I don't deserve it! You have given me everything! You have been so faithful, so loving, and so forgiving. After all I have done, I do not deserve mercy. Let me die. I deserve death."

Hosea continued, "I know you don't deserve mercy based on what you have done. But I would rather die so that you can live. I don't love you because you deserve it. My love for you is unconditional. It always has been. I don't love you because of how faithful you have been. If you only knew and believed how much I love you it would change everything. I have always loved you, I love you now, and I will always love you. There is nothing you could ever do to change that. I would lay down my life for you. I will take upon myself what you deserve so that you can be free. If only you could see how beautiful you are in my sight. Go now, before the police get here!"

Gomer was in shock. She couldn't believe what was happening. It was too good to be true. How could anyone love like this? She had never known a love like this. She jumped in the car with Sam. As the car pulled away from the scene, Gomer looked back to see the police arriving and Hosea dropping to his knees, with his hands on his head. He surrendered. He was not taken, he freely gave himself up. Hosea was quickly taken to jail, and eventually sentenced to death for the murder of that young woman who lost her life that night. Six months later, Hosea was put to death by lethal injection. He freely gave his life for Gomer. No hesitation. No second thought. His instinct was love. He loved Gomer to death, and freely gave up his life so that she might live.

Gomer had a life-changing experience that night. She encountered a love better than life itself. It was too good to be true. HE was too good to be true! How could He be so good to her? She cheated on him more times than she could count, and yet all he had ever done was remain a faithful husband and provider. He never stopped pursuing her. He never gave up. Never lost hope. She deserved to die. He deserved to live. He was so good to her. Unconditional love changed her life forever that night. She had never known a love like this, and it was this love that brought her back to life. She started to believe her life mattered. One scandalous act of mercy wrecked her in the best way possible. Inexplicable grace was not an excuse for her to continue down such a destructive path, it became the very reason she wanted to get well. His love gave her a reason to wake up in the morning, and do the hard work to find healing. Gomer started going to counseling, AA meetings, and Celebrate Recovery meetings on a regular basis. She finally started to see the sunrise after a lifetime of darkness. She found the strength to face her past. She stopped escaping the abuse she endured as a child and found the courage to forgive and accept forgiveness. But it all started with a spark. A spark that lit a fire in her heart. She felt dead inside before that night.

Unconditional love had ignited a flame in her heart that would grow the more she let love in. Opening up to let love in was like throwing gasoline on the flame that was ignited inside of her. She began to trust that God loved her, and she mattered. She was loved and forgiven. She was able to make amends with the family of the young woman who tragically had her life taken that night. Did it bring her back? No. But she was able to ask for forgiveness and make amends the best she could. She told them the truth. She told them that her husband gave his life for hers. He took the punishment she deserved. Forgiveness doesn't erase the past, it changes the future. Hosea was pleased. He was with his Father in

Heaven. No sadness. No regret. He would check in on Gomer from time to time. Watching her progress. It brought tears to his eyes to see her finally let love in. She had shut Him out for so long. But now, she was finally learning to love again. Open to love. Open to grace. Open to mercy. Open to forgiveness. Letting go of the past. Trusting in the future. Letting go of bitterness and resentment. Love had won. Not a cheap love. A love that stopped at nothing. A love that cost Him everything. He would do it all over again just for her. To see her come to life. It was worth it all.

God the Father looked over at his Son and said, "Ya' done good Son," with a grin on his face.

The Son replied, "WE did good, Dad."

"You're right Son, WE did good." The Father whispered as he wrapped His arm around His Son.

You are the bride. You are Gomer. I am Gomer. We are Gomer. We are ALL Gomer. Don't take this personally. You are a whore. "Wait a second," you must be thinking to yourself. "Who the hell do you think you are calling me a whore?!?" You don't know me! I know exactly who you are. In order to fully grasp the goodness of God, we must fully absorb the weight of our own treachery. Otherwise, all you are left with is a kiddy pool of grace when there is an endless ocean of God's love which knows no bounds and has no end. Somewhere, hidden deep in your consciousness of the depths of your betrayal, you will find the priceless jewel of unfailing love. But you must let go of your need to be presentable. You are a whore. In the same breath, you are a whore that is deeply loved by God. This is where religion has gone astray. Organized religion is predicated on control. Many times this manifests itself in extreme black and white thinking. "Either/or theology," as I call it. We have to clearly define and control everything. Doctrine. Heaven. Hell. And Even God himself. Well, good luck with that. Trying to clearly define and control an infinite God seems pretty stupid and illogical to me. Religion goes through extreme pendulum swings. From one extreme to the other. It's either "this" or "that." God is "this" or "that". This is either a "sin" or it's not. Blah blah blah. True religion embraces profound mystery and wonder. Many times there is no black and white response. It's usually not an "either/or" scenario. It is usually a "both/AND" situation. We are neither holy OR wretched. We are both holy AND wretched. We are broken AND whole. We are righteous AND have a sinful nature. We are sick AND healed. God seems to live in divine tension. Hiding in plain sight. Profound paradox. Mystery. We cannot fully grasp or understand just how wonderful He is.

Religious people cannot stand paradox and mystery because they don't have control. We are not in control of the mystery and wonder of God. We are not in the driver's seat when we acknowledge we do not have the answer. There is not always a simple answer. There isn't always a cookie cutter Bible verse we can throw at children getting cancer, or homelessness, or mental illness, or natural disasters, or suffering. We have to sit in the tension and stop trying to control what is happening. We don't control shit. That's the truth. You are not God. Let go. It's a lot easier to throw a shallow Bible verse or prayer at something instead of sitting with someone in the divine tension and pain they might be in. Stop trying to control everything. Don't fight your powerlessness, lean in to the Divine Mystery.

The truth is that you have run to the arms of anything and everything you could get your hands on to find fulfillment besides God. I know the truth hurts, but we need to face the truth. "For all have sinned and fallen short of the glory of God." The Bible says that God searched the whole world for a single person who was righteous and he could not find one, no, not even one. Not even YOU. The love story of scripture is not how beautiful the bride is. Nope. That is not how the story goes. The Gospel message is that humanity as a whole is so wicked that God came to earth, and we are so messed up, that we murdered God. You and I spit in his face. We mocked him. We betrayed him. We have all gone astray and became enemies of God. At the very moment where our sin and treachery reached its pinnacle, He poured out his life for us so that we might live. As Jesus was hanging on a cross being tortured, humiliated, mocked, spit on, pierced, and murdered by us, his last dying breath was: "forgive them Father, for they know not what they do." He took upon himself what we deserve so that we could take upon ourselves what He deserves. He didn't wait a couple hundred years to get over His bitterness and resentment. At the very moment of the greatest betrayal in history, He cried out for mercy.

This is not a love story of a good-looking bride. This story is, and has always been, a story about a God who would pursue His bride no matter the cost. No matter how far she runs from Him. He would stop at nothing to bring her back home. He withheld nothing from us. He poured out His own life so that we may live. He loved us to death. He is still loving me to death. He still pursues me no matter how far I run from Him. No matter how many times I forget Him, He has never forgotten me. This love is not an excuse to keep making poor choices. His love is better than life itself. It is a love worth dying for. It is the very reason I breathe. The reason my heart is beating. Every breath I take is mercy. Every beat of my heart is the lover of my soul choosing me. At any moment, if He were to stop choosing me, I would cease to exist. He is sustaining my life. No matter what I do, His love never fails. Stop fighting your identity. Don't resist the role you play in the greatest love story ever told. You are a whore. You are a whore that is deeply loved by the creator of the heavens and the earth.

I will end with this. Hug the cactus. Allow me to explain. Robert Downey Jr. was accepting an award for best actor in a motion picture and told a profound story as he accepted this prestigious award. He had a long standing and very public battle with drug addiction and spoke of his experiences, what he had learned during that time, and what changed his life. He almost lost everything, including his life. He went on to say that in the pit of his addiction, Mel Gibson reached out to him. Mel Gibson had some struggles of his own and gave him some profound life advice. Robert Downey Jr. said his life was spiraling out of control, losing everything, and he couldn't seem to find a way out. He said Mel Gibson taught him how to love himself. Self-hatred and shame were consuming him. Mel Gibson urged him not to give up hope, and find his faith, which must be rooted in forgiveness. He told him he needed to embrace those parts of himself that were "ugly." He called it "hugging the cactus." Mel encouraged Robert that if he "hugged the cactus long enough, he would become a man of some humility and it would change his life forever." Hugging the cactus looks like embracing our identity as a whore. A whore who has prostituted ourselves to anything and everything but God at times to find fulfillment. Not trusting Him to be good enough to fill our souls, we have turned to money, sex, power, possessions, religion, control, drugs, alcohol, codependency, relationships, porn, cars, houses, social media, fame, fortune, patriotism, nationalism, and our own worship of self. Forgive us God. Forgive me. It is when I sink deep into the reality of my brokenness that I discover my belovedness. You must have total depravity in order to have real mercy. Otherwise, we just have God affirming our awesomeness. Embrace the reality that you, like everyone else, have gone astray, yet He will never give up on you. Nothing could keep Him from bringing you home. You are not the hero in this story. Allow yourself to be rescued. As you face your own shadow self, may you come to know just how wide, how long, how deep, the love of God is for you, which surpasses all human understanding. His love is not meant to contain, but to get lost in. May you find yourself lost in the wonder of His goodness.

FILTHY
RAGS

Chapter 12

FILTHY RAGS

We are experts at "cleaning the outside of the cup," as Jesus would call it. I am much less spiritual than Jesus, so I just call it "polishing the turd." Here I am writing a book for grown-ups, using potty talk. Sheesh. But seriously, we consistently try to polish the turds in our life. Instead of actually removing the turd, we just try to polish it and pretend it doesn't stink. 1 John 1:8 says that if we claim we have no sin, we are deceiving ourselves. When we are in denial with shit all over our shoes, we might be fooling ourselves, but everyone around us smells it. You might fool some who don't know you very well, but those who actually know you a bit deeper can smell it a mile away. Sorry to be the one to break it to you, but your shit does, in fact, stink. It smells pretty bad. Join the club! But here is the good news; we all have shit on our shoes and it all stinks! Everyone! Even your pastor. You are in good company.

Jesus did not die for you to remain the same creation. We are not supposed to remain the same creation and simply try to clean up our behavior. The purpose of the cross was not to make me a more moral person. Jesus died so I could have a brand new life. More specifically, He died so that I might experience resurrection life. He died so that I could die with Him, be resurrected with Him, and experience life as a brand new creation in Christ Jesus. We have traded transformation for manipulation. Instead of allowing Jesus to transform the core of who I am, we have settled for shallow behavior modification. It's not surprising because in order to experience resurrection life I need to die. God cannot resurrect someone who refuses to die. The Gospel is, and will always be, death and resurrection. We have been trying to find a way to skip over the cross to find resurrection. It doesn't work that way. Jesus did not pick up His cross so that I would never have to pick up mine. He called us to "pick up OUR cross and follow Him." The only way to become a new creation in Christ Jesus is through the Cross. True transformation is found in death and surrender. The Apostle Paul said he had to die daily. This is what we are declaring when we get baptized. We are dying, we no longer live, and we have been raised to new life in Christ. This isn't meant to be some sappy religious exercise. This is supposed to be an external demonstration of an internal reality that is happening inside of us. Yet many of us are fighting that grave. I mean seriously, who wants to die??? Nobody. Ever.

True transformation will cost you everything. Since nobody wants to die to find new life, we had to try and manufacture another way. There must be a different path. A shortcut, maybe. Can we take a detour around the cross? Maybe we can just skip over this whole death part and try to pretend like we are a new creation. Maybe if we act like a new creation, we will somehow morph into a new creation. Let me get this straight. Have you ever seen a cat bark? If the cat barked long enough, would it transform into a dog? Sounds pretty silly, huh? Jesus said it this way in Matthew 12:33, "Make a tree good and its fruit will be good, or make a tree bad and its fruit will be bad. You brood of vipers, how can you who are evil say anything good? For from the overflow of the heart the mouth speaks. A good man brings good things out of the good stored up in him, and an evil man brings evil things out of the evil stored up in him." Holy cow. Jesus just dropped the mic on our shallow behavior modification. We cannot make ourselves holy, no matter how hard we try. Jesus was rebuking religious leaders for trying to polish the turd. He was rebuking them for cleaning the outside of the cup. Jesus straight up tells them it is impossible for them to say ANYTHING good! What? They CAN'T produce good fruit. Impossible. No amount of polishing the turd will ever be enough. We cannot clean the outside of the cup good enough to ever make the inside of the cup clean. Jesus wants to come in and make the inside of the cup brand new, which will produce good fruit. Does an apple tree have to think or try really hard to produce apples? Of course not! It just produces apples because it is an apple tree. That's what it does. Sometimes we look as silly as a cat trying to bark our way into becoming a dog. Or we are an orange tree trying really hard to produce apples. Good luck with that. Even when you produce some sort of fruit that might resemble an apple, it will be rotten inside.

As I mentioned earlier, we are experts at "cleaning the outside of the cup." Clearly, Jesus wasn't a huge fan of behavior modification. Probably because Jesus knows us better than we know ourselves. We are a bunch of addicts with obsessive compulsive behaviors so we just trade one addiction or obsession for another. We are completely helpless to clean the inside of the cup. No matter how strong our willpower may be. "If righteousness could be gained through the law (behavior) then Christ died for nothing!" Galatians 2:21. Even if we try to do the right thing, many times we have the wrong motives. I'm unable to change my own heart, mind, desires, and thoughts. It is much more difficult to submit myself to God and allow Him to completely transform the very nature of who I am. Which is probably why most people hang out in the shallow end of the pool and simply try to manipulate people's behavior. The only problem is, no matter how many times you spit-shine the outside of the cup, it will never be enough. The Pharisees polished the outside of the cup better than anyone could imagine, and still Jesus looked them in the face and called them "brood of vipers, sons of hell, and whitewashed tombs." In Jesus' day that was hardcore profanity. How startling it would have been to overhear a respectable Jewish Rabbi speak to other Jewish leaders this way.

Let me share with you a fascinating part of Scripture that I have never heard spoken about. Circumcision. Snip snip. Sorry, I know this is getting a little weird, but stay with me. You've made it this far, don't quit reading now over a little foreskin. Circumcision was a commandment from God to the children of Israel. So why in the world would Paul insist to the church in Galatia if they "allowed themselves to be circumcised that they would be cutting themselves off from the grace of God" (Galatians 5:2-5)? Does this make sense? Is Paul undermining God? Historically, circumcision was a commandment from God to mark his children; a trademark of the people of God. So, why then would Paul instruct the Galatians not to do this?

Paul preached the radical Gospel of grace to the Gentiles in Galatia, and as a result, many encountered God. After Paul left Galatia, a group of pious religious Jews went behind Paul's back to undermine the Gospel of grace he had just preached. The Gentiles received salvation by grace through faith in what Jesus had just done for them, something they could never do for themselves. These Jews could not accept that God would just welcome in these second-class citizens. Nobody hates the Gospel more than religious people. They can't stand it. So, they decided to tell these Gentiles that if they wanted to be saved and accepted as children of God, they needed to get circumcised! What? These are grown freaking men. It's pretty gruesome to circumcise a baby, let alone a grown adult! That's insane. My wife was so traumatized when we had our son circumcised that she told me she would never do it again if we had another baby. I guess it's a good thing we were done having kids by that point.

God instructed the church in Galatia, through the Apostle Paul, not to be circumcised for one reason; because he knew they would be missing the whole point of the Gospel! He knew if they felt the need to be circumcised in order to be in right standing with God, then they did not understand what Jesus had just accomplished for them! If they allowed themselves to be circumcised then they would be putting their faith in what they were doing for God, not in what God did for THEM! This is the definition of "self-righteousness." Self-righteousness is when our security comes from what we bring to the table. What makes you feel "safe" or "right" with God? Is it your list of good deeds that you have compiled? Is it because you go to church every Sunday like a good Christian? Is it your 10% tithe? Is it because you don't drink, or cuss, or sleep around? Is it because you carry the title of "pastor"? Is it because you are in full-time ministry? Is it because you went to Bible College? Is it your infinite knowledge of the Bible? Is it YOUR love for God? Is it the fact that you were a virgin when you got married? You see, there is a reason God told us in Scripture that our "good deeds" are like filthy rags (Isaiah 64:6). Our "good deeds," which we cling to for dear life become our security blankets in our relationship with God. Our security blankets are actually suffocating the life out of us. We will never be free until we let go of all of our filthy rags and experience the scandalous grace of God, which has absolutely NOTHING to do with what we have done to deserve it.

The single greatest obstacle standing in our way of experiencing the goodness of God is our own perceived "goodness." A saint is not one who is good, but one who experiences the goodness of God! This sounds crazy, but only in my wretchedness will I discover my belovedness. Paul had harsh language for those who sought righteousness through "good Christian behavior." Paul told the Galatians that if they allowed themselves to be circumcised, they would be "cut off from grace, and they would be alienated from Christ." Wow. Sounds serious. Notice how he didn't say if they murdered someone they would be cut off from grace, or if they slept with their neighbors wife they would be cut off from grace. Nope. Paul reserved harsh language for those who jumped through a religious hoop, thinking somehow that if they were a "good obedient Christian," they would be "saved." This is the enemy of the Gospel. This is anti-christ. Putting your confidence in YOUR own righteousness rather than

His righteousness. Can you imagine if God told you to stop your "good Christian behavior"? Doesn't that sound crazy? What if Jesus told you to stop "going to church"? Wait a minute, put the pitchforks down. Hear me out. What if, deep in your soul, you are finding a false sense of security and identity in your relationship with God because of all of your "good behavior"? What if we have constructed our identity as a follower of Jesus based on our own self-righteousness? Is it possible? I would say it is much more than possible. I would say it is even "probable." I know I am not the only one to struggle with this. Search out your own heart. Be honest. Isn't there a little part of you deep inside that feels worthy because you go to church, tithe, or read your Bible? What if God wanted to blow up the shallow, self-righteous glass houses we are all hiding in with His grace. What if He wanted to open your eyes to see that your righteous deeds, which are security blankets that make you feel worthy of love, are actually filthy rags to Him? What if He wanted you to lay down all of your good deeds in order to discover His love for you, which has nothing to do with your good deeds?

Throughout my life, I have fallen into two different temptations, which are actually two sides to the same coin. I have either thought I was "following God pretty well" or "failing God miserably." On one side, when I thought I was doing all of the "right" things and avoiding all of the "bad" things, that became my security. I felt safe or secure in my relationship with God because of what I was doing for God. In other words, I felt safe because I wasn't drinking, smoking, cussing, or sleeping around. I also felt safe because I was reading the Bible, going to church, leading worship at youth group, going to Bible College, spending time in prayer, and "witnessing." This way of thinking is a trap many Christians have fallen into today. We have become enamored with what WE do for God, not the other way around. Scripture is very clear about this basic concept, but somewhere down the road we get sucked into a life of self-righteousness, and it will eventually choke the life out of us! Our relationship with God must NEVER begin with what WE have done for God, it must always begin with what God has done and is still doing for us! "This is love: not that we loved God, but that he loved us and sent his Son as an atoning sacrifice for our sins," 1 John 4:10. It doesn't get much clearer than this. We get so caught up and proud of all of the sacrifices we make for God and what we do for Him. Our pride gets carried away and we soak in the praises of others telling us how godly we are. Don't pretend you are above this; the moment you think that you are above falling into this temptation is the moment you should look in a mirror and realize this IS you.

The other side of this coin is when we experience failure and lose our sense of security or love we feel from God. I can't tell you how many times throughout my life I have ridden this roller coaster of "works" in my relationship with God. I can't tell you how many other people I have witnessed struggle with the exact same thing. When we fail, we feel so distant from God. We feel like God can't love us anymore and His affection for us has changed. Again, in this example, our relationship with God begins with what WE do for God, and in this case it leads us to shame and self-hatred. This causes us to distance ourselves from God. God does not distance himself from us. We hide from Him in shame and isolation. This goes all the way back to the Garden of Eden, when sin and brokenness first entered the world. In the beginning, Adam and Eve sinned, they hid from God, and we've been hiding ever since. Man, that sounds all too familiar for me. When our relationship with God begins with what WE have done for God rather than what He has done for us, we are left with one of two emotions: shame or pride. Both are poison. One is no better or worse than the other. Both are equally toxic poison in the well. No matter which side of the coin we are talking about, anytime our relationship with God begins with what WE do for God, we are set up for catastrophic failure. We will not experience the freedom found only in the love of God. The perfect love of God, which John says "drives out fear." I never experienced unconditional love until God peeled back the layers of my self-righteous "security blankets." I wrapped myself in my filthy rags and clung to them for dear life. They allowed me to feel safe for a time, but they were never enough. They felt comfortable and harmless at first, but soon I realized they began to suffocate me. Freedom is found in the Scandalous Love of God, and in this place alone will we be made whole. Lay down your filthy rags. It's terrifying, but trust me, they will end up choking the life out of you. This is the most terrifying and liberating thing you will ever do.

THE BONDAGE OF INNOCENSE

Chapter 13

THE BONDAGE OF INNOCENCE

"Until you see the cross as that which is done by you, you will never appreciate that it is done for you." - John Stott

I love this quote. I was talking to someone years ago about this idea of scandalous grace. In a conversation I brought up the fact how we all, meaning all of humanity, are so messed up that we murdered God. Wrap your mind around that. Crazy. The person's immediate response to this was; "I didn't murder God. I wasn't there." Geez. How desperately we attempt to dodge our identity as guilty. What he was really saying is, "I'm innocent. I would never do such a thing. I would have hung on a cross right next to Jesus and died for my own sins!" To say this is to avoid the very foundation of the Gospel message. How do we miss what is in plain sight? "For all have sinned and fallen short of the glory of God," Romans 3:23. We are all guilty. Just in case you still don't believe me, here is more evidence. "There is no one righteous, not even one. There is no one who understands; there is no one who seeks God. ALL have turned away; all alike have become useless.

There is NO ONE who does what is good, not even one," Romans 3:9-12. Seems pretty clear. Not one. NOT EVEN YOU!

We must not cling to an identity of innocence any longer. The path of innocence will suffocate you to death. The definition of hypocrite simply means to wear a mask. The mask that hypocrites tend to wear is a mask of self-righteousness and innocence. Righteousness simply means "right standing" with God. Our position with God has absolutely nothing to do with what we have done for God, but everything to do with what He has done for us. Now THIS is love: "Not that we love God, but that he first loved us." I think many of us forget this simple truth. We have been Christians for a very long time, been a part of Church leadership, maybe even have a formal Christian education and become enamored with the ways WE love God. We feel so devoted. So obedient. We volunteer at church and other ministries that love the poor. We feel pretty dang good about ourselves. We feel worthy of love. We feel entitled to HIS love. Our righteousness is filthy rags. The path of innocence will beat you to death with guilt and shame. Nothing you ever do will be good enough. You will never measure up to the standard which was set by God himself when he commanded us to "be Holy just as I am Holy." What? How in the world am I supposed to be Holy like He is Holy? "This is impossible," you might be thinking to yourself. You're right, it is impossible. The irony is that we are hiding behind a law which is testifying of our guilt; the law is shouting from the rooftops that we are condemned and worthy of death.

Some people have misunderstood the words of Jesus in Matthew 5:27 to be a challenge to strive for greater righteousness on our own. This is the passage where Jesus says to the religious elite if they have looked at a woman with lust they have already committed adultery. Jesus goes down the list of the Ten Commandments and raises the bar. "You've heard it said, 'thou shall not commit murder,' but I tell you that anyone who is angry with a brother or sister is guilty of murder. You've heard it said 'thou shall not commit adultery,' but I say anyone who looks at a woman lustfully has already committed adultery in his heart.'" It feels as if we just completed a marathon and Jesus was waiting at the finish line, daring us to keep going. The Pharisee in us wants to man up to this challenge and kick the law's ass! "I accept this challenge and will prove my strength!" Oh, what silly hypocrites we are! When I hear these words come from the mouth of Jesus, all I hear Him saying is "you are all guilty." Jesus' words were not meant to be a challenge to us; they were meant to expose us. The law was not meant to rescue us; it was meant to reveal us.

Jesus was addressing an audience whose perspective was through the law. This was the lens through which they saw the world around them. From their perspective, only some were guilty. The murders, adulterers, and thieves are guilty. Surely we are not like "them." This message is intended to set those who have committed adultery free, and those who have not physically committed adultery free, from the bondage of the law. This neutralizes the playing field between those who commit literal murder and those who harbor anger and bitterness in their hearts. They are both held hostage by the curse of the law. "How can this be?" you might ask. One is innocent and the other guilty. How can the one who is innocent be held hostage by a law they have not broken? Oh, how God longs to free us from the bondage of thinking we are innocent. How He longs for us to plunge into the depths of our wretchedness to discover our belovedness. To know we are all guilty, and all dearly loved! If we refuse to face our wretchedness, we are robbing the redemption story of its beauty, and we will never experience true joy. We need not toil any longer clinging to an identity of innocence. What a weary and vain pursuit, wearing a mask of innocence to conceal our true identity. This is not who we are, and this is not the condition in which Christ offered up His life for us. "Yet when we were sinners Christ died for us."-- Romans 5:8.

One of the common ways we continue to wear a mask of innocence is by measuring our brokenness against our neighbor. As we mentioned earlier, the religious elite differentiated themselves from "sinners." They used the law as a means of hiding their own brokenness. "Those people" are the guilty ones, and "we" are not like them. This is very subtle and very dangerous. The very fact that I can separate myself from those who I deem "guilty" affirms my false identity of "innocent." You do it all the time subconsciously. Don't believe me? We all do. Trust me. I have been the king of this kind of thinking. I justify my destructive behavior and sin by measuring it against someone else who I perceive to be worse off than I am, which diminishes the severity of my own brokenness and enables me to stay in denial of my own junk. It helps me to sleep at night knowing "at least I'm not as bad as my neighbor, because he is really messed up. I mean, he beats his wife. I just watch a little porn occasionally. I'm not that bad." See how I elevated myself? Notice how I subtly differentiate myself from my neighbor? I am now better than someone else. Different. Special. I am not like "him." My junk is now somehow not as bad. Jesus told a story in Luke 18:9-14 that paints this picture vividly:

> **"9** To some who were confident of their own righteousness and looked down on everyone else, Jesus told this parable: **10** Two men went up to the temple to pray, one a Pharisee and the other a tax collector. **11** The Pharisee stood by himself and prayed: 'God, I thank you that I am not like other people—robbers, evildoers, adulterers—or even like this tax collector. **12** I fast twice a week and give a tenth of all I get.'

13 "But the tax collector stood at a distance. He would not even look up to heaven, but beat his breast and said, 'God, have mercy on me, a sinner.'

14 "I tell you that this man, rather than the other, went home justified before God. For all those who exalt themselves will be humbled, and those who humble themselves will be exalted."

My mind exploded when I read this. First of all, the writer goes out of his way to point out the audience Jesus is speaking to. It says Jesus was speaking to "some who were confident of their own righteousness and looked down on everyone else." Jesus is laying the smack down on these guys. Jesus is laying the smack down on ME! He is calling us out! Jesus knows us better than we know ourselves. He sees our hearts. He knows our thoughts. He sees our motives. He sees you and He knows you completely. Nothing is hidden from Him. He knows our tendency to do this. The psychological gymnastics we perform to escape confronting the reality of our own brokenness. This story is mind-boggling. The Pharisee is so puffed up about himself and so arrogant, he actually prays, "Dear God thank you that I am not like 'that guy over there.'" Unbelievable. Who do you see yourself as in this story? Please don't tell yourself that you are the humble sinner in the back of the room. Kind of how we tell ourselves we are all the

Samaritan in the story of the Good Samaritan. None of us would have walked by a person in need, even though we all do it everyday. I know we always read the Bible and see ourselves as the hero, but humor me for a moment, and consider the possibility that you might not be the hero in this story.

This religious man is directly measuring himself against other people who he is desperately trying to disassociate himself from. He's not like "those people." He's not like the "other people —robbers, evildoers, adulterers—or even like this tax collector." No, those are the guilty people. He is innocent. Blameless. He even goes on to toot his own horn and brag: "I fast twice a week and give a tenth of all I get." This is fascinating. Don't skip over this. Sit with me for a moment here. Can you see how you do this? Can you see the Pharisee inside of you? I see him in ME. He is in us all. You see a homeless person shooting up heroin, and deep in your subconscious it helps you feel better about your own junk. Suddenly, your crap doesn't look so bad. I drink a little too much sometimes, but "thank God I'm not like 'that guy' over there." Sure I may have a porn issue, but at least I'm not like the guy at work who actually cheats on his wife. See what I'm doing? Just like the Pharisee. I may be super greedy with my money, but just like the Pharisee, we boast in our deeds. "But I give a tenth of all I get," we tell ourselves. And just like that, magically I am innocent and everyone else is guilty. "Those people" need to get their act together. Surely I am not like them. We don't say this audibly. We speak it to ourselves internally to justify our sin. God desperately wants to free this religious man from the bondage of his shallow facade of innocence. He desperately wants to set the Pharisee inside of you free as well.

> "If we claim to be without sin, we deceive ourselves and the truth is not in us. If we confess our sins, he is faithful and just and will forgive us our sins and purify us from all unrighteousness. If we claim we have not sinned, we make him out to be a liar and his word has no place in our lives."
> 1 John 1:8-10

You are a hypocrite. If that triggers you, it might be exposing how you are still resisting your identity as guilty. You might be in denial if you are still fighting the reality of the Pharisee living inside of each one of us. I am a hypocrite! I say it loud and proud. I am no longer manipulating the narrative of my life to make myself the hero in every situation. I am not the hero. This is who I am. I am not a sinner or a saint. I am a sinner and a saint. I am "both and" not "either/or." I am a jumble of paradoxes. I am both holy and helpless. Righteous and broken. Strong but weak. Blameless and filthy. Everyday I want to maintain the humble posture of the man in the story Jesus told who beat his chest and asked for His mercy that is new every morning. I want to be the one in the story who goes home justified before God. I don't want to be the self-righteous a-hole who looks down on everyone else to make myself feel better about my own junk. I've been that guy way too long.

It's time. It's been way too long. Take off the mask. Lay down the facade of innocence. You are not innocent. You are neither the victim or the hero. I know this is terrifying, but the miracle of the gospel is when you embrace your identity as guilty, He gives you a new identity. He declares you innocent. Wait, I thought the whole point of this chapter was laying down our identity of innocence? It is. YOU are not innocent. You are innocent because you have been rescued. You are not the hero. But there IS a Hero and His name is Jesus. He declares you innocent because of the blood of Jesus. Not because you go to the temple and pray like the Pharisee and give a tenth of all your money. No. Not YOUR righteousness. He gives you His righteousness. It is a gift so that no one can boast. He took upon Himself what we deserve so that we could take upon ourselves what He deserves. As we come out of denial and lay down our mask of self-righteousness, He gives us His identity.

> **"8** For it is by grace you have been saved, through faith— and this is not from yourselves, it is the gift of God— **9** not by works, so that no one can boast. **10** For we are God's handiwork, created in Christ Jesus to do good works, which God prepared in advance for us to do." -- Ephesians 2:8-9

This is the Gospel. This is Good News. You are guilty. Don't avoid it. Don't repress it. Don't deny it. Embrace it and you will hear Him declare "You are righteous." NOT BY WORKS! Not of yourself. It is a sheer gift. It is extravagant mercy. It is scandalous grace. It is the most scandalous love story ever told. We murdered God. We spit in God's face. We stripped Him naked and publicly mocked Him. We drove nails through His hands and drove a spear through His side. You did. I did. Humanity, which was created in the image of God, murdered the very One who created us. "Yet, when we were sinners Christ died for us." I AM guilty. But He has declared me "not guilty." Jesus has declared me to be holy, righteous, blameless, white as snow, chosen, called, and dearly loved. Thank you, Jesus, for doing for me what I could never do for myself. I am eternally grateful and offer my life as a response of gratitude for what You have done, and continue to do for me. This is a love worth dying for.

THE SCANDAL OF JESUS

THE SCANDAL OF JESUS

Jesus has become quite the confusing historical figure. People have done and said a lot of terrible stuff in the "name of Jesus" throughout history. This has not only given Jesus a bad rap but really confused people about who Jesus really was. I don't really get riled up when people are awful, but man, sometimes I really just want to go off on people that are awful "in the name of Jesus." Seriously, if you are going to be a dick, can you please just leave Jesus out of it, for God's sake?!? You do you. Go ahead and be awful, but please don't drag Jesus through the mud with you. Jesus said that the world would know Him by the way WE love one another. Well, let's just say that we have done a piss-poor job at showing the world what Jesus looks like. Some people have rejected Jesus because he is judgmental, petty, unforgiving, white, middle class Republican. Well, to those who have rejected THAT Jesus, so have I! I don't want anything to do with that Jesus, either.

And to others, Jesus is this passive, Norwegian softy carrying a baby lamb with him wherever he goes. He never offended anyone and just talked about rainbows and sunshine. I'm really baffled sometimes that we forget that we actually brutally murdered Jesus! You do realize that, right? Who Jesus was and the crazy stuff he said got him killed. Don't you think he stepped on a few toes on the way to the cross? Do you think he would have been crucified if he just walked around tickling everyone's ear? I don't think Jesus was crucified for telling people what they wanted to hear, or playing nice with everyone. No, he wouldn't have been killed for that. He pissed off a lot of really powerful people! We hated his sermons so much that we had to silence him for good.

The Gospel is a paradox. The Gospel literally means "good news," and it is really, really Good News. Don't get me wrong. But, at the same time it is really, really bad news. The Gospel is a death sentence to our ego and our flesh! Our ego and flesh squirm with every word Jesus speaks. Our flesh doesn't go down without a fight. Some of the things that Jesus said would send us into a literal rage against this truth. We fight the truth kicking and screaming.

Before He was even born, the scandal of Jesus began. His lineage. His family tree was pretty jacked up. It was scandalous. A prostitute in the lineage of God?!? What?!? How scandalous can you get? Was this an accident? Or is there a consistent thread underneath all of scripture that we have been missing? Let's take a glance at the beautiful family tree of God himself. Abraham had such little faith in God that he knocked up his servant to try and make the promises of God happen on his own. Jacob was a thief and a liar, Solomon was an idolater, and David was an adulterer and a murderer. Tamar was the daughter-in-law of Judah, who tricked him into sharing her bed as an act of revenge. Rahab was a prostitute who became famous for lying. Ruth was a foreigner from Moab whose entire race was a lasting reminder of the incest committed between Lot and his oldest daughter. Bath-Sheba was an adulteress whose husband was murdered at war while she was shacked up with another man. And you think your family is screwed up??? Get in line. Jesus could "one-up" whatever dysfunctional family you grew up with. Why in God's name would he allow his only Son to be born into such a dysfunctional family? Wouldn't God want to try and preserve a bit of his Divine dignity? Why would He allow, better yet, choose to be born of this lineage? We are missing it. We are missing the current underneath the story of God. It is found in Genesis all the way through Revelation, and we've missed the message that is leaping off of the pages of Scripture. He LOVES to redeem what seems to be lost. What the world deems ugly, broken, and discarded, He sees as an opportunity to put His goodness on display. Even family.

And then to top it off, the King of Kings, and Lord or Lords, the Messiah, the all powerful Omnipotent God, born in a stable for animals. How can this be? You do realize that God could have chosen for Jesus to have a triumphant entrance to the world and rode down from Heaven on a white horse or something right? Every move God makes is on purpose. He doesn't accidentally let things unfold that catch him off guard. Especially the birth of His one and only Son. Don't you think if He wanted a different entrance for Jesus He would have done so? But He CHOSE for Jesus to come to earth in humility. He could have chosen a palace for the birth of His Son. Even the palace would not have been worthy of the Son of God. Even a palace would have been God humbling Himself on earth. No throne on earth is worthy of Him. Just the fact that God chose to come to earth is the most scandalous act of humility in history. Yet He takes it a step further. Actually, He took it more than one step further. He takes it abundantly further. Just the mere fact that God would come to earth in a body is impossible to wrap my mind around. Yet, He chose the most humble of beginnings for even a human. Unbelievable. He comes to earth in an environment only suitable for animals. This is God. If that doesn't shatter your religious ideas of who God is, I don't know what will.

And his mother was "allegedly" a virgin. So right off the bat His family had a sex scandal. The whispers of who Mary hooked up with when Joseph wasn't looking. What's a good story without a juicy sex scandal, right? She couldn't really be a virgin. I can only imagine the conversations that were happening in their village behind their back. Let's be real, if someone in your circle of friends claimed to be pregnant with a child and still a virgin, I think we would be slightly "skeptical." That's not true. We wouldn't be skeptical. We would be trying to get this woman on antipsychotic medication and institutionalized for severe mental illness. Plus, we would be talking smack behind her back for sure. Christians are some of the best crap-talkers I've ever met. What in the world was God thinking when He dreamed up the birth of Jesus? What kind of story is God telling? What is He revealing about Himself in this story? Born in the wrong family, in the wrong place, at the wrong time. This is the story of Jesus. The birth story of God Himself. Messy. Scandalous. Divine.

Then we get to His FIRST miracle. Of all of the things He could have chosen to be the very first demonstration of His power to perform miracles. And He chose in John 2:1 to bring more booze to a party that had been going for days already at this point. Again, I would urge you to begin to recognize that all of these events are not random and accidental. I hope you begin to see what God is up to. Here we have Jesus, again in the wrong place, at the wrong time. I'm offended that my dignified God would even show up to such a party, let alone provide more wine to keep the party going! Some people literally cannot accept THIS Jesus as their savior. They have convinced themselves that the wine back then didn't really have alcohol in it because the thought of their Jesus doing this is too much to bear. This messes with their polished religion. So they smooth out the rough edges of Scripture that they are uncomfortable with and perform their own miracle and turn wine into holy grape juice! I guess they can sleep better at night knowing that their Jesus would never do such a thing! Now their gospel is suitable for children. Thanks to us, Jesus is now acceptable to our religious intellect. Jesus made a late night beer run when the party was fading. Is Jesus beginning to push your buttons? I mean, your "I'm offended" button? Are you having trouble wrapping your mind around this beautiful, offensive savior? This is not the Sunday school Jesus you learned about as a child.

Jesus had a reputation of hanging out with sinners, drunkards, prostitutes, tax collectors, etc. but He was God. This is hard for people to fathom. If you want to know what God looks like, look to Jesus. This bothers some people, but gives me great comfort as I begin to discover who Jesus actually was. He was so full of mercy. There was no barrier that could keep Him from those that were lost. Take the encounter with the woman at the well, for example. Jesus crossed every racial, geographical, ethnic, social, and gender barrier that existed in this day to encounter this woman. Jesus, being a Jewish man, should have never even been on that side of town to associate with gentiles, let alone a woman. This woman had such a scandalous reputation in her community that she would have to go to the well to get water later in the day when nobody was around to avoid ridicule. Most women would fetch water from the well in the early morning, but not this woman. Jesus lays His own reputation on the line to touch this woman. Make no mistake, this was a scandalous encounter. This would be like one of the most respected well-known pastors today going to Las Vegas and meeting with a prostitute at a whorehouse.

No respectable Jewish man would have a conversation with a woman like this, let alone a Samaritan. He goes to the wrong side of town, at the wrong time of day, speaking to someone of the wrong gender, and of all the women he could be caught speaking with, it's the town whore! What is Jesus thinking?!? This would have created quite the buzz in this town and I can only imagine the rumors that could have begun circulating about Jesus because of this. Again, Jesus was murdered. Let's just say the masses didn't love Jesus so much. You think people didn't talk crap about Jesus back in the day? Of course they did. And this is exactly why. I bet the whole town was spreading rumors about this Jewish Rabbi who was having "inappropriate relations" with the woman at the well. They definitely didn't like her, so I'm sure they would have no problem piling on and trashing both Jesus and this woman for this scandalous encounter.

Man, I love Jesus. Despite all of this, He would not let anything stop Him from showering this woman with mercy. He didn't let the fear of what others thought about Him keep Him from performing these scandalous acts of mercy. Even though He knew that this was the kind of stuff that was going to get Him killed, His love was relentless. Nothing could stop him from setting this woman free. What a powerful revelation about what God looks like. What a prophetic picture of the love of God. There is no scandal that could keep Him from you. He will lay His reputation on the line for you. He could care less what the rest of the world may think about you. He's not like us. He doesn't disassociate with those the rest of the world hides from. In fact, it appears that He is usually doing quite the opposite. You want to find God? Here is a little test. If you want to find Jesus, why don't you find the ones that the entire world is trying to disassociate themselves from and go spend some time with them; and I bet you just might find Jesus along the way. You might just run into this rebellious Jewish Rabbi in the most unexpected places. What is hilarious to me is that even though we have a written down record of who Jesus was, somehow we think that He completely changed over time. As if Jesus isn't the same yesterday, today, and forever. I think if Jesus were alive in flesh again today, walking among us, I think He might be doing and saying the exact same things He was doing and saying 2,000 years ago. Just in a different language.

How about when Jesus hung out with a wealthy scumbag? Zacchaeus was one of the most despised people in town. He was a Jew, but sold out his own people and collected taxes for Rome from his own oppressed people. Way to keep it classy, Zacchaeus. How low can you go? You can imagine why everyone hated this guy. He was the ultimate sellout. Not only was he not poor and suffering along with his other Jewish brothers and sisters, he was making his wealth from helping oppress his own people group! Dirtbag. One day, Jesus was making His way through Jericho and the crowds were so intense that Zacchaeus had to go and climb up a tree just to get a look at Jesus. In front of the multitudes that surrounded Jesus, He calls out to Zacchaeus by name. This is a profound interaction. The entire crowd surrounding Jesus would love to beat the piss out of Zacchaeus, and here Jesus is calling this man out of the crowd. He calls out to Zacchaeus in front of everyone "Quick, come down! For I MUST be a guest in your home today!" What?!? This was such a scandalous exchange. I am confident that Jesus had this interaction in public intentionally to make a statement. Bring me your despised. Bring me your outcast. Bring me the ones that you believe are "out." I need to let all of you know that the ones you think are "out" are actually "in" My Kingdom! The upside down, offensive, scandalous Kingdom of God. Most people don't like this kingdom.

When Jesus calls out to Zacchaeus, it says that he came down immediately with excitement and joy, but not everyone was excited about this exchange. You see, the kingdom of God brings unspeakable joy to some, but for others brings out uncontrollable rage. The crowds grumbled: "He has gone to be the guest of a notorious sinner." The multitude was not pleased. Man, I love Jesus. For Jesus to go to Zacchaeus's house to eat a meal is no insignificant act. For Jesus to do this, He is telling the world that Zacchaeus is "in." Not only that, but in front of the multitudes Jesus tells Zacchaeus: "Salvation has come to this home today, for this man has shown himself to be a son of Abraham. And I, the Son of Man, have come to seek and save those like him who are lost." Just pulls the ultimate mic drop that Zacchaeus is "in." In front of everyone, Jesus tells the crowd that Zacchaeus is a son of Abraham. That is the ultimate "in crowd" for Jews. To be a part of the lineage of Abraham is to be a part of the "in" family. Bring me your notorious sinners. Jesus has a bad habit of welcoming notorious sinners like me into His Kingdom. Not the respected. Not the popular. Not the honorable. The losers. The broken. The sick. The poor. The lame. The drunk. The homeless. The addict.

Jesus is saying the same thing to us today. Bring me your notorious outcasts. Bring me the town whore that you love to gossip about. Watch this. She is "in" and you are "out." Does that piss you off? Does the kingdom of God piss you off? It wouldn't be the first time Jesus pissed someone off. He pissed off so many powerful people they murdered him in the most horrific way possible. Apparently, the kingdom of God wasn't very seeker sensitive. It was pretty offensive to people. Otherwise, Jesus never would have been killed.

One of my favorite stories of Jesus is in Luke 7:36-50. Jesus was having a meal with a respected group of the religious elite. I think this meal was a set-up by Jesus. Again, I don't think Jesus gets caught off guard by events, I think He intentionally arranged for this event to unfold exactly how it did. He was setting up these Pharisees to get a taste of the scandalous Kingdom of God. Lo and behold a certain "sinful woman" heard about this little dinner party and just had to crash it! She brings one of her most valuable possessions and heads over to this house. She has a beautiful jar filled with expensive perfume, walks in this house unannounced, and kneels down beside Jesus, and begins wiping his feet with this expensive perfume. She begins to weep and continue to anoint and kiss his feet with this perfume and her tears and wipe them with her hair. This is beyond scandalous. This is borderline pornography at this point. This is completely inappropriate. I bet you could hear a pin drop in the room.

The Pharisee who was hosting this religious ego stroking dinner party couldn't believe what he was witnessing. The Bible says that he saw what was happening and said to himself, "This proves that Jesus is no prophet. If God had really sent him, he would know what kind of woman is touching him. She's a sinner!" Obviously, we have another example of a "notorious sinner." She didn't even need to introduce herself. As soon as she walked in the room, everyone knew exactly who she was. Her reputation was securely intact. She was such a "sinful" person that the entire town knew about it. It doesn't say in this particular text what exactly her sinful reputation was for, but you can let your imagination run wild.

Then Jesus does something pretty funny. He responds to the Pharisee's thoughts. That's gotta freak the guy out. Can you imagine thinking something to yourself and having someone respond to what you just thought in the privacy of your own head?!? That's crazy! Again, Jesus is awesome. Jesus doesn't stop the woman. He doesn't correct her for disrupting this prim and proper religious gathering. Not only is this inappropriate for a respectable woman to do what this woman is doing to Jesus, it's a notoriously sinful woman to top it all off. Here we have again Jesus throwing His reputation out the window for this woman. Allowing himself to be ridiculed and mocked in order to show mercy to a notoriously sinful woman. So powerful and so beautiful.

Jesus does not correct or rebuke the woman, but He does correct and rebuke the elite religious Pharisee. Again, Jesus flips the narrative and tells them that this notorious, sinful woman was "in" and they are "out." He doesn't rebuke her, He rebukes them. He tells them, "Look at this woman kneeling here. When I entered your home, you didn't offer me water to wash the dust from my feet, but she washed them with her tears, and wiped them with her hair. You didn't greet me with a kiss, but she has kissed my feet again and again from the time I first came in. You neglected the courtesy of olive oil to anoint my head, but she has anointed my feet with rare perfume. I tell you, her sins, and they are many, have been forgiven." She is right, YOU are wrong. She is IN, & YOU are out. The first are last and the last are first. The head of the table is the end of the table and the lowest seat at the table is the most honorable. Are you beginning to see a consistent pattern?

The cross. Does it get more scandalous than this? God chose to die. Jesus was not killed. He freely gave up His life. No heroic death on the battlefield. He chose to die a sinner's death. This was the most humiliating death imaginable. What the heck? My savior cannot be this weak! Peter could not bear this thought. He tried to lash out to protect Jesus and cut off a soldier's ear who came to arrest Jesus because this reality was too much to comprehend. His messiah could not be tortured to death in public. And what did Jesus do? Fight back? Call down fire from heaven to consume his enemies with fire? Nope. He healed the man who had His ear cut off. Could He still be the Messiah if this happened? This can't be. God himself surrendering His life to die a shameful death. He who had no sin became sin. God was stripped naked in public. God was mocked. We spit in God's face. We publicly tortured God to death. We drove nails in His hands. Blood gushing from His side as we drove a stake through His side. A crown of thorns served as a cherry on top of this great humiliation. Remember, we did not kill God. He freely gave himself up for us. He could have stopped us at any moment. God chose to die this excruciating death. He allowed it. He had gone mad with passion for you and me.

This is the most scandalous moment in history. The very ones He was dying for were the very ones driving the nails in his hands. The hands that were physically beating Him to death were the very hands that He was dying for. Every single one of the 39 lashings He endured just for you. Every insult that was spoken to Him on that bloody day He took upon Himself so that you might live. Every time He was spit on and mocked, He had you on His mind. He was bleeding for the ones who were spitting in his face. He was suffering for those who were laughing at Him as they put a crown of thorns on His head and mocked him as "The King of the Jews." Have you ever felt humiliated? Mocked? Abandoned? Alone? Suffering? Ridiculed? Hurting? You have no idea. Here is the God who is well-acquainted with suffering. He died for us. He suffers alongside us. He weeps with us, and over us. A man. A God. Who said His soul was crushed to the point of death as He shed tears of blood. For you. Only you. It was all for you. Even if you were the only one on the planet, He would endure it all over again just for you. That is what He would tell you.

The whole earth was silent as Jesus hung on the cross. Naked. Beaten. Bloody. Bruised. Whipped. Sweating. Shaking. Humiliated. Alone. All of history was hanging in the balance. As His friends looked on. Hoping before Jesus took His last breath that a white horse would come down from heaven and Jesus would transform into some kind of angelic figure that resembled Zeus or something, and He would crush His enemies. No. That is not how the story unfolds.

The birds stopped singing. Creation stood still. The earth was shaking. And with His dying breath, the Son of Man belts out one last cry. What would He say? What is going to happen? And with His last breath, He cries out from deep within his soul: "Forgive them Father, for they know not what they do." WHAT?!? Forgiveness! This is bullshit! How could you plead for forgiveness for the very people that are murdering you? Torturing you! Mocking you! Spitting on you! Cursing you! You could crush them with a single word. In the same way that you spoke us into existence, speak a word, and we would die. Utter the words and our lives would end. No. Not an eye for an eye. Mercy. Forgiveness. Unspeakable Grace. How can this be, that you would save a wretch like me. He didn't wait a couple hundred years to get over His resentment and forgive us. No. In the moment of the greatest betrayal in history, we see the most powerful act of mercy the world will ever know.

On the surface, this appears to be the weakest move in history. Little did we know that the greatest power is found in surrender. Little did we know that Jesus would submit to sin and death and defeat it from the inside out. He conquered death not by avoiding it, but taking hell's best shot and crushing it under his foot. That's all you got? Death could not hold Him. A tomb could not contain Him. Hell could not keep Him. I could not imagine a more violent scandal than this. Murdered by the very ones He loved. This is the scandal of Grace.

We can't forgive someone who cuts us off on the freeway. We can't let go of resentment for unwashed dishes! Let alone betrayal. Infidelity. Murder. Lies. Deceit. Stealing. That's a whole different ball game. Some of us will hold on to that bitterness till the day we die. We just can't let go. Could you imagine if someone killed your only child? This possibility is too much for us to wrap our minds around. Too scandalous for us to comprehend. I can't fathom enduring such a heinous betrayal and immediately, without hesitation, extending mercy and forgiveness. Yet this is the Gospel. This is the love story that is written about us all.

I am a grateful recipient of the Scandalous love of Jesus. I will never understand or comprehend why He continues to love me. Why He hasn't bailed on me. Why He forgives me over and over and over again. His love makes no sense. It is too wonderful for me to understand. Too great for me to wrap my mind around. My love is so limited and conditional that it is truly impossible to comprehend the reality of truly unconditional love. Seriously. No conditions. Nothing we could ever do. Do you get that? Murder. Rape. Incest. Adultery. Porn. Drugs. Alcohol. Meth. Heroin. Lies. Child abuse. Self-righteousness. Prostitution. Legalism. Idolatry. Materialism. Pride. Think of the most heinous act. Fill in the blank. HIS love is greater.

That really pisses off some people. That would explain why we killed Jesus. We could not accept unconditional love. We want certain people to "get what's coming to them." Don't we? We want everyone to get what they deserve…except us. When the reality we cannot escape is that we ALL deserve hell and death. That is not my opinion. That is what the Bible actually says. Everyone. No exceptions. Romans 3:10, "No one is good-not even one. No one has real understanding; no one is seeking God. All have turned away from God, all have gone wrong. No one does good, not even one." Romans 3:23, "For all have sinned and fallen short of the glory of God. Yet now God in His gracious kindness declares us not guilty!" The wages of sin is death. That is what I deserve. That is what you deserve, but HE, by His gracious kindness declares you NOT GUILTY! If this doesn't make you jump out of your chair and sing and dance, then I would venture to say that you do not know the Good News. And the Good News has a name. And His name is Jesus. I love Jesus. But Jesus first loved me. And His Love is so much greater. In the words of Saint Augustine, "Quia amasti me, fecisti me amabilem." This is Latin for "In loving me, you made me lovable." I am worthy because He says I am worthy. I am lovable because He loves me. This is the scandal of Jesus. Romans 5:6, "When we were utterly helpless, Christ came at just the right time and died for the ungodly. Now, no one is likely to die for a good person, though someone might be willing to die for a person who is especially good. But God demonstrated His great love for us by sending Christ to die for us while we were still sinners." My prayer for you is that you would sink deep into the scandalous love of God for you in Christ Jesus.

YOUR SCANDAL

Chapter 15

YOUR SCANDAL

So here it is. Your story. Your story is my story. My story is your story. Me casa es su casa. I am thou. You are unique, but you are not unique at the same time. What I mean by that is this. Because you are unique, your brokenness will flesh out a bit different than anyone else. However, we are all exactly the same, in that the root of all of humanity's brokenness is EXACTLY the same. At the root of our brokenness is a disconnect between humanity and God. In the beginning, God was in the garden with us and our relationship with him was perfect. Sin and shame had not entered the picture. We found our identity and value from the One who made us. We were whole. No insecurity. No hiding. No shame. No covering up. We were fully exposed before God and others and we felt no shame (Genesis 2:25). Our self-worth was wrapped up in God. We were completely secure in our identity as his children that were deeply loved. God walked among us in the Garden of Eden. In Genesis 3, sin and brokenness entered the world. The Scriptures say that our eyes were opened, we saw that we were fully exposed, and we were ashamed and hid from one another and God. In the beginning Adam and Eve hid, and we've been hiding ever since.

Sin created a disconnect between God and humanity. It clouded our vision. We could not see clearly our identity as sons and daughters of God that were deeply loved. We began to look at ourselves and feel shame and insecurity. The story of Scripture is a God who loved us relentlessly and rescued us in spite of our brokenness. He loved us to death. Literally. He died to restore this relationship.

Unfortunately, we are still broken. This is a paradox. We are both broken and whole. We are both healed and sick. It's not one or the other. It's "both and." People have waged theological warfare for centuries over this. Religion hates paradox. It hates mystery. We like black and white. We want to be in control and black and white answers allow us to feel a false sense of control. Our sickness manifests itself in a plethora of different ways, but it all boils down to this. Our identity, self-worth, and value are meant to come from God. That relationship is not perfect. HE is perfect. His love for us is perfect. But our own sin and brokenness distort our perspective of reality. His love and affection for us is not changing. Restoration and hope are always right in front of us, but sometimes our bad choices lead us to a place where we can't see truth when it's right in front of our face. Sin does not have the power to separate me from God. What it does is pervert my perspective of God and myself and lead me to a place where I might no longer believe that He loves me because of what I have said or done. This is simply not true. The enemy cannot change the cross, the only power he has are lies. There is a reason he is called the "father of lies." He cannot remove the power of the cross, but if he can get me to stop trusting and believing in what Jesus has done for me, he is accomplishing the same goal. I lock myself in hell. God doesn't put me in hell, I put myself there. I punish myself. He said Himself: "I did not come to condemn but to set you free." But I'm pretty dang good and condemning myself! When I get in that place, I am essentially saying that the cross was not enough for me. This is the scheme of the enemy.

I am left restless. My identity, self-worth, and value are not wrapped up in God 100% of the time. So I am left feeling bankrupt and unsettled at times. What is our natural response to this feeling of restlessness? I am convinced that we are all addicts. We are like addicts who desperately need a hit of something to curb the unsettledness deep in our soul. Temporary as it may be, we will take a hit of anything or anyone to make us feel an ounce of self-worth, even if for only a moment. This root disease is driving all of your thoughts and behaviors all day long, whether you are aware of it or not. Think of it this way. We are all infected with a disease. It is a sickness deep in our bones. No surgery could remove this sickness. This disease deep in our subconscious tells us we are not worthy, we are not good enough, we are not valuable, we are not loveable, we are not good, we are not beautiful enough, we are not successful enough, we are not obedient enough, we are not holy enough, and on and on. This mental illness has infected us all. Every single human ever born is infected with the exact same disease.

Here is my version of "attachment theory." We have a disease and it cannot survive without a host. Infections need a host to survive. We will attach to anything and everything that will give us a temporary sense of identity, self-worth, or value, or at least numb the craving. Our career, our house, our car, our spouse, our kids, our bank accounts, our anxiety medication, drugs, our religion, our political party, alcohol, sex, porn, self-righteousness, or fill in the blank with whatever you want. It genuinely doesn't matter. God does not differentiate between one drug and the other. WE do. We have a sickness, an infection, a disease that desperately needs a "host" to survive. Our sickness cannot survive without a host to carry the disease. It is not a matter of whether or not you are "attaching" to something or someone, it is simply a matter of "what" or "whom" you are attaching your self-worth and identity to. When we do not cling to Jesus for our self-worth, identity, and value, we are left shipwrecked. Every other "host" that you attach yourself to will leave you bankrupt. No spouse will ever be able to calm that obsessive unsettledness in your soul. No amount of children will be able to subside the craving deep in your bones for your life to matter. Desperate for your life to have significance and purpose. That you are worthy. That you are loved. No amount of money can cure your disease. Like any addiction, this disease is a progressive one. The insanity of this illness is the more we have of what we are longing for, the more we crave more of it. The more money we have, the more unsettled we feel and the more money we crave. The more success we have, the more we crave more success. The more sex we have, the more we need to quench our addictive thirst. I know this intimately. The more I drank in my life, the more I had to drink. Ask anyone who has been addicted to a physical substance and they will tell you that the more drugs or alcohol you consume, the more drugs and alcohol you will need to consume to get the temporary sensation of relief. Well, that is not unique to drugs and alcohol.

Some of you who are piss drunk with money and success need to hear this. It will never be enough. Some of you who are piss drunk on religion need to hear this. There is no amount of moral superiority that will ever be enough. In the words of the Apostle Paul in Galatians, "If righteousness could be gained through the law then Christ died for nothing!" YOUR righteousness is filthy rags. No amount of good deeds could ever accumulate to justify you before God. Some of you who are piss drunk on your image and physical appearance need to hear this. No matter how physically attractive you are, it will never give you the sense of self-worth or security that you are desperately longing for. No amount of plastic surgery will ever be enough. You will never have peace about what you see in the mirror until you hear the one who made you tell you "you are beautiful" and "I knit you together in your mother's womb and you are fearfully and wonderfully made." You cannot manipulate your appearance to find what you are looking for in Him. Some of you are piss drunk in your career and perceived success. No amount of power or control will ever be enough. No matter how large you feel your tiny kingdom is, it will never be enough. Your tiny kingdom will always be an anthill compared to the Kingdom of God. You will never build enough wealth to curb your obsession for more wealth. No amount of success can ease the craving in your spirit for more. Some of you who are piss drunk on social media need to hear this. No amount of Facebook "friends," "likes," or Instagram "followers" will ever be enough. You will always obsess for more, just like an addict. You know why? Because you are one. Sorry to be the bearer of bad news. Don't shoot the messenger. Although it wouldn't be the first time we murdered someone who delivered the Good News.

No matter your drug of choice, it will ALWAYS come up void. No other "host" that we attach ourselves to will ever give us life. They will always leave us shipwrecked and bankrupt. Jesus is the only voice that has the power and authority to calm that obsessive thing deep in our soul and give us peace. Just like the time Jesus commanded the storm to cease, He has the power to calm the raging seas inside our souls. He brings peace to the internal storms we all experience. He is the only "host" that, if we continue to attach ourselves to Him, day by day will quench our thirst. He can calm the obsessive and addictive behavior. He is the cure for our disease. This is exactly what Jesus told the woman at the well in the Gospel of John. In John 4:13-14, Jesus told this woman "Everyone who drinks 'this' water will be thirsty again, 14 but whoever drinks the water I give them will never thirst. Indeed, the water I give them will become in them a spring of water welling up to eternal life." Jesus is speaking directly to that sickness deep inside us all. He is calling us out. He is telling us a universal reality. Drink from "this" well and you will be thirsty again. Fill in the blank with whatever "well" you are drinking from. Success, money, fame, fortune, physical appearance, religion, ego, drugs, alcohol, or sex. Drink from "that well" and you will be thirsty again. This I promise you! You cannot escape this reality. I rarely speak to things that I refer to as universal realities, but this is one of them. Test me. Try it out and tell me if I'm wrong. Life has a way of teaching you things that are universally true. We like to think that we get to choose our "truth." Unfortunately, no matter what you think about the sky, it is blue and remains blue whether or not you believe it.

The first step in recovery is to admit you have a problem. I desperately want you to find healing. But if you don't first admit that you have a problem, you will never be healed. People who don't know they are sick don't go to a doctor. If you don't know you have cancer, you won't get chemo. I want to expose our disease. Call it what it is. Put it all out in the open. This is fertile soil to encounter God. Just like in recovery, you cannot totally help someone who is in denial. It is the only prerequisite to getting well.

Speak it out loud. I am sick. It's okay. We all are. You are not alone. We are all in the same boat, whether we like it or not. This really pisses people off who think they are on a yacht, and "those people" are floating in the ocean on an inner tube. They can't swallow the reality that we are all in this together. I am sick. You are sick. And we desperately need a cure. I hope that this book is food for your soul. I hope as you read the stories of Scripture, you find comfort in knowing that you are not alone in this screwed up journey of following Jesus. If you have had one too many Jerry Springer episodes in your life, guess what? Welcome to the freaking family. Most of the time, the people who are not willing to admit that are more screwed up than anyone. You fit right in. Your junk fits right in with the rest of the dysfunctional family of God. You are not different. Or more screwed up. I am thou. Stop hiding. All of creation is groaning for the bride to be revealed. Blemishes and all!

My scars tell of how great HIS love is! This is the beauty in my story. My blemishes preach the goodness of God. They put the power of God on display for the world to see! Your scars are beautiful. That is what makes the story of Scripture so beautiful. He is beautiful. This is the greatest love story ever told. Unfailing love. A love that conquered sin and death. A love that held nothing back for you. He was dying to love you back to life. Literally. What makes your story so beautiful is not you. It is Him. It's always been Him. My story is not how wonderful I have been. Our story is that no matter how far we have veered off the path, He has been pursuing us. No matter how far we run from Him, He has been chasing us. His love is beyond any sin I have ever done or will do. We are meant to stand in awe and wonder at the goodness of God. Not contain it. Not box it up and put it on a shelf. It is an endless ocean we are meant to sink deep in. There is no beginning and no end. You cannot find the bottom of this ocean floor. He is too good for your mind to comprehend. Sink deep.

Unfortunately, in order for us to genuinely embark on this journey we need to first sink deep in our own wretchedness. Step one. Admit I am sick. Our ego and insecurity fight this step tooth and nail. Yet, this is the very thing that will set us free. As I expose the scandals of my life, I hope you begin to see the love of the Father coming forth like light bursting through the cracks of a mason jar. Nobody wants to be broken. But if we allow ourselves to be broken, light will burst through the cracks of our broken lives. In the words of Jesus, "Unless the seed is broken and dies it will die alone, a single seed. But if you allow yourself to be broken and die your death will give life to many."

I wrote this book for two reasons. Number 1: for me. This is a journey that I have been on for years that God has been using to liberate me. Writing this book is setting me free. If nobody reads this book, it has served its purpose. Number 2: for you. I desperately want the world to know just how good HE is. I want you to know that the Good News is actually Good News! HE is much better than we think! My purpose was to deconstruct the false perceptions and judgments that we have placed on God so that we could reconstruct a more accurate depiction of who God really is. Most people I have encountered who reject God are simply rejecting the evangelical projection of who God is. And my response is usually, "I don't believe in that God either!" What is completely ironic to me is that if you actually read scripture and the gospels you will find that these false projections of God that are masquerading around our culture could not be further from who we see Jesus to be in scripture. Jesus has been completely lost in a religion bearing his name. I would encourage you to denounce the American Jesus. But I would also encourage you to embark on a lifelong journey of discovering the One who made you. The One who loves you. The One who loved you to death. The One who cares for you. He is patient. He is kind. He is forgiving. He is compassionate.

Brennan Manning tells a profound story of a nun who is having visions of Jesus. She is consistently having powerful visions of Jesus during her prayer time. Word begins to spread that this Catholic nun is having visions of Jesus. So the local archbishop decides to pay this woman a visit (because we simply can't have people in our churches having visions of Jesus). The archbishop finds this woman and confronts her. He is skeptical and almost condescending to her. He asks her sarcastically, "I heard you have been having visions of Jesus. Is this true?"

The woman replies, "Yes."

The archbishop continues in his condescending tone, "Well, the next time you have a vision of Jesus, I want you to ask Him something for me."

The woman replies, "Okay. What would you like me to ask Jesus next time I see Him?"

The man says, "The next time you have a vision of Jesus, I want you to ask Him what the last sin I confessed was."

The elderly nun replied, "Okay."

The archbishop leaves and some time had gone by. Word continues to circulate that this woman was still having these profound visions of Jesus. So, the archbishop decides to pay her another visit. He finds the woman and confronts her a second time.

Still in his cynical attitude, he asks the woman again, "I heard you were still having these visions of Jesus, is this correct?"

She replied, "Yes."

He continues to push her. "Did you remember the question that I asked you to ask Jesus for me?"

She replied confidently, "Yes."

The archbishop was insistent now, "Well, what did he say?!?"

The old woman took the archbishop's hand in hers and gently replied, "I asked Jesus what the last sin you confessed was, and His exact words were 'I don't remember.'"

He is MUCH better than we think. This is a liberating reality. There is nothing that can ever separate you from the love of God in Christ Jesus. Nothing. Death could not hold you. Sin could not keep him from you. No matter how ugly life may have gotten, you are NOT beyond redemption. No matter if you were the victim or the perpetrator. The enemy cannot remove the resurrection power of the cross. All he can do is lie. Years ago I was hanging out with a friend of mine who happens to be a pastor. We went over to his house, and at the time he had 2 young children. His oldest daughter Ava, was about 5 years old. I will never forget this. I looked at his refrigerator and there was a coloring held up by a magnet on his refrigerator. Nothing out of the ordinary here. However, this particular coloring was hideous. No joke. His daughter Ava had colored this for him. I remember thinking to myself "Dang, that's a terrible drawing, your kid can't color worth squat." Of course I didn't say that out loud. This picture was so bad it was as if someone went out of their way to make the worst coloring possible. She used the ugliest colors in the box of crayons. And boy, did she color outside the lines of this coloring page. I mean, she hardly got anything INSIDE the lines at all! I remember my friend looking down at that drawing and he had this stupid grin on his face. He looked up at me and said, "This is terrible." And we both laughed. But he still had this stupid grin on his face. He looked down at this coloring again, after we cracked some jokes about how terrible this coloring was and how his daughter wasn't going to be an artist when she grew up. When he looked down at the coloring again with that stupid grin on his face he said to me, "But she did it for me." A stupid grin on his face from ear to ear. This was the stupid grin of a Father who takes delight in his kids. He had ZERO concern for how well she colored. ZERO concern for the fact that she used the wrong colors and couldn't color inside the lines. His affection for her was not dependent on whether or not she went "outside the lines." This is no different than the love of our Heavenly Father. My friend in this story is definitely not a perfect father, by any stretch of the imagination. How much more does our Heavenly Father love us?

However, we routinely believe the lies that tell us that we have colored outside the lines one too many times and God cannot love us. Yet, God is that Father with the stupid grin on his face from ear to ear saying, "But I love that you are coloring for me." Some of us have stopped coloring altogether. Suffocated by the fear of failure. Terrified of disappointing God and those around us. Not living in the fresh reality that we are loved, we always will be loved, and nothing we could ever do will make him love us less (or more). His affection for us is not based on how well we perform for him. We are good because he says we are good. He took upon himself what we deserve so that we could take upon ourselves what he deserves. When God looks at me, He sees Jesus. No blemish. Totally forgiven. Completely loved. Accepted. Whole. The more I begin to believe this and trust it, the more I begin to walk in who I already am. I live FROM this identity. Our identity shapes our beliefs, our beliefs shape our thoughts, and our thoughts become our behavior. I cannot attain what I already have. And what I have is the affection of the Father. This love and acceptance does not become an excuse to keep sinning, it becomes the very reason I wake up in the morning. My life is not an attempt to gain love and acceptance, my life becomes a response of gratitude for the fact that I am already loved and accepted by the creator of the universe. I begin to live more like a son of the King who is deeply loved and accepted. Most of the time we live out the narrative we believe to be true about ourselves. If you believe that you are a piece of shit, you will probably behave like a piece of shit.

The question is: "What narrative are you believing to be true about your story?" The more you read the Bible, you will begin to see that your story isn't as messed up as you think. You are not the only person in history to experience failure, sin, shame, fear, doubt, or regret. The very things that the enemy is trying to kill you with, the Father is using to bring you home if you allow it. I used to have deep resentment towards God for my alcohol addiction. The more that I grow, the more I stop fighting my story and start to "lean in." How is God using this to redeem me? The truth is, if it weren't for my addiction, I wouldn't be writing this book right now. I'd probably be some self-righteous asshole pastor somewhere, doing the very things that I condemn in this book. God has used my alcoholism to set me free. The very thing the enemy is using to destroy you is the very thing the Father is using to liberate you. I know that sounds contradictory, but hear me out.

God is in the business of death and resurrection. Alcohol was my path to the cross. It was painful and bloody, but resurrection is always on the other side of the cross. I always tell people, if you feel like you're dying, you're probably headed in the right direction. Jesus was the only one who didn't mince words when he described the journey of following Him. "Pick up your cross and follow me." "If you hang on to your life you will lose it, but if you lose your life for me you will find eternal life." The Apostle Paul said he "died daily." That's the most accurate description of what it looks like to follow Jesus that I have ever heard. Baptism is a demonstration of this reality. We are identifying with Christ in his death and being resurrected to new life with him. But that involves death. The death of Jordan. This hurts. It's painful. Humiliating. If I surrender to this process, I will discover that He is setting me free.

Whatever your journey has been, I believe that beneath it all is a loving God who is leading you home. His intent is to draw you unto himself. Because He knows just like I mentioned earlier in this chapter, that He is the only thing that will quench our thirst. He is the cure. It all leads to Him. Not what He can do FOR me. He, Himself, is the answer to our prayers. Not what He can DO, but the person of Jesus himself IS the answer. Sometimes we pray for God to change our circumstances, not realizing that our circumstances at times are designed to lead us to Him. If I hadn't wrestled with alcohol addiction throughout my life, I would not know God the way I do now. Think about that. Isn't that crazy to realize? Did God make me an alcoholic? No. Does He want that for me? No, of course not! He did not cause my sin. He did not intend for that to be my story. That is simply the product of living in a broken world as a broken individual. But in a mysterious way that I will never fully understand, He is bigger than my sin and shame and can use it to redeem me in profound ways. God does not create evil. He does not murder children, or give people cancer, or orchestrate car accidents so that we will suffer and cry out to Him. That is stupid. Sin and death were never God's original intent. He grieves over us and with us when we go through these things. It breaks His heart. He weeps with us. He did not cause those things to unfold. But in the midst of these tragedies, He is bringing new life and rebirth.

Lean in. Lean in to your story. Do not allow your story to shape your perception of God. It requires great courage to allow the character of God to shape your perception of your story. Donald Miller once said in his book 'Searching for God Knows What': "In the beginning God created man in His own image, and man returned the favor." We have a tendency to shape and mold who God is based on our limited life experience. This has happened all throughout history. Different cultures and people groups fashion a God around what they are experiencing. This is not always a bad thing. This is why we have wonderful hymns like Amazing Grace that were written during a time of slavery. A group of people were suffering and held as prisoners and slaves, so they wrote songs about a God who would deliver them. God became a God who would break their chains and set the captives free. However, this tendency to shape the character of God around our life experience can be dangerous and harmful. You can see how one could easily paint a picture of a mean, cruel God if they allowed their tragedies to shape and mold their perception of God. This is extremely difficult for those who have suffered great loss or tragedy, especially at a young age. Sometimes, we need to cling to the truth and the character of God, even though we don't always feel it. Until we begin to see our story through His eyes. If we put our ear to the ground long enough, we will begin to hear the faint heartbeat of the Father. It is constant. We will begin to see the journey beneath the journey. We will see His hand and provision even when we feel abandoned. We will see Him holding us when we lay on our apartment floor in the fetal position, weeping uncontrollably. We will see Him right next to us, weeping alongside us. He never left. He never bailed on us in our time of trouble. You will begin to encounter the risen Jesus just as I have, even when the stench of alcohol is still on your breath. You will see the nail-scarred hands wrapped around you, holding you tight. Even when I locked myself in hell, He was right there with me.

Religion has caused many of us to lean out. We have leaned out because we have not been able to reconcile our messed up story with the Story of God. Religion has not equipped followers of Jesus for real life. We were left without any tools to navigate the muddy waters of life. We could interact with Jesus on some level when we felt good about ourselves and life was still somewhat "inside the lines." But the minute the shit hit the fan, we were crushed. Paralyzed. Unable to cope. Not knowing that our story falls perfectly in line with the Story that has been unfolding since the beginning of time. He is making all things new. Even you.

So here you are. What are you going to do? I would plead with you to get off the sidelines. You have not been disqualified because of your past. Your mistakes do not define WHO you are. HE defines you. You were never qualified based on what you had done to begin with. That includes anything good or bad. You weren't qualified because of what you did "good," in the same way you are not disqualified for what you may have done "bad." You are qualified because of what HE has done for YOU that you could never do for yourself. Get in the game. He took upon himself what you deserve so that you could take upon yourself what He deserves. When God sees you, He sees Jesus. You are perfect. Welcome to the victorious limp. Welcome to The Divine Scandal.

TABLE OF CONTENTS

INTRODUCTION

Becoming a superhero isn't as easy as it used to be. Supervillains, like **Dr. Deathmask**, are a lot smarter than the previous generations of evildoers. It takes a different breed of hero to rise up and beat back these new threats to humanity. Those daring enough to take up the noble calling need more than strength of steel. You will need to understand the scientific principles that govern how everything works. That's what this book is all about. Study and learn, because saving the world requires knowledge. **Bolded** words have added definitions in the back of the book if you want more details on those terms.

The vast majority of superheroes are humanoid, with bones and muscles just like you and me. They didn't become super by sitting on the couch all day chomping on potato chips. Superheroes stay in peak physical condition by working hard and working smart. These defenders of justice understand the science behind exercise, physics, aerodynamics, weaponry, and social interaction so they can reach the apex of their potential.

Learn and apply the basics and one day you too may find yourself elevated to the ranks of the revered champion.

SECTION 1:
TRAINING LIKE A SUPERHERO

Some superheroes got lucky and can move via telekinesis, teleportation, super speed, or wingless flight. But most have to travel the old-fashioned way: with muscles.

There are different types of muscles: smooth

muscles like those in your stomach and around your veins; cardiac muscles that make up your heart; and skeletal muscles that attach to your bones and allow you to move. We will focus on skeletal muscles because without those you couldn't run, jump, or be a superhero.

Muscles pull but can't push. That is the reason most skeletal muscles team up to form **antagonistic pairs**, where one muscle contracts and the other relaxes. These muscle pairs work together, enabling us to move our arms and legs. The quadriceps and hamstrings, the pectoralis major (chest muscle) and latissimus dorsi (lower back muscle), the biceps and triceps, are all examples of antagonistic pairs.

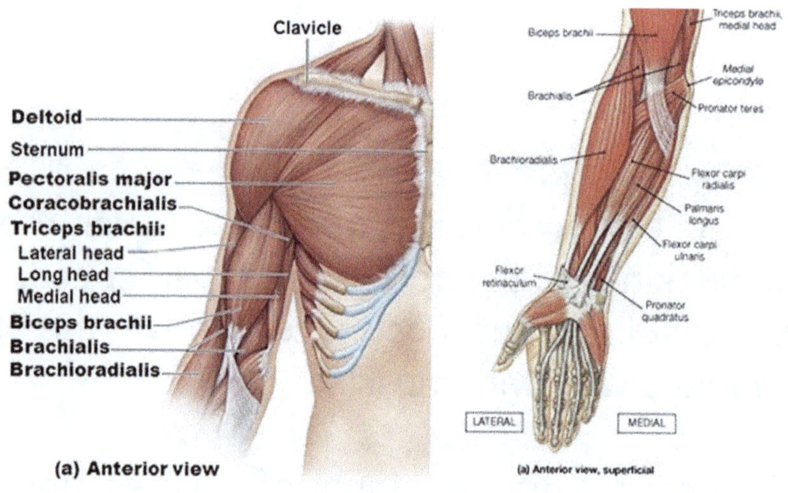

MUSCLES

Our brains automatically send signals all over our bodies, coordinating our movements whenever we want to perform an action, like punching through a legion of supervillains for the sake of justice for all mankind.

We want those punches to inflict maximum damage on those bad guys when we get the opportunity someday. Therefore, we need to prepare our bodies so we can increase the strength of our muscles and deliver those well-

deserved blows. When we exercise, we work our muscles, allowing them to become bigger and stronger.

Exercise helps keep your muscles strong and flexible. If you don't use your muscles they can **atrophy**, or shrink, and become weak. This is why the best superheroes exercise consistently. You can't stand toe-to-toe with the biggest bad guys on the planet without making sure your body can put up with the rigors of saving the world.

ENDURANCE TRAINING

Endurance, or the ability to continue fighting past fatigue or other discomforts, is a key component of being a superhero. You'll have to be able to run, jump, and punch long after you're too tired to move. Building up your endurance will help you be ready when disaster strikes your city in the form of a giant robot or genetically engineered super-lobster.

Running is an extremely useful exercise for future superheroes. Especially since you will often need to chase the enemies of peace and justice as they flee before your superpowers. Running incorporates several muscle groups to apply force into the ground. That force propels the body forward. If you want to run faster, all you have to do is apply more force with each stride and reduce the amount of time your foot remains on the ground.

The concept is easy to understand but difficult to do well. That's why the great paragons-of-virtue train hard. It would be really embarrassing to let the bad guy get away because you couldn't keep up. The more you run, the better your brain becomes at coordinating all those muscle groups, and the stronger your muscles are, the more force you'll apply with each contact.

Muscles also get stronger when they struggle against a resisting force. The entire earth is resisting your muscles as you run because of its gravitational pull. Gravity works against your muscles and forces them to gain strength.

So how can you increase the resistance to your legs while you are running? One way is to run up a flight of stairs at your local sports arena. You're working against gravity as you run upward, which makes things more difficult. Gravity is constant and will always work against you, but there are ways that you can make things easier for yourself when dealing with this eternal force. For example, if you try to climb directly up a wall you will use a lot of effort, but if you have a ramp that goes up to that same height, walking up that distance will be far easier.

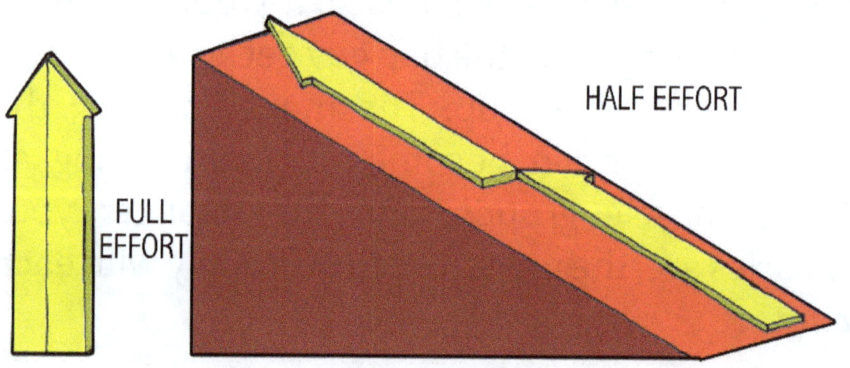

There's a trade-off between the distance you move, and the effort required to move that distance. The ramp, or **inclined plane**, reduces the effort by half when the distance doubles. The inclined plane has many applications in science, and the would-be superhero needs to understand how it works.

It just may save your life one day.

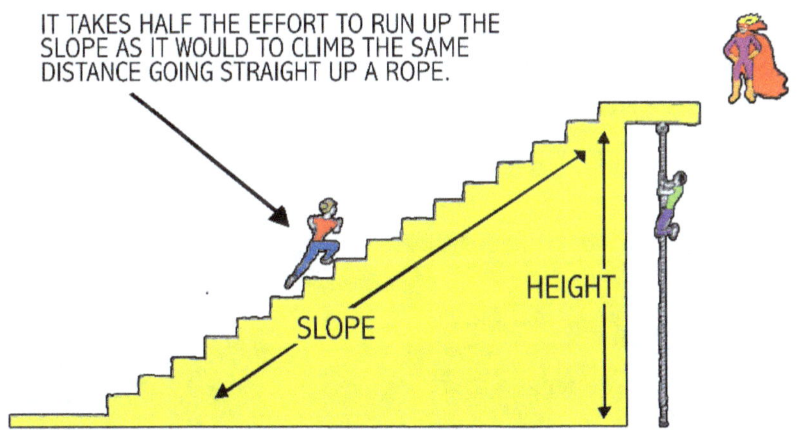

Flights of stairs or a hill are all inclined planes. If the distance of the slope (how far it is to the top) is twice the distance of the vertical height (how tall it is), then the effort required to run up the slope will be *half* of what it would take to climb straight up. Arriving at the peak requires the same amount of work, but heroes that haven't been blessed with flight can save a lot of effort by choosing a different route.

Science is full of trade-offs, though. Less energy is required to run up the slope, but you'll need to travel a greater distance.

Another form of resistance training to increase muscle strength is weightlifting. Weights add extra resistance to your muscles that you couldn't get without them. When you lift weights, you're actually straining the muscles and tearing their tiny fibers. When the body heals the damaged muscles, the fibers fuse and get bigger. That's how you gain muscle mass.

You may be tempted to bulk up for those photo ops with the mayor after you catch a bad guy, but lean muscle mass is much more useful to the everyday superhero.

Muscle is good for lifting things, but the more you have, the less flexible you are. Flexibility (your body's range of motion when you move and stretch) is something else you'll want to consider. Being flexible can get you out of many dangerous spots where muscle won't help you, so keep that in mind.

PARKOUR

Those pesky villains never seem to be captured easily and you will often find yourself in pursuit. Practicing Parkour is a fantastic way to stay fit and prepare for future foot races. Parkour is about efficient movement, increasing your speed when clearing obstacles while minimizing your energy loss.

Imagine being able to jump off a second-story balcony, land on the grass while tucking into a ball, and not get hurt! That is what Parkour is all about: training you to use your body's flexibility to safely jump, scale, and land in otherwise dangerous situations.

Parkour was created in the late 1980's as a form of acrobatics used in cities. The purpose is to find the fastest and most efficient route through any and all environments. This can involve all kinds of movement like running, jumping, swinging, vaulting, climbing, swimming or any other mode of travel you can think of. It's even been used in movies like the James Bond series and Batman!

Since Parkour is all about efficiency, it's

perfect for your superhero training.

A wall-run converts linear (forward) momentum into vertical (upward) momentum, allowing you to climb walls with great speed (imagine Spider-Man). You accomplish this feat  by running at a wall head-on. As you approach the wall you jump and bring your leg up in front of you, planting your foot on the wall.

You can then use the wall as a sort of springboard to push your foot against and instead of pushing back, you boost yourself upward. At this point, you will extend your arms above your head to reach for the top of the wall. Hopefully, you have enough momentum to clear the top in one fluid motion.

If the wall is too high for that, your best bet is to grab onto the top and pull yourself up and over.

This maneuver is not as easy as it looks. You may want to incorporate a regular pull-up routine into your exercise sessions.

Another good use of Parkour is if you ever need to jump off a building. Under normal circumstances, jumping off anything higher than a few feet isn't something you'd want to do, but if you're chasing your arch nemesis across rooftops, it may become

necessary. If you do it wrong, you could easily break an ankle or leg...but do it right and you might just have a chance of capturing your enemy.

When jumping off a wall straight down, the force of the impact has nowhere to go but into your body. Now, while ounce for ounce, bones are actually stronger than steel (yes, really), it still only takes about 25 pounds of pressure to break ankle bones or tear ligaments. Unless your bones are literally made of iron, you're going to want to know how to land properly. That's where Parkour comes in.

Instead of landing flat on your feet, jump out as far as you can and execute a safety roll upon landing. This spreads out the impact-force your body absorbs and increases the time that force travels through your body, which actually decreases your chance of injury. This requires training, but luckily for us superheroes, Parkour classes are offered in every major city in the country.

HAND-TO-HAND COMBAT

One thing we know for sure about bad guys is they don't play nice. A wise superhero will allocate a portion of her exercise time to the study of hand-to-hand combat.

There are various forms of martial arts to choose from depending on your interests. It is recommended you choose one that compliments your superpowers, whatever those may be.

For would-be heroes who can't catch a bullet between their teeth, finding the right fighting style to match your needs is especially important.

Next up is a list of different martial arts that come in handy in the superhero game. Pay close attention to which would work best with your personality and goals as a hero. As your skill grows and you gain mastery over your chosen form of martial arts, it may be necessary to study and perfect multiple forms to better equip you to deal with whatever situation comes your way.

Karate

Karate is a very popular form of martial art that originated in Japan. Used primarily as a defensive fighting style, Karate does employ offensive moves as well, all with the goal of taking down your opponent as quickly as possible.

Jiu-jitsu

Also from Japan, Jiu-jitsu focuses on using your body's center of gravity as leverage against your opponent. It includes everything from punching, kicking, and grappling, to locking your attacker's joints and even biting.

Taekwondo

Taekwondo isn't so much about violence as it is self-mastery. This martial art is meant to develop a greater bond between a person's body and mind. Self-defense is the goal, while helping students gain peace with themselves and others.

Aikido

If Taekwondo is all about peace and understanding, Aikido takes that even further. In Aikido the goal is to stop your opponent while doing as little harm to them as possible. It trains students to find weaknesses in their adversary and exploit them without causing injury.

Krav Maga

Created in Israel, Krav Maga is meant to be used in real-life scenarios where ending the threat is paramount. If an attack gets violent, students of Krav Maga know how to use everything in their environment to defend themselves. Krav Maga is used by specialized commandos and anti-terrorism units around the world.

Each of these arts will serve a different function depending on what type of hero you decide to be. Whether you want to hit hard and never let up, or disarm your opponent without hurting them, there is a martial art that will serve your needs. Which you choose will say a lot about the type of hero you are.

Choose wisely.

ENEMY WEAPONS

Have you ever seen someone lay on a bed of nails? I can think of better ways to sleep. Although it would be uncomfortable, it likely would not cause serious injury because the force of gravity is spread out over each nail.

The result would obviously be much different if there were only one nail. The force would be the same, but the area where the force is applied is drastically reduced, causing much greater damage to the body.

One nail will pierce the skin, but many nails grouped together will support your body's weight and not hurt you. That's the principle behind a bed of nails.

The same theory can be applied to weapons of all types.

One of the most basic weapons is your fist. Just as the example of the single nail, your middle knuckle is the point where all the force is concentrated in a punch. The **force application**, or the amount of strength or energy you use, does not need to be high for a punch to do a lot of damage. So, watch out, a malevolent henchman can still hurt you even without a laser cannon in-hand.

Before you can face off against an evil overlord, you will have to go through the henchmen first. And they have an annoying habit of carrying knives wherever they go.

A knife behaves the same as an inclined plane, specifically a form of the inclined plane called a **wedge**.

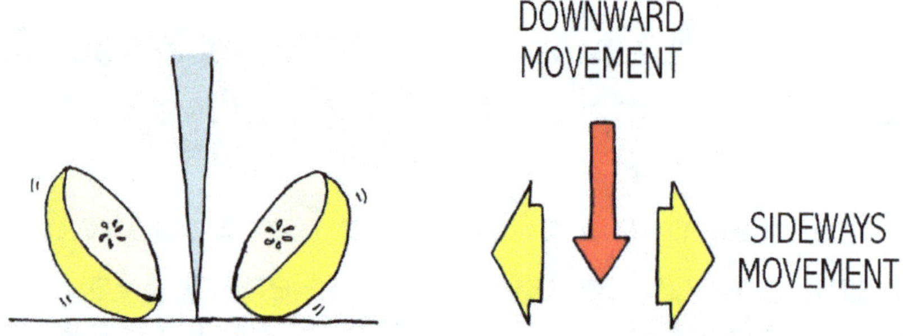

Knives use the principles of an inclined plane to reduce the amount of effort required to cut through objects. The downward motion of the blade, or wedge, creates a strong lateral force to cut something, like a piece of fruit, in two.

THE DANGERS OF GLASS

Since we're talking about knives as wedges, we should take a moment to talk about how glass works in the same way.

Movies and video games constantly show heroes jumping through glass windows and coming through the other side with barely a scratch. While it may look cool, this is not what happens in the real world.

Glass is heavy and sharp. If you were to jump through a closed window, the injuries you would sustain would be life-threatening, even in the best of circumstances.

This is something you'll want to remember so you can avoid injury while saving the day. Take the time to open the window before charging through. It may not seem as dramatic when you're trying to catch a world-conquering despot by surprise, but it will save you a trip to the hospital.

LEVERS

Another standard thug weapon is a club. Clubs act as third-class levers when swung at a protector of peace. What's a 'third-class lever,' you ask?

Excellent question!

Before we can answer it though, we need to learn about levers in general. Then clubs and third-class levers will make a lot more sense. The next two examples are both first-class levers. They are perfectly balanced, but they're not the same, as you'll see.

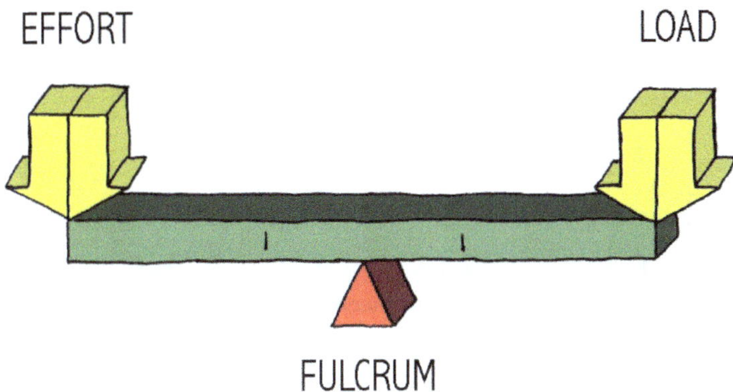

With the fulcrum in the center (like the see-saw below), the effort to move the object is the same. When the fulcrum moves closer to the load, the effort on the opposite side becomes less.

The first is a standard lever with the **fulcrum** (the place where the lever rests or is supported) in the middle, spaced exactly between the load (the object you're trying to move) and the effort (the force you'll use to move the object). When you move the fulcrum to half the distance between the load and where the force is applied, the effort required to move the load is cut in half.

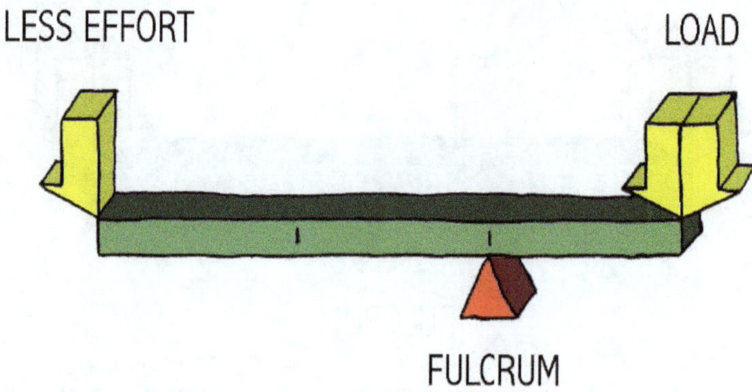

Move the fulcrum closer to the load (the object resting on the lever) and suddenly you need less effort to lift it.

This is the beauty of levers! Half the effort means you'll have more strength left over to thwart your nemesis.

Examples of first-class levers include a seesaw, scissors, pliers, and a crowbar.

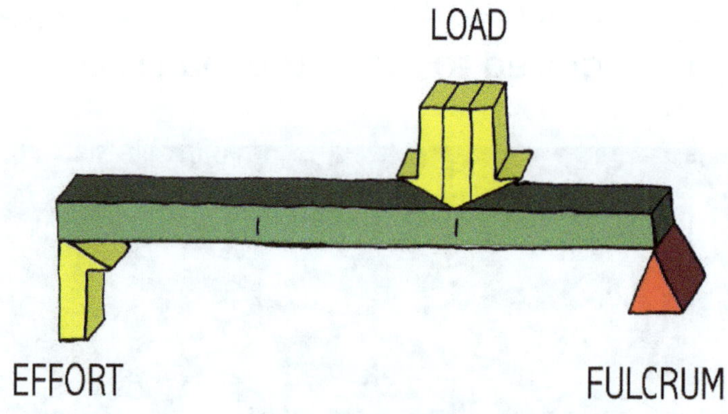

Second-Class Lever

A second-class lever has the load situated between the effort (the force needed to move the object) and the fulcrum. Examples include a wheelbarrow, fingernail clippers, and bottle openers.

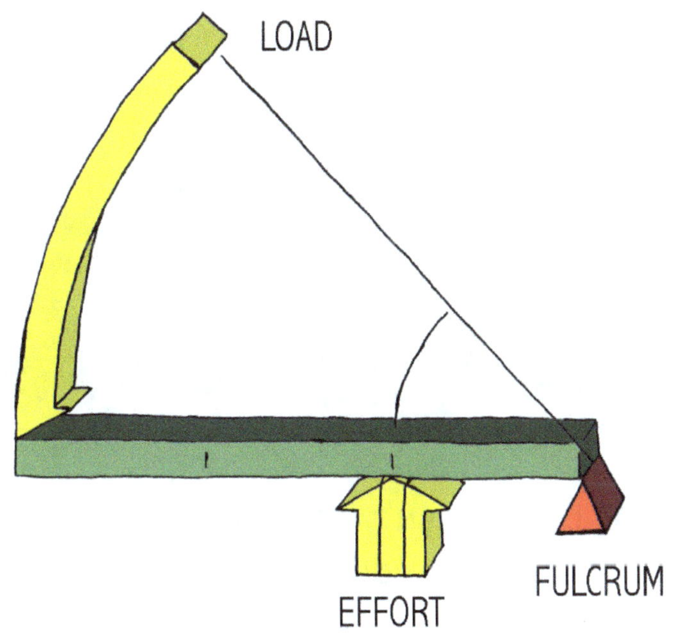

Third-Class Lever

A third-class lever reverses the position of the effort and the load, while the fulcrum remains in the same position. The end of the lever sweeps in a wide arc to move the load. Common Examples include sweeping with a broom, hammering in a nail, or swinging a baseball bat. Even your forearm is a third-class lever when performing bicep curls with dumbbells.

Alright, now that we have levers figured out, let's get back to the example of a club. An evil minion applies effort at the handle to swing the club, providing an opportunity to strike at a greater distance. The trade-off for the increased range is a reduced impact force.

That usually isn't a big deal to the common goon because the reduced force still hurts. If your maniac is particularly maniacal, they could increase the amount of damage by adding a wedge to the end of their lever. Remember, a knife is a type of wedge, so we're talking axes, hatchets, or cleavers.

A hatchet is a wedge fixed at the end of a club and can be thought of as a sharp third-class lever.

Heroes beware of the villain that combines scientific principles to inflict pain!

GUNS

Not all superheroes are bulletproof and should be on the lookout for firearms. They can be incredibly destructive to heroes without impenetrable flesh, as well as civilians caught in the crossfire.

Handguns fire projectiles called bullets. An unfired bullet has four basic parts: a case to hold all the components, a primer, a powder charge, and a bullet, or slug. A bullet by itself isn't all that dangerous, but a gun can turn a small bit of metal and powder into a deadly force.

Understanding and respecting firearms will help us avoid fear and misconception.

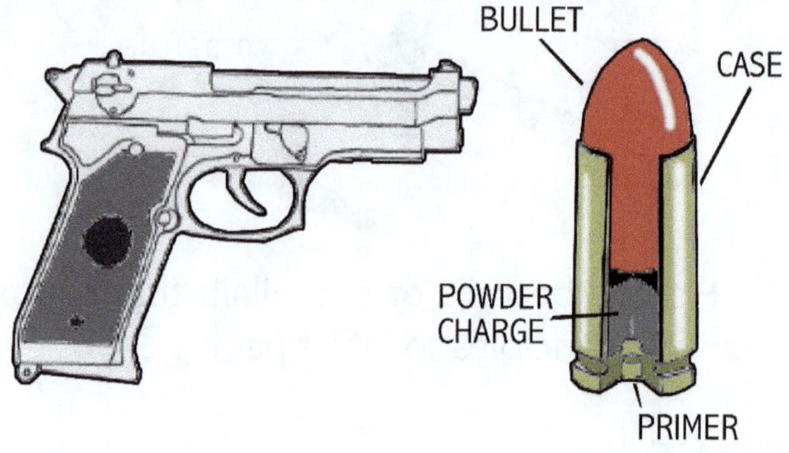

When the trigger is pulled, a firing pin is released and strikes the bullet where the primer is located. This creates a spark that ignites the powder charge. The chemical reaction produces rapidly expanding gas which drives the bullet down the barrel of the gun at great velocity.

Most handguns allow the wielder to fire multiple bullets in rapid succession. This level of threat should never be taken lightly.

If you ever come in contact with a gun, even if it's just sitting on a table, you need to treat it with the proper respect. Don't pick it up or point it at anyone. Make sure you let an adult know what you've found. Guns are a tool, like anything else, but if not properly understood, they become a destructive one. Understanding them is key to eliminating fear and unnecessary danger.

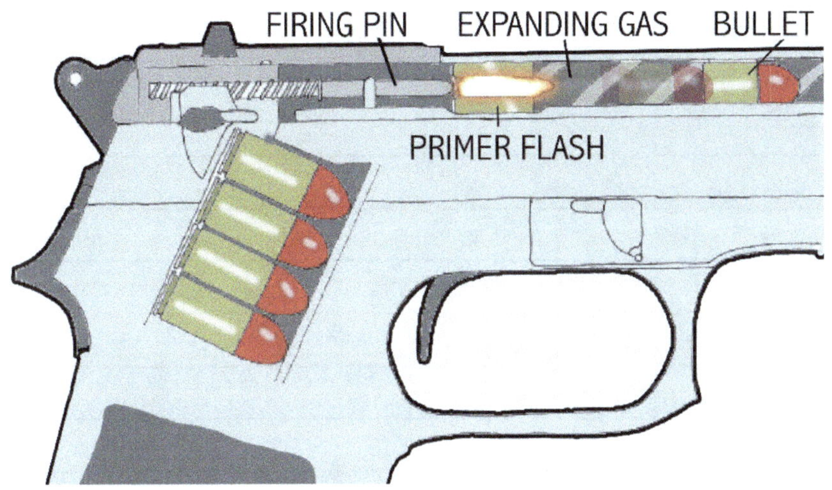

Training isn't something that ever ends, particularly for a superhero. Villains are always trying to outsmart their adversaries, so you need to stay one step ahead.

Now that you understand incline planes, how muscles work, martial arts styles, and how weapons function, you're ready to move on to the next stage of your super-scientific journey!

SUPERHERO PLANNING:

What can I do to train to become a better superhero?

____

____

____

____

____

____

____

____

____

____

____

____

____

____

____

____

____

SECTION 2:
CRISIS SITUATIONS & SAVING THE INNOCENT

Every superhero eventually faces a crisis situation where innocent bystanders are at risk of mortal injury. When that day comes, the burden will fall upon your super-shoulders to rescue those in harm's way. It is helpful to know about some of the most common scenarios you will encounter.

You may think you can just fly over and save an airplane falling from the sky without knowing anything about aerodynamics or the laws of physics.

Think again!

One wrong move and that plane will fly apart. You need to know your science before you can rescue a 747 in freefall.

GRAVITY

No discussion of super-heroics can begin without an understanding of the most basic force on earth: gravity.

What goes up must come down. That's the fundamental idea behind gravity. It's the force that attracts a body or object toward the center of the earth, or toward any other physical body having mass. We talked about this principle a bit when discussing endurance training, but we'll get into it more here.

The more **mass** something has, or the more material it's made out of, the more gravity it will have. For example, the sun is massive...so massive that it has enough gravity to hold all the other planets in its orbit. Earth is the same way. It's big enough to hold everything to its surface, including you.

What this means for you is that unless you can fly, you will never be able to escape gravity's pull. You can exert force to temporarily overcome gravity, like throwing a ball or an airplane flying, but no matter what, gravity will eventually take over and pull you or the object down.

It's a basic principle, but one that influences everything you do in our physical world.

THE LAWS OF MOTION

There are three basic laws of motion that will come into play when you're trying to save someone.

#1: *Objects at rest will remain at rest, and objects in motion will remain in motion at the same velocity, unless the object is acted on by an external force.*

This means that a baseball lying in the grass will stay there unless someone picks it up and throws it. The ball won't move by itself.

Or put another way, if Dr. Deathmask throws the Mayor off a building, she will continue to fall until something stops her. That could be you saving the Mayor in midair like the hero you are, or the ground ending her fall with a splat.

#2: The forces acting on an object are equal to the object's mass multiplied by the acceleration of the object ($F = M \times A$)

This means that the bigger something is, and

the faster it's moving, the harder it will hit. This law of motion is particularly helpful when thinking about a really big supervillain throwing a powerful punch. The hit will have a much greater force than a punch delivered by little Megan, the 4-year-old down the street.

#3: *When one object exerts a force on another object, the second object exerts an equal and opposite force on the first.*

Or in other words, if you punch a wall, even as hard as you can, the wall will exert equal force back, likely breaking your knuckles.

The same is true when saving the Mayor as she's falling from the building. If you try to catch her by flying right up and grabbing her, your force will hit hers and she will likely be injured. You would first need to match the speed of her fall and slowly decelerate so the Mayor isn't hurt.

These laws of motion govern every interaction, so understanding them will make your job easier and safer. Remember, you're becoming a hero to save the day, and that means knowing HOW to save the day.

AERODYNAMICS

Aerodynamics is the study of how air flows and interacts with objects moving through it, like airplanes. Understanding aerodynamics is what allowed us to learn how to fly in the first place.

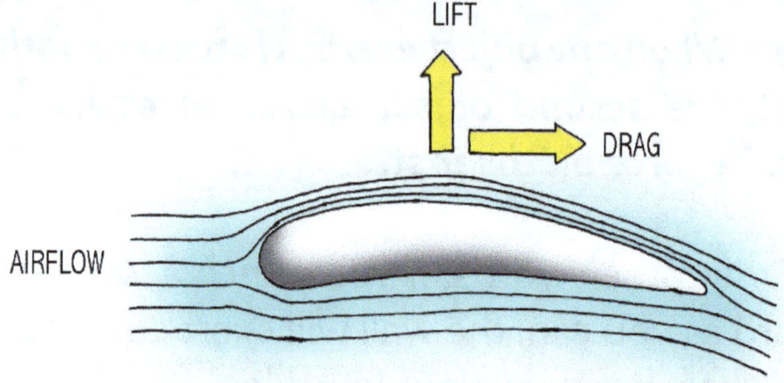

Air flows over and under a plane's wing. The design creates more pressure beneath the wing, which causes lift.

The airfoil (the cross-section of a wing) has a special shape that forces the air above the wing to flow faster than the air below. This creates a suction force we call **lift**, which allows the plane to fly. The air moving across the wing also creates a drag force.

Wings don't always meet the airflow head-on. The angle of attack changes the lift and drag forces on the wing. By adding the lift and drag together, we can understand the total force, or

resultant force, on the wing. As you can see in this example, the resultant force is not straight up or forward. This is helpful to know if you want the ability to control a plane in flight, or if you need to catch one as it's falling from the sky.

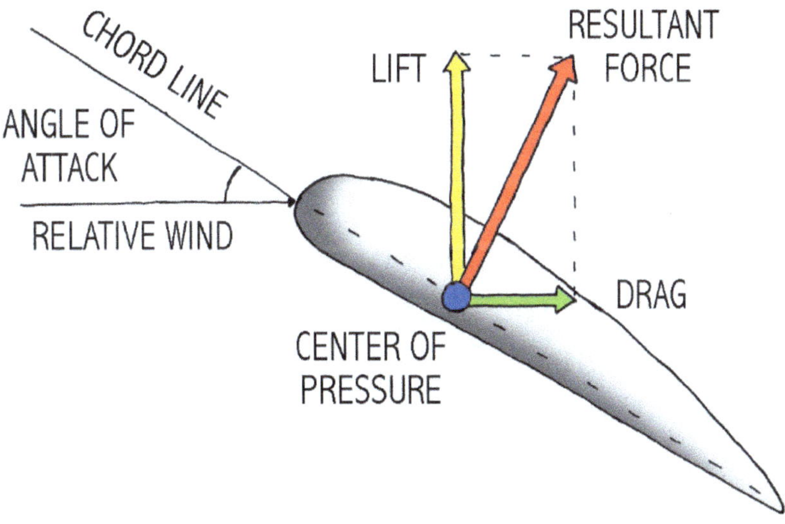

This cross-section shows how a wing interacts with all of these forces while taking off from the runway, climbing, cruising or landing.

Now let's say you want to have a jet as a part of your superhero arsenal in the shape of a crescent moon, or with the wings jutting forward at harsh angles because it looks cool. It may not be the most practical design, but there are lots of planes that have forward swept wings and fly just fine. In fact, fighter jets are intentionally designed unstable, which enables them to perform sharper turns. As a result, they are much more difficult to fly and a great deal more dangerous.

We can make lots of impractical shapes fly, but you'll want to keep in-mind that the crazier the design, the harder your plane will be to control.

Most airplanes have engines that provide thrust, wings that generate lift, and control surfaces such as ailerons (wing-flaps), elevators, and rudders, for the plane to roll, pitch, and yaw (the ability to turn). Planes also experience drag force and the force of gravity that must be overcome to achieve flight.

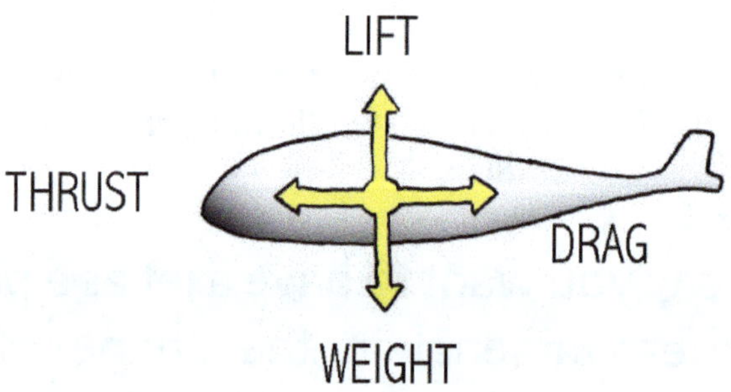

Pilots understand all the forces acting on the plane and how each control surface can be manipulated to take off, fly, and land the aircraft safely.

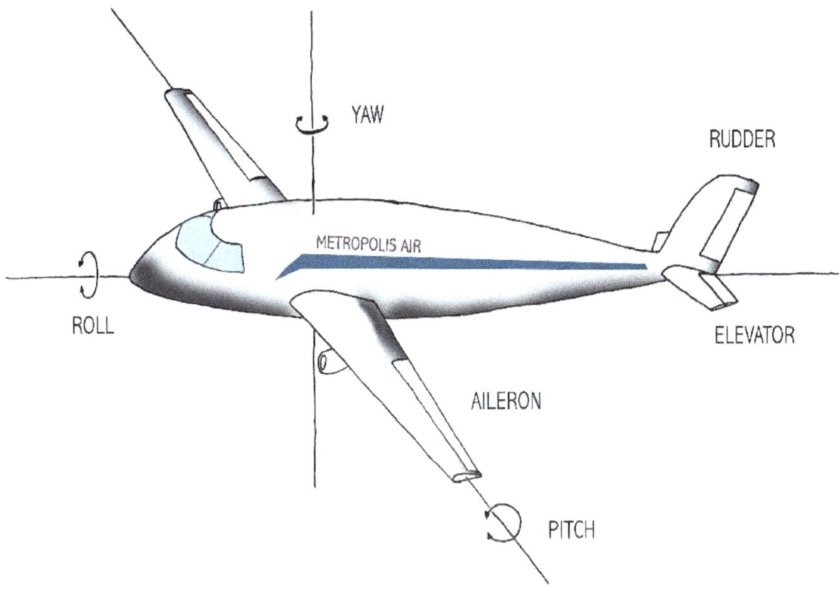

Overcoming these forces is no trivial matter, as evidenced by our relatively recent invention of the airplane. And when things go wrong, they can go wrong in a big way.

For example, Dr. Deathmask could decide to unleash his nano-fusion pulse bombs on an unsuspecting airliner, destroying an engine and tearing off one of the wings. The remaining engine would cause the plane to **yaw** or turn continuously. The lack of lift on one wing would make the plane roll out of control. The passing superhero would have to balance these forces to save the passengers from certain doom.

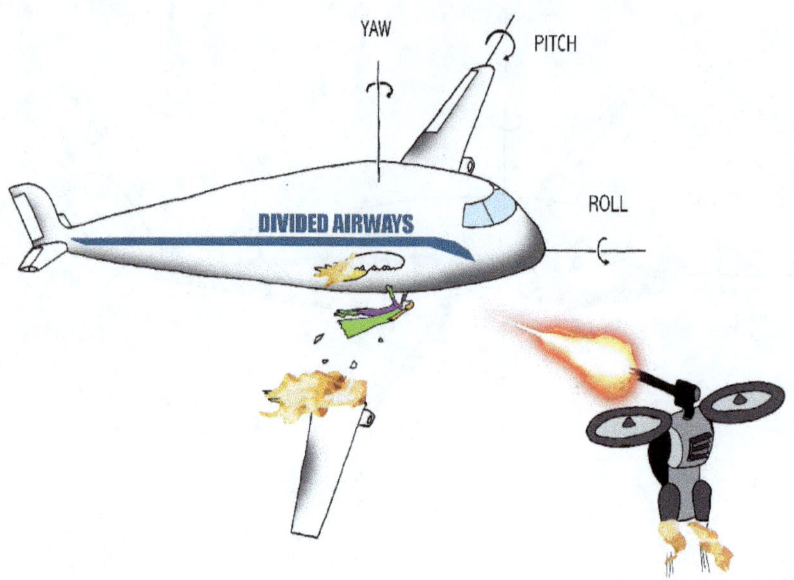

You couldn't simply slam into the front of the plane to get it to slow down. All of these same forces would be in-play and you would need to overcome all of them, balancing, pitch, yaw, roll, and gravity, to land that plane safely.

Aerodynamics doesn't just apply to the sky either.

Surprisingly, water and air act in similar ways, so many of the same rules apply when working with submarines and boats as with airplanes.

A disaster at sea can be just as devastating as a plane crash. Fortunately, boats and planes have a number of things in common. Boats have rudders to control yaw, or the way the boat turns.

A boat also has a propeller, similar to smaller planes, that provides thrust for the boat. These large vessels are also shaped in a way that displaces water. The water, in turn, pushes back against the ship and enables it to float.

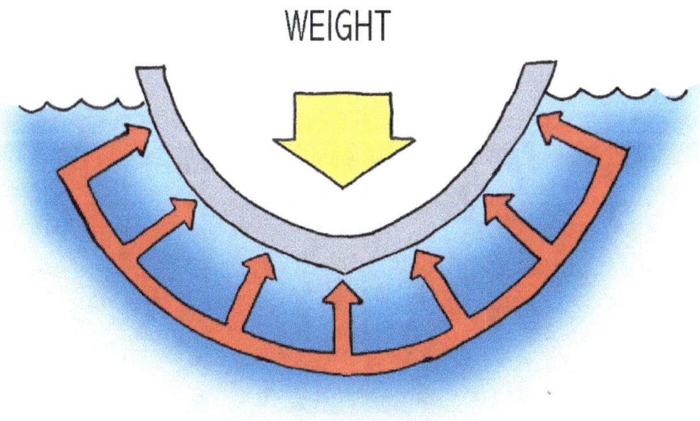

The propellers that drive ships forward have a shape you should recognize, looking very much like the cross-section of a plane's wing.

Airplane and boat propellers use the same principle to move each through the air or water.

The propeller spins through the water, forcing the fluid to flow in front and behind the blade. The shape of the spinning blade creates a suction force (similar to the lift generated by an airfoil) that propels the ship forward. The faster the propeller spins, the faster the boat goes across the water's surface.

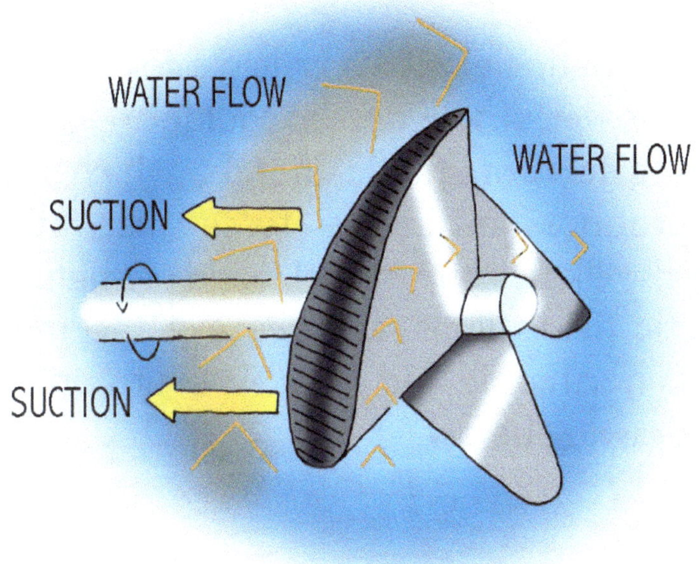

The boat propeller spins, creating suction, which pulls the boat through the water.

Since air and water respond similarly, many of the same principles apply between the two. Flying through the air would be comparable to swimming underwater if you ever developed the power to defy gravity.

Knowing these principles of aerodynamics will help you in your next rescue and allow you to avoid some of the pitfalls that come with not understanding these simple principles.

MAGNETIC FIELDS

A magnetic field is an invisible force and can be very powerful. Magnets of course are naturally occurring **ferromagnetic metals**, which means they produce an innate force that attracts materials like iron, nickel, and cobalt. The magnetic field's lines of force exit the magnet from its north pole and enter its south pole, like in the drawing below.

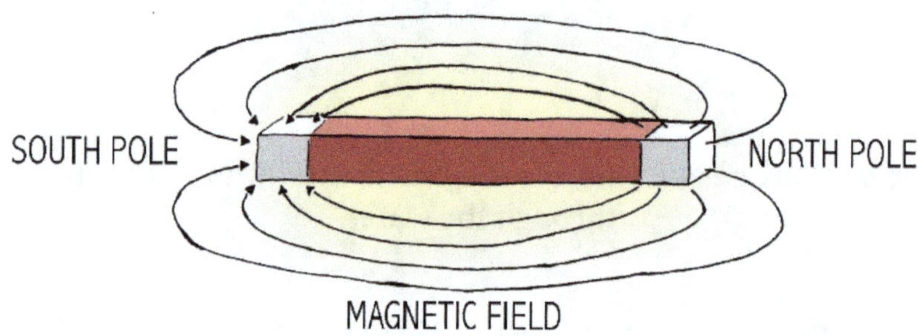

Curved lines are often used to depict how the magnetic force behaves, traveling from one "pole" of a magnet to another. The force can push or pull on any material with a molecular composition that aligns with the force, typically metal alloys similar in composition to the magnet itself.

One of the ways heroes (and villains) have used magnetism to their advantage is in the creation of **electromagnets**. An electromagnet is a man-made magnet where the magnetic field is produced by an electric current.

You can create your own electromagnet by running an electric current through a wire. This is because charged particles like electrons are what produce a magnetic field in the first place. Since an electrical current is generally made up of moving electrons, that current will magnetize the metal as long as electricity continues flowing.

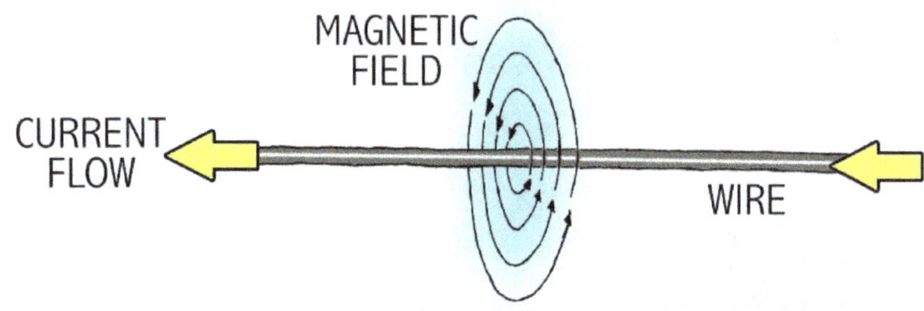

One small wire will not create a large magnetic field unless you alter its shape, though.

A coiled wire allows the field to build off itself and generate a force similar to what is produced by a bar magnet. The field can further be concentrated by placing an iron core in the middle of the coil, creating an electromagnet. Electromagnets can be powerful enough to lift cars, levitate trains, and launch roller coasters at high speeds.

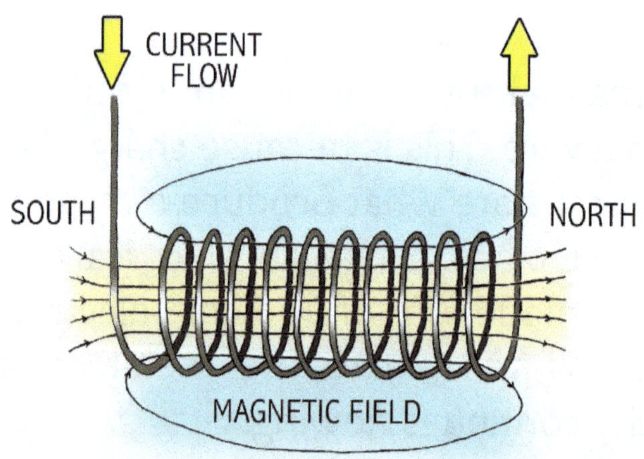

Mechanically, electromagnets are pretty simple to create and can be incredibly powerful. This is important to know if you're planning on using superhero armor made of steel or iron. A villain using a simple electromagnet could spell your doom!

Copper wire wrapped around a metal cylinder is basically all you need to create an electromagnet. Once electricity is introduced (through a battery

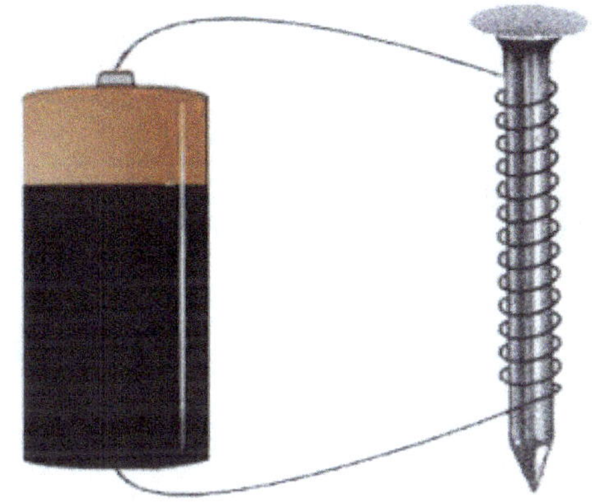

for example) a magnetic field is created just like natural magnets. Once the power is turned off the magnetic field dissipates. So, if you ever find yourself battling someone like the evil Magnatron who uses electromagnets as their primary weapon, remember to focus on cutting off their power source and you will be victorious.

You may not realize it, but magnets and magnetic fields play a big role in the technology-driven world of today. Simple objects like the bell in your school that rings between classes, use magnets. Electric power generators also use magnetism. When you move an object through a magnetic field, electricity is created. Power plants use different types of fuel to create heat. That heat boils water and produces steam, which rises and turns a turbine between the poles of a large magnet, which in turn creates electricity.

Wind turbines use the same principles to generate electricity. In fact, this is how all power plants work. Even electrical devices that contain no magnets at all would have a hard time charging up without magnetism!

ATOMIC FORCES

Superheroes can be found waging battle on a grand, intergalactic stage with the fate of humanity hanging in the balance. However, this is not an everyday occurrence. More often than not, our heroes are serving locally, training their bodies, and hitting the mental dojo to stay sharp. A great place to start your studies on your path to becoming an interstellar warrior is on a much smaller stage with the basic elements.

The Atom

Everything in the universe, from the biggest planet to the smallest insect, is made up of tiny particles called atoms. Every solid, liquid, and gas is a collection of trillions of atoms all packed together.

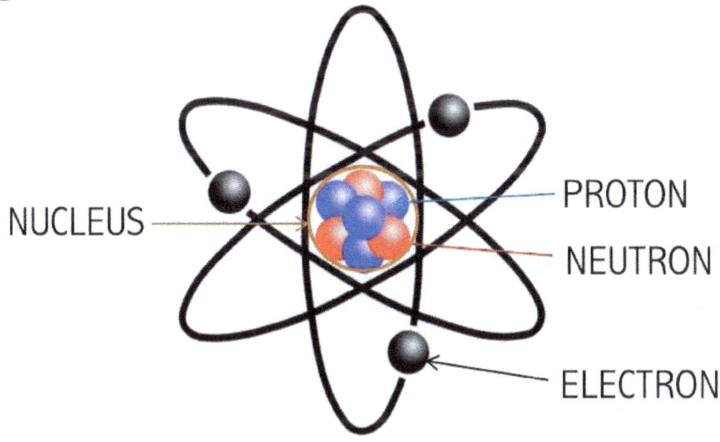

Atoms are made up of three parts: Protons (particles with a positive electrical charge), Neutrons (particles with no electrical charge), and Electrons (particles with a negative electrical charge).

The planetary model of an atom (as seen above) has the ability to catch the eye, but unfortunately, doesn't represent what an atom actually looks like. Electrons don't orbit the nucleus like planets orbit a star.

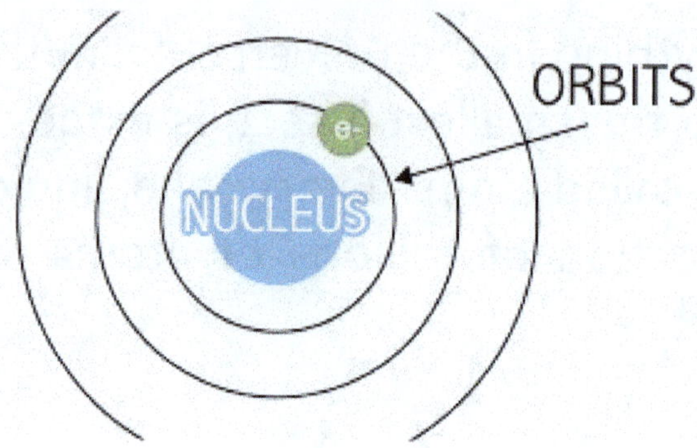

The Bohr model (pictured above) teaches us how an electron can instantaneously shift between orbits depending on its energy level. This model helped us gain a better understanding of how electrons behaved, but still didn't accurately depict an atom.

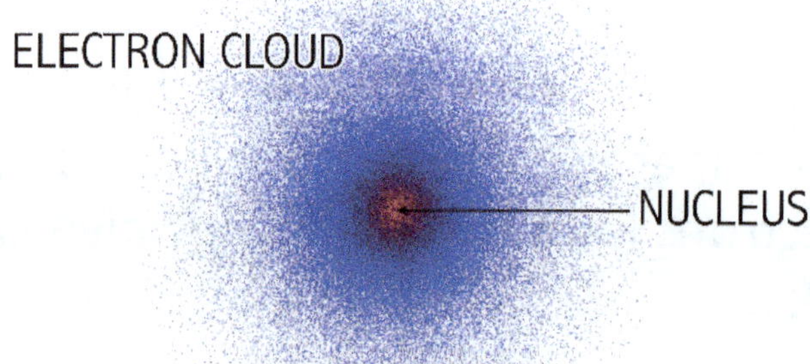

The electron cloud model (pictured above) does a better job of portraying what we observe when we examine atoms in real life. We now know that electrons can be in many places at the same time!

You may have heard the term **molecule** before. A molecule is a group of atoms bonded together, representing the smallest fundamental unit of a chemical compound that can take part in a reaction.

By themselves, atoms can't do much, but bring them together and everything is possible.

Atoms can interact with other atoms. They share electrons, or even steal them from each other. The protons and neutrons of atoms can break apart and re-combine into different atoms. Some of these changes are harmless, and we may not even realize anything is happening at all.

Other changes can be quite disruptive. A nuclear **chain reaction** occurs when one reaction causes one or more subsequent reactions in rapid succession. This process, when applied to the right kind of atoms, can create nuclear power...or a nuclear explosion.

A nuclear bomb exploits this process to generate massive amounts of heat in a very short period of time. The bomb contains a hollow sphere of a specific kind of atom found in uranium, or plutonium (both radioactive).

Radiation is the emission of energy as electromagnetic waves, heat, or as moving subatomic particles. A candle actually produces radiation in the form of heat from its fire, but that type of radiation isn't harmful unless you touch the flame and get burned.

Radiation from uranium and plutonium is a bit different and more dangerous. This radiation emits fractured atomic particles that can pass through materials and our bodies. When these tiny fragments hit a person at high speed, they can break down chemical bonds in the body and cause us to get sick.

This is one of the components of a nuclear explosion that can cause harm long after the bomb itself has exploded.

A remote device is used to trigger the detonator inside the bomb, which releases neutrons into the center of the sphere. The sphere is then crushed around the neutrons, forcing them into contact, which initiates the chain reaction that produces the explosion.

A uranium sphere surrounded by blocks of neutron-reflective tungsten carbide.

There is no going back once the detonator is triggered. The explosion is deadly, but the radioactive fallout can spread through the atmosphere, poison the land, and ravage the bodies of anyone exposed, for years to come.

Therefore, a superhero's best chance of thwarting the villainous plans for a nuclear explosion is to remove the remote device from their evil clutches. You will also want to secure the bomb in order to prevent any future threat.

Understanding these atomic forces will allow you to get the upper hand against your next supervillain. Plus, if you ever get shrunk down to subatomic size, it's good to know what type of universe you're dealing with!

SUPERHERO PLANNING:

How can I use the laws of physics to help those in need as a superhero?

____

____

____

____

____

____

____

____

____

____

____

____

____

____

____

____

SECTION 3:
EVERYDAY INTERACTIONS

Fortunately, the would-be superhero doesn't have to face off against villains like Dr. Deathmask every day. There are moments of reprieve between battles. That time is well spent in training, but there is much about the hero life that is quite normal. In order to keep the mental edge, champions of peace often study the science behind everyday objects as well. You never know when this knowledge could be applied to a life or death situation.

CREATING HEAT AND COLD

Take a villain like Mega-Freeze for example. He uses a simple compression unit from a standard freezer like you have in your kitchen to shoot ice particles at superheroes. Knowing how his technology works in advance can help you to stop him the next time he escapes from Super-Max Penitentiary.

Simply put, refrigerators and freezers move heat from inside the cooling unit to the outside by utilizing the process of evaporation. The more molecules vibrate, the more energy, or heat, they have. When molecules move from a liquid to a gas, they take that energy, or heat, with them. This leaves the liquid in a cooler state because it has lost heat.

Refrigerators and freezers use this process to cool themselves. Inside a freezer (usually where you can't see it) is a series of copper or steel pipes that contain a refrigerant gas. These gasses are designed in a laboratory to evaporate and condense at specific pressures and temperatures.

Freezers use a compressor (or high-pressure pump) to move refrigerant around a pipe with an electric motor to compress the refrigerant gas at high pressures. Compressing the refrigerant gas causes it to condense into a liquid and release heat (get hotter). Then the pressurized, very hot refrigerant gas is sent through a condenser outside the freezer to allow the gas to cool to room temperature.

After the refrigerant has flown through the coils of the condenser and cooled, it is forced through a small valve or hole into a low-pressure chamber inside the cold area of the freezer known as the evaporator. Inside the evaporator, the refrigerant liquid rapidly expands into a gas because it is no longer under the pressure required to keep it in a liquid state. The evaporation of the refrigerant causes it to suck up the heat from its surroundings, freezing everything in sight. Then it flows back through the evaporator and the compressor again and the cycle repeats.

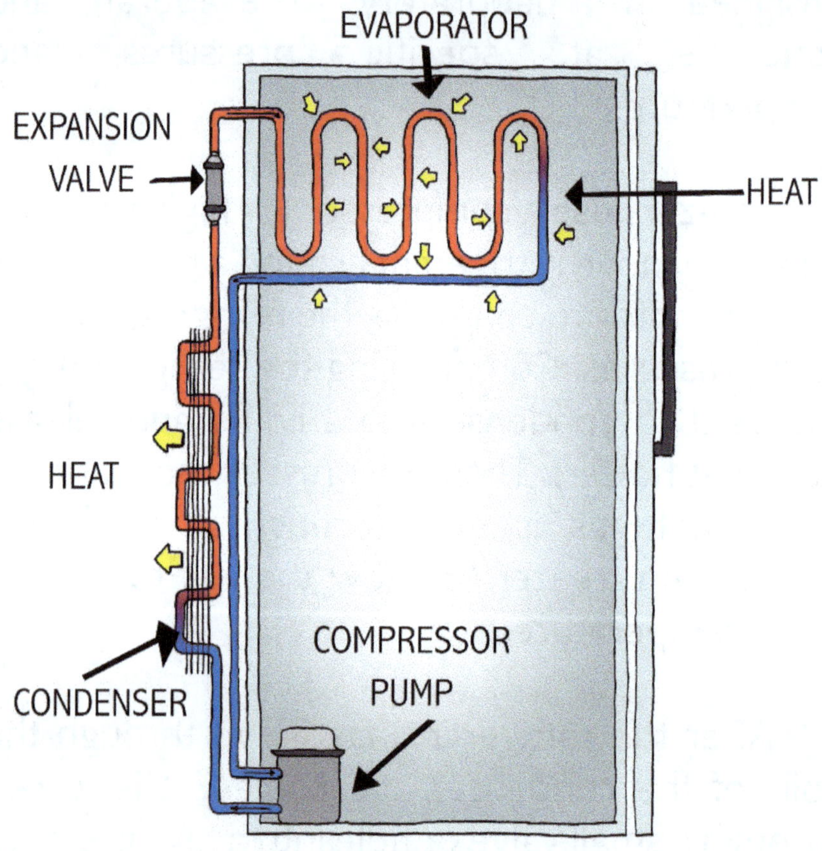

So, if you find yourself in a fight with Mega-Freeze, you can focus on the compressor where the gas is compacted. Once the compressor is broken, Mega-Freeze's ice cannon will be about as dangerous as a squirt gun.

SURPRISING TOOLS

We often take our silverware for granted. It is easy to overlook the power behind the spoon, especially when it is delivering mouthfuls of ice cream. Simple items like spoons can a help heroes in numberless ways. If you understand how and why they work the way they do, you can use them in hero-ing situations to disarm a foe or rescue a civilian.

The tip of the spoon acts as a wedge, allowing you to separate a small amount of ice cream from the container. The handle of the

spoon acts as a lever, making it easier to pry portions of delectable goodness from the rest of the frozen dessert. Can you figure out what class of lever the spoon is?

It's a third-class lever, like the swinging of a baseball bat.

Now, in a superhero situation this can come in handy. Imagine needing to pry open the door to a locked room where a group of hostages is being held. Now that you understand the lever and wedge aspects of the spoon you could use one to help open the door. Knives, forks, crowbars, or anything else can be used as a first-class lever as well. You're only limited by your imagination and the materials at hand.

Scissors are used on a daily basis in school and for art projects. They combine multiple principles to achieve the desired result of cutting something. The first is the wedge. In this case, there are two wedges moving toward each other to create a shear force on the material you are trying to cut. The wedges are connected at a single point, creating a second-class lever.

It's been said that the pen is mightier than the sword. In a lot of ways that's true, particularly if you look closely at how they work.

Most pens utilize **capillary action** to take advantage of a pressure differential. Capillary action causes a fluid to flow into a small tube and stay there because water is naturally sticky (yes, water is actually sticky! Try getting it off you the next time you're wet).

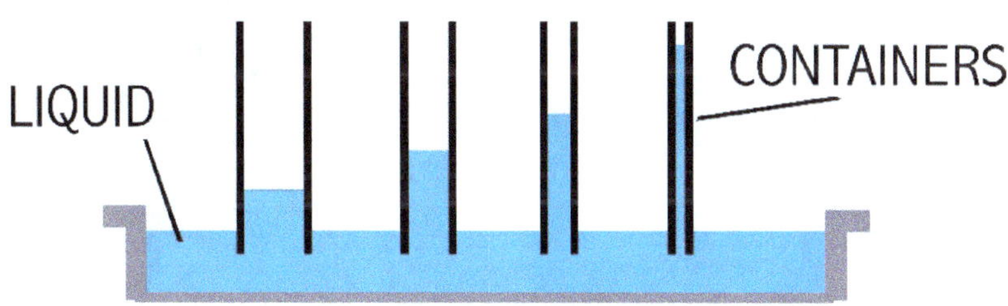

The tighter the container, the higher the liquid will be forced due to capillary action.

This is thanks to the forces of **cohesion** and **adhesion.** Cohesion is a natural phenomenon that pulls molecules together, and adhesion makes them stick once they are close to each other. Water molecules follow these principles and stick not only to themselves, but to foreign substances as well.

What all of this means is that when you put ink into a tight cylinder the pressure of the liquid in the small space will force the ink up, even if gravity is pulling it down. That's why the ink comes out of the pen without you needing to squeeze or exert force on the tube.

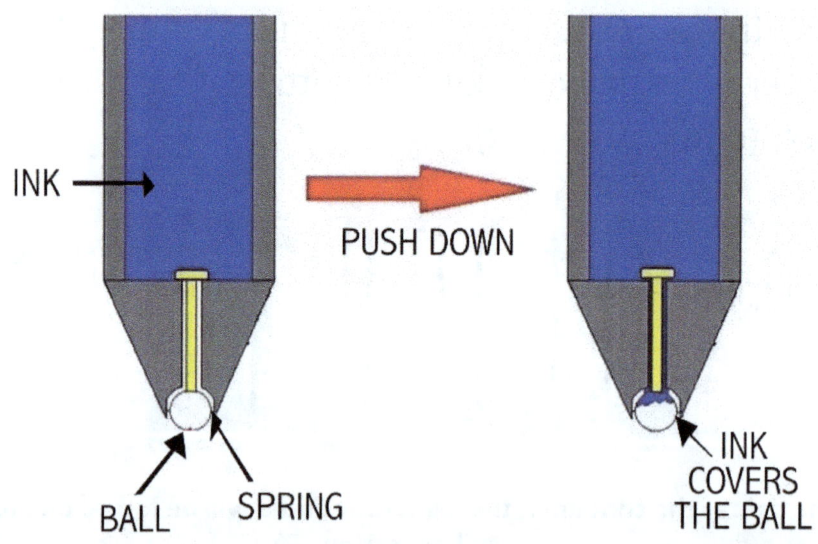

The inside of a pen contains a small tube of ink, that flows onto the paper through capillary action. Some pens use a felt tip to transfer the ink. Others have a metal ball that "rolls" the ink onto the page. These types of pens were only invented about 200 years ago, so they're relatively new.

The ability to write things down has more potential to thwart supervillains (and superheroes) than you may think. Remember, words have power. Imagine if Dr. Deathmask discovered your secret identity and decided to share it with everyone using the biggest newspaper in the city. He would have the power to destroy you with a simple article.

You couldn't punch your way out of that one, but maybe writing a response and using your own words to combat his could make an impact. You'd need your pen ready so you could battle evil and help salvage your reputation.

Plus, capillary action is actually really important in our bodies too. Without a liquid's ability to push against gravity our cells wouldn't be able to absorb water and would dry out and die.

Who knew you could learn so much from a pen?

SUPERHERO HYGIENE

Keeping clean is incredibly important for a superhero. If you ever find yourself covered in toxic waste after fighting Captain Sludge, you'll know what I mean.

Nobody needs a shower worse than a superhero fresh off the battlefield. Showers may be the best invention of the modern era. You have to feel bad for those poor superheroes from the Dark Ages who never knew about indoor plumbing.

Water flows through pipes due to a pressure differential. The difference in pressure can be provided by gravity since water naturally flows from a higher elevation to a lower elevation. Water towers help to create that pressure differential. Pumps can also be used to get the water flowing.

Opening the water valve allows the water to flow. Cold water comes straight from the source pipe, but the warm water stops off at the water heater first. The warm and cold-water pipes meet and mix at the shower valve before pouring out of the showerhead in a cascade of refreshing

and relaxing droplets. Just be sure to test the water before stepping into the shower. Nobody wants to be scalded after surviving a vicious battle for freedom.

Stopping unseen **germs** and **bacteria** is another aspect of being clean that can't be overstated. Germs and bacteria are microscopic organisms that can get inside your body and multiply. Depending on the type of germ, they can cause all kinds of sicknesses.

You wouldn't want to face this beast without soap.

If you had the power to shrink yourself down to microscopic size, you would see a very different world where giant bacteria try to wreak havoc in your body. Defeating these monsters with a punch would be all but impossible, but a little bit of soap will end their reign of terror before they can even get started.

SOUND WAVES

When an object is struck, waves of energy transmit vibrations through solids and even the air. We hear these vibrations as sound. The science of sound has allowed us to design instruments to take advantage of the different ways sound is transmitted. Most instruments are classified as string, wind, or percussion.

Different instruments produce different sounds, but the vibrations all travel to your ear in the same way.

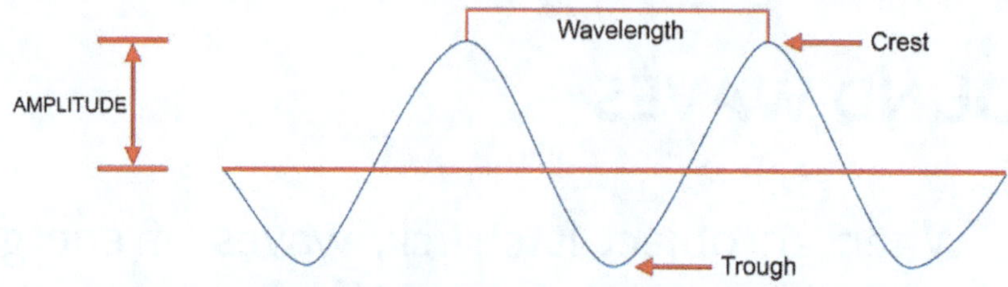

When the crest and trough of the sound wave are pulled close together the sound becomes higher pitched, like a siren.

The sound waves from musical instruments or any other noise, enter your ears and cause your eardrums to vibrate. The vibrations get passed to the inner ear where they are converted to an electric signal and transmitted to your brain. Your mind perceives the sound as music, a cry for help, or an explosion from across town.

Some sounds are loud and high pitched, others are low and booming. Some sound waves can't even be heard, but you can *feel* them! Imagine using these sound

waves when you're fighting crime. You could rattle your enemy with the power of sound, and no one could hear it.

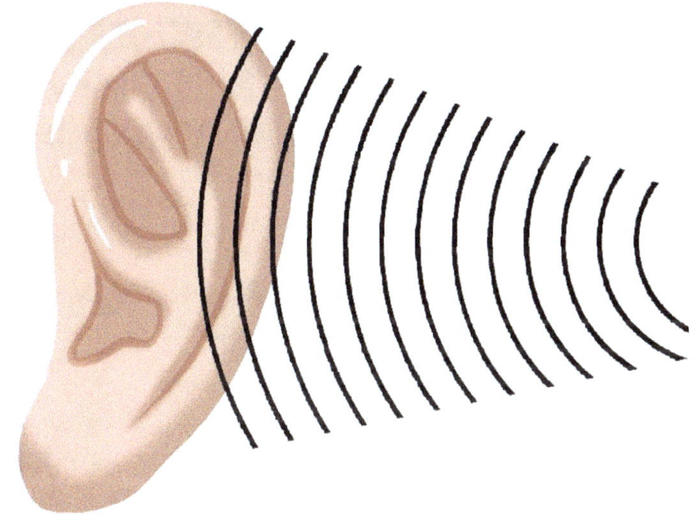

Sound waves hitting your ear.

Sound waves can interact with each other too. When one sound wave is out of phase from another sound wave, the two cancel each other out. This is the scientific concept behind noise-canceling headphones. A microphone samples the incoming sound signal and produces the corresponding out-of-phase signal to cancel out the noise.

When two sound waves interact with each other that are in phase, they combine and get louder.

Using a magnetic field (remember those?)

you can transfer sound through speakers (both audible and waves you can't hear). That's right, stereo and television speakers, headphones and earbuds all use electromagnets to help produce the music you enjoy.

Earbuds allow you to hear your music privately while you train. They are essentially a miniature loudspeaker that fits comfortably in your ear. The signal travels to a wire attached to a diaphragm (the part of the speaker that vibrates to make sound) sitting inside a magnetic field. The vibrations create a sound wave that reproduces the digital signal.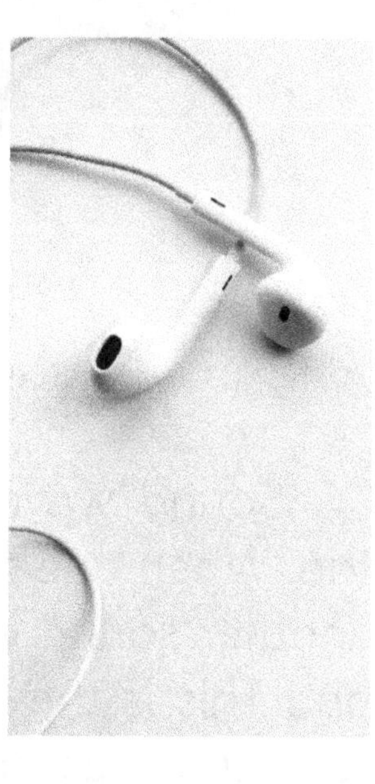

Recording equipment can transform an acoustic sound wave into a **voltage** (the electrical force that drives a current between two points). It can then be digitized and saved, which allows it to be played later. Many enemies of evil take advantage of these digital signals to listen to music while training...or issue their demands to an entire city!

You can use them too, by recording when a villain decides to monologue their entire plan to you. It happens more than you think. Villains LOVE to monologue.

Sound waves are useful for more than just recording and listening to music though. They can also bounce off surfaces, warning you of an impending ambush. You can also listen in on devious conversations, spoiling an evil plan before it can be put into action.

That principle is used in nature all the time.

Bats actually use their big ears for what's called **echolocation**. They screech while flying at night and listen for the sound of their cry to bounce off objects around them. When the sound  returns to their ears, they have a pretty good idea of the environment and what surrounds them. Echolocation allows the bat to 'see' in the dark. It's a very cool (and completely natural) superpower.

There are even blind people like a man named Daniel Kish who have learned how to use echolocation themselves. Daniel listens to how the sounds of the world bounce off objects around him and can 'see' them in his mind, even though he is blind. Amazing!

Daniel Kish may be blind, but he's learned how to use echolocation and can navigate the world like a bat would. In fact, he's been dubbed 'Batman' because of his ability.

X-RAYS

Some waves can be heard, others can be seen, and some are beyond our ability to sense. But that doesn't mean those waves can't interact with our bodies. X-rays are a good example of this.

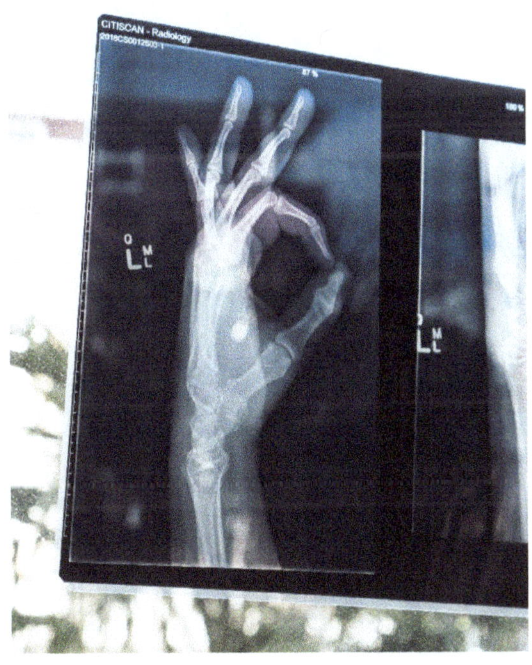

An X-ray of a hand.

X-rays are types of electromagnetic radiation best known for their ability to see through a person's skin. While under an X-ray machine images of the bones can be clearly seen. Advances in technology have led to more powerful and focused X-ray beams that allow us to do more than just see through things. We can image tiny biological cells and structural components of materials like cement, all the way to using focused X-rays to kill cancer cells.

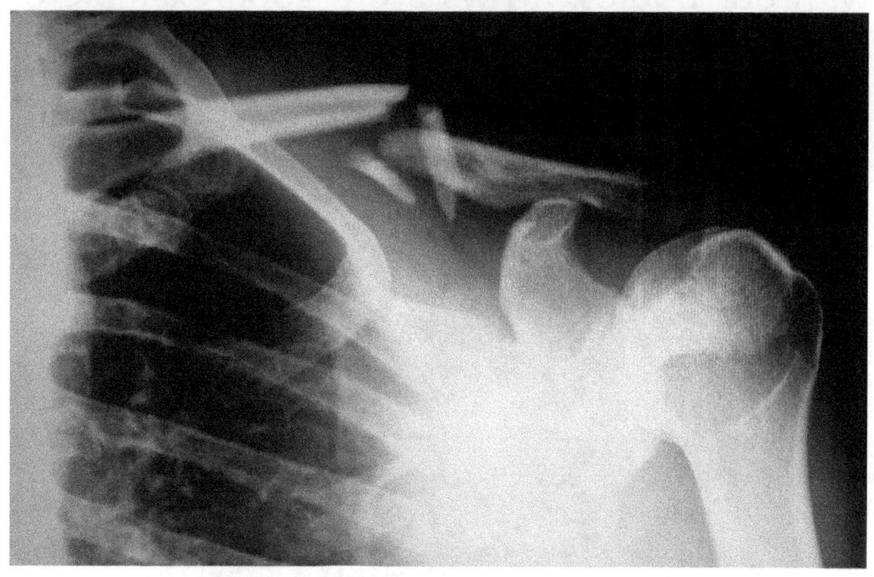

An X-ray of a broken collar bone.

There will be times where a confrontation with Dr. Deathmask or his goons goes south. For those occasions where you don't break any bones but are injured nonetheless, an MRI machine will help you figure out the specific problem that troubles you.

MRI, or Magnetic Resonance Imaging, is a

type of scan that uses strong magnetic fields and radio waves to produce detailed images of the inside of the human body. An MRI scanner is a large tube that contains powerful magnets. You lie inside the tube during the scan. Magnetic and radio waves resound through the tube, allowing doctors to see everything going on inside. MRIs are harmless, unlike X-rays, but the machine does produce a very loud noise while it's scanning. It's pretty wild, but an amazing tool, especially if you've received some blunt force trauma while saving the day.

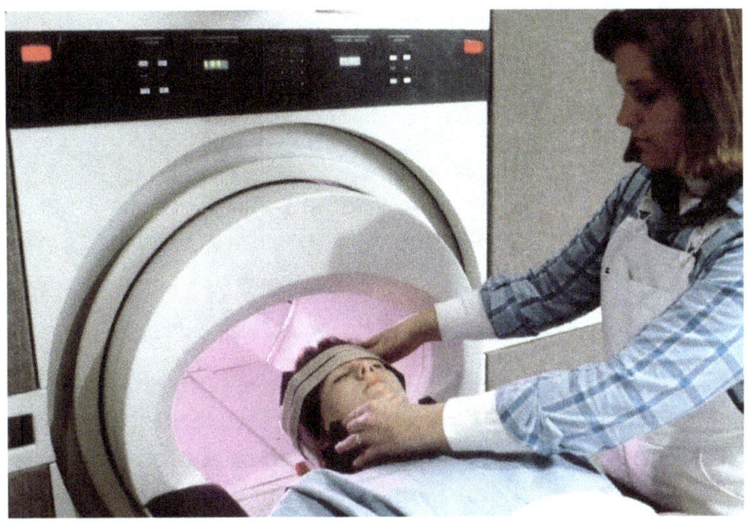

A doctor about to put a patient inside an MRI Scanner. The patient must remain as still as possible for the machine to get a clear picture of what is going on inside their body.

LIGHT WAVES

Our eyes can sense the difference between the frequencies of light rays. This makes the world appear to be filled with vibrant colors. What we are actually seeing is a reflected light frequency not absorbed by a surface. The material properties determine which colors are absorbed and which get reflected.

Sunlight is made up of every color all at once. Only the color you see is reflected to your eye. All other colors are absorbed by the object. Some types of light are already filtered or shine at a specific wavelength and don't contain every color.

Your brain processes more information gathered from your eyes than any other sensory organ. They are THAT important. Light reflecting from the costume of a rival enters your eye and passes through a lens that focuses the inverse image on your retina. The information is transmitted to your brain via the optic nerve, so you can react appropriately to the threat.

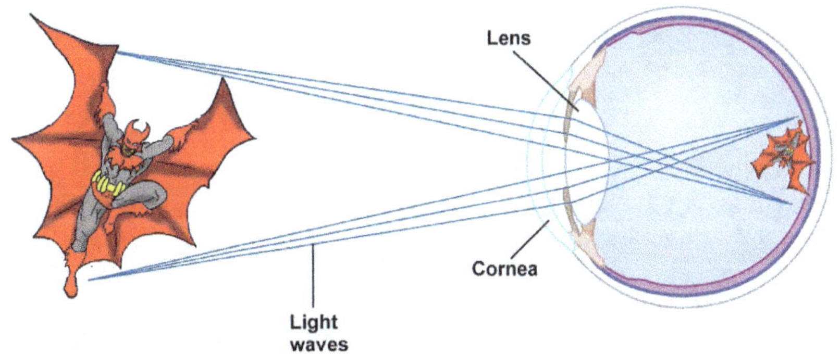

When light hits your cornea, the image you're seeing is flipped upside down. Your brain then flips the image back right side up.

HEAT WAVES

As a superhero, understanding heat radiation is incredibly important. If you're rescuing civilians from a fire, you'll need to know how much heat your skin can take before burning, as well as if your protective gear can stand up to the temperatures.

You may have seen ripples of air rising from the street on a hot day. Those are actually waves of heat contorting the molecules in the air. Sometimes it will look like there is water on the road even when the pavement is dry. While you can't see heat itself, you *can* see its effects on the world around it.

Waves of heat look like water on the roadway.

Conduction is heat transfer in solid objects. One side of an object is heated, causing the molecules to vibrate faster. The vibrating molecules collide with other molecules and transfer the energy. Thus, heat is conducted from one side of the solid object to the other.

Convection is heat transfer in fluids (liquids

and gases). A fluid contracts and sinks when cooled or expands and rises when heated. A heat source in a fluid causes some molecules to heat and rise, creating a difference in temperature which moves the molecules around and spreads the heat.

Fire is an excellent source of heat and produces infrared rays.

Sources of heat radiate infrared rays (light we can't see), which can travel through empty space until they strike cooler objects. That contact transfers the energy, and the objects warm up through convection or conduction.

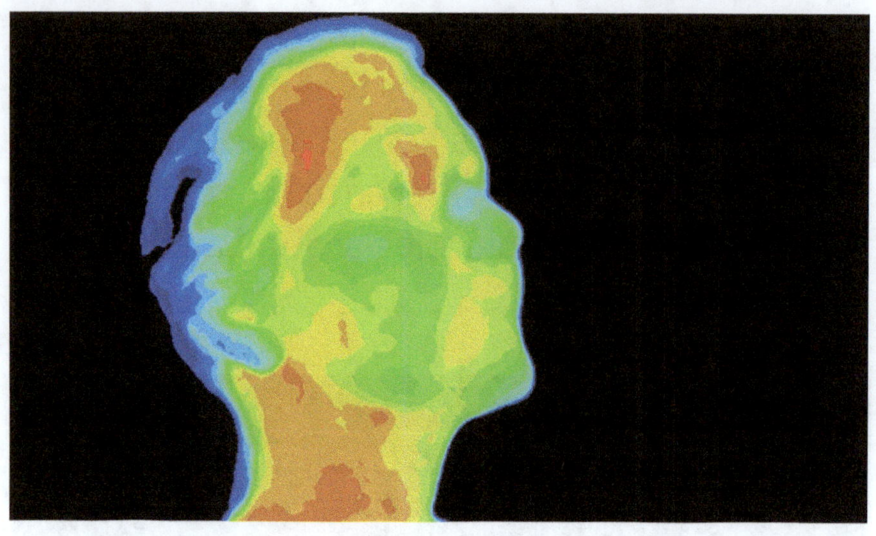

Infrared images show hot and cold spots on our skin.

Heat also affects your body. The more you move the more your body lets off heat. Our sweat helps to cool us down, but without replenishing that liquid through drinking water and even salt, we can become overheated and end up in the hospital.

That being the case, it's a good idea to have extra water with electrolytes hidden on your utility belt. It may not seem like something you'd want to carry while out on a patrol, but trust me, you don't want to get **dehydrated** (run low on water in your body) in the middle of a battle with a brood of angry henchmen.

A COUPLE OTHER HELPFUL TOOLS

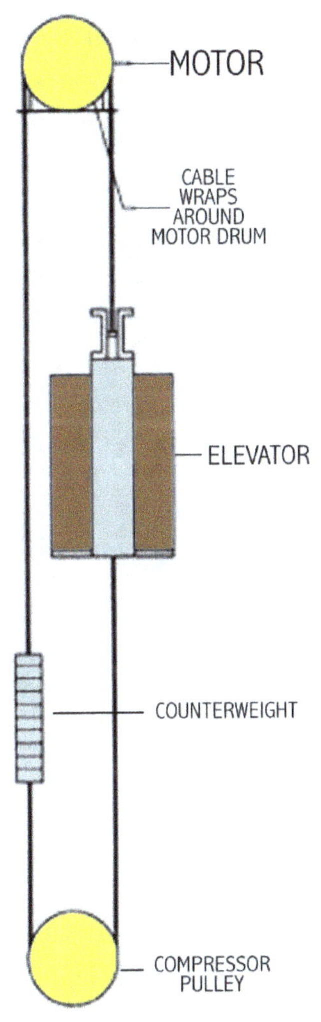

After a long day of fighting crime, the last thing you may want to do is climb several flights of stairs to get to your apartment. Thank science for the elevator. An elevator car is raised and lowered by a cable running over the top of a pulley and balanced by a counterweight. An electric motor is attached to the pulley and powers the motion of the car.

Cellphones are another great tool for fighting crime. First off, if you have an assistant or sidekick, you'll be able to stay in contact with them. Second, modern cellphones have numerous apps for recording video and audio that could allow you to gather evidence against your arch-rival.

Smartphones are actually miniature computers that can execute different programs for various functions or apps (applications). You can download crime statistics to track Dr. Deathmask and his team's movements while texting "Happy Birthday" to your dear, old grandma.

How it does all that is pretty ingenious. Cellphones send out signals to a local base station or cell tower. The Base Station routes to a Mobile Exchange (where calls are passed along to other phones or towers depending on the distance between callers), which connects to a main exchange within the cellular network. If needed, longer distance calls utilize relay towers or an international exchange that use satellites and undersea cables, depending on the application.

All of this happens almost instantly so you don't even realize anything has happened at all.

You have so many tools at your disposal as a superhero, from phones, to X-rays, to the sounds that enter your ear. Understanding all of them will take time. Don't try to master each one. Instead, pick which ones you think would work best with your superhero identity and go from there. Remember, your hero persona is as unique as you are, so focus on what interests you and you'll have more luck saving the day!

SUPERHERO PLANNING:

How can using everyday objects and principles help me to be a better superhero?

____
____
____
____
____
____
____
____
____
____
____
____
____
____
____
____
____

SECTION 4: SUPER-SLEUTHING

One of the core elements of superhero life is detective work. Supervillains are so named for a reason. They don't make it easy for you to uncover and thwart their mischievous scheming. You will need to hone the craft to become a super-sleuth. This section will get you started.

DETECTIVE WORK

A detective is someone who investigates and solves crimes. This can be a police officer, or someone trained to look at clues and understand patterns at a crime scene. Talking to witnesses and informants, collecting physical evidence, or searching records on computers and paper files are all ways detectives solve crimes.

LOGIC TECHNIQUES

Detective work isn't easy and requires dedication and a lot of patience. Clues don't just come together and solve themselves like in the movies. The detective must put pieces together, pay close attention to detail, and listen carefully.

Using **Deductive Logic** (the process of making a rational argument based on observable facts) allows you to move from a general premise to a specific conclusion, given the evidence you've collected. *Fact A* combined with *Fact B* ultimately leads to *Conclusion C.*

For example, let's say you are investigating a robbery where the burglar set fire to the building to cover his tracks. You have a testimony of a witness that saw the crook exit the building with a bag over his shoulder and deposit the bag into a nearby car. He then ran back into the building. Soon after, smoke began billowing from the windows. The same man ran out again dragging a second bag in one hand and shaking his other hand as if in pain.

You could deduce that he injured his hand during the second trip into the building, possibly burning it while setting the fire. You could then search for a man with a burned hand.

Inductive logic (the process of using examples and observations to reach an assumption about an event) allows our brains to make general conclusions based on experience. For example, all the thugs you've come across that work for Dr. Deathmask had a "DM" tattoo on the inside ring finger on their left hand. You could conclude that all Dr. Deathmask's lackeys have that same tattoo in the same location. This may or may not be true, but you now have a framework when searching for bad guys.

Observation/Curiosity

A natural curiosity will be a tremendous help. You can also increase your skills of observation with training. Ask yourself if there is anything abnormal going on around you, especially things that would normally go unnoticed. Of course, it helps to have an understanding of how things normally work on a day to day basis.

This is where curiosity comes in.

Ask lots of questions about everything you can. Learn from experts when you have the chance so you can gain from their experience. You never know when one of these details will alert you to the beginnings of a sinister plot.

INTERROGATION

One other key technique for detectives is the **interrogation**. This is where you talk to a suspect, ask them questions, and see if they contradict themselves or the evidence you've gathered. You can learn a lot from interrogating witnesses and suspects.

You never know who will have that little tidbit of information that unlocks the secrets of a case. It could be the mayor or the gas station attendant. You need the ability to converse easily with individuals you've never met.

Questioning Techniques

You will need to learn to ask lots of questions that follow a logical flow. You also need to be able to circle back and ask questions in different ways when you think people are hiding something from you.

Here is an example of asking follow-up questions:

You: *What did the assailant look like?*

Witness: *She was 5' 6" with blond hair and blue eyes, probably in her thirties.*

You: *Do you remember anything else about her appearance that would help me identify her?*

Witness: *She wore a black leather jacket, but I could see she had tattoos just under the sleeves at her writs.*

You: *Anything else?*

Witness: *Yeah, she had a scar on her left hand. It looked like a bad burn that had long since healed.*

By asking follow-up questions, you went from an average looking Caucasian female suspect with average build to a specific set of characteristics that few people share (tattoos, scars, height, etc.). Your search pool went from potentially millions of people to a small handful of suspects.

The Problem with Eyewitnesses and Human Memory

It is important to note that an eyewitness account of a situation isn't a guarantee that events unfolded exactly as described. The human memory is imperfect and can be contaminated by other sources of information. Our brains don't capture every detail, so they fill in the holes by drawing on our past experience. In some cases, the brain will produce a false memory based on the individual's limited exposure to the actual event. It is preferable to have video footage of an incident because the camera doesn't lie. In the absence of footage, you should question each witness separately to get a picture of what happened without biasing the witnesses.

Detecting Deception

Not everyone you talk to will tell you the truth. Some may intentionally deceive you in an attempt to throw you off their trail. These dishonest individuals can be spotted, with practice, by observing their non-verbal cues. This is based on the premise that lying causes emotional or cognitive stress on the individual. It manifests in different ways that you can look for, such as a long pause, a change in behavior, or involuntary micro-expressions in the face. You may not have conclusive evidence that the individual is attempting to deceive you, but you will likely get the impression that something isn't right.

Trust your gut and verify the information whenever possible.

Follow the clues and you may stumble upon your criminal!

EVIDENCE

The interrogation will only get you so far though. You need **evidence** to convict a supervillain. Physical evidence, also known as forensic evidence, are objects left behind at the scene of a crime, like a footprint, drops of blood, fingerprints, or a gigantic plasma cannon. You'll need evidence before you can lock your nemesis away. Justice isn't served until you can prove someone committed the crime. You may have a gut feeling, but without evidence you can't send someone to jail, no matter how evil they seem.

Look for Clues

Dr. Deathmask may be an evil genius but his minions tend to be dim and have a habit of leaving behind evidence of their dealings. You don't need a magnifying glass to search for clues but you should definitely bring your smartphone or a high-resolution digital camera so you can refer to important photos later. Latex gloves and resealable bags are helpful to have when collecting any evidence.

Thoroughly inspect areas of high interest. Pay attention to little details. Does anything look out of place? Is something gone that should be there? You should always take photos in case you miss something.

Take notes

Unless you have super memory, you will want to take notes of your interviews and findings to refer to later. You will likely find a clue down the road that will fit with the rest of your case in a way that unravels the mystery.

Once you've investigated a crime scene, document everything in the room using notes and photographs. Everything is a possible clue, so look closely and try to determine patterns, like how a robber may have moved from one part of the room to another by how things fell on the floor, or how big a person might have been

based on deep footprints in the carpet. Remember: everything is a possible clue.

You'll also need to investigate **records** in order to help close a case. These records could be police documents with fingerprints and mugshots (photographs of suspected criminals), computer files with statistics on crimes, surveillance camera footage, and anything else that will give you enough data to catch Dr. Deathmask.

BASE OF OPERATIONS

All great superheroes have a place of refuge where they can think in peace while they connect the dots. Be sure to set up a secure location where you can store your evidence and clues.

A futuristic base with tons of cool tech would be amazing, but maybe start with something simpler first...

This could be a room in your home where you can get away from everyone else, OR you could go full superhero and build your own lair!

Constructing a clubhouse or secret hideout requires plenty of material and hard work, but you can ask for scrap material from construction sites easily enough or scavenge what you

can from your neighbors. People are always willing to help when a superhero is in need!

You'll want to start with a foundation of a few cinderblocks and wood, like in the photo above. You can make the base as big or as small as you want, but you'll need to measure everything out to make sure things nail together properly.

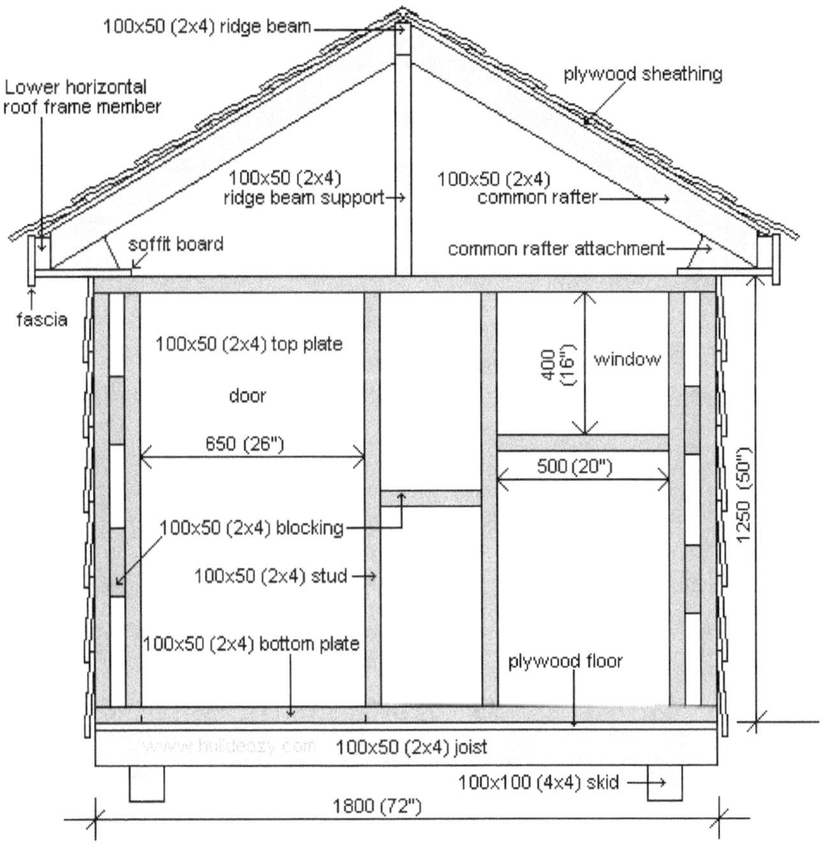

This is a basic blueprint for a clubhouse. Feel free to design it anyway you like, so long as you have approval from your parents on where it will go in the backyard.

Once you have your foundation built, you'll need to add walls, windows, secret entrances, whatever you need.

Measure twice and cut once. Your lair can come together surprisingly quickly if you dedicate a Saturday to building.

You could even build using old wooden pallets from warehouses and stores. This doesn't have to be an overly complicated project. Use your imagination and you can accomplish anything!

Be sure to ask people you trust for help, after all, this is going to be your base of operations and you don't want any villains learning its location.

Supplies you'll need: Forty (40) 2x4s, ten (10) sheets of plywood, four (4) 4x4 beams, eight (8) cinderblocks or bricks, nails or screws, roofing shingles, hammers, screwdrivers, measuring tape, skill saw, and a ladder.

It's hard work, but once your base of operations starts coming together, you'll know your superhero career is about to take off.

Once complete, your clubhouse can serve numerous functions that will help you make the world a better place.

When the structure is complete, you can paint it to match your superhero identity. Are you dark and mysterious? Colorful and hopeful? Your hideout should complement who you are.

FINDING A SIDEKICK

Some heroes like to go it alone. It's a respectable choice, though we recommend you find someone to join in the detective work. Even superheroes are stronger together. Plus, you will find you solve a great deal more crimes and mysteries when you have someone to help carry the load and share ideas.

But what makes a good sidekick? That will depend on each person individually, but there are a few traits that you'll want to look for in your superhero partner.

BRAVERY is key. If someone wants to fight by your side, they'll need to have the courage to stand firm no matter the threat.

STREET SMART. Having a sidekick that knows their way around the city, along with a few good criminal contacts that could help you solve crimes, is a huge bonus.

LOYALTY. Supervillains will do anything to corrupt a sidekick. You'll need someone that won't betray you for anything; a true friend.

HUMOR. Things can get dark in the detective and superhero world. A partner that can make you laugh and lighten things up a bit will make all the difference when you're facing down disaster.

WEARING DISGUISES

Last but not least, there are times when you don't want to advertise your superpowers by wearing your costume.

A proper disguise is in order when you need to move through enemy territory without being noticed.

Don't over-think it. A simple trench coat and hat or pair of glasses, maybe a fake mustache or beard, can be enough to make you less noticeable. All you need is to blend in with the crowd. That way you can easily sneak around in search of clues or make a hasty departure when necessary.

A trick real detectives use when hiding their identity is to have one very memorable aspect of your disguise, like a fake scar on your cheek or a bright red scarf, that will draw attention away from the details of your face. This way Dr. Deathmask's thugs will be less likely to identify you when asked about the quiet intruder.

Developing your detective and disguise skills will allow you to be one step ahead of your enemies. Sometimes you'll need more than that to win the day, so don't slack off now! Our next section will give you a few more advantages that could make a huge difference in your superhero career.

SUPERHERO PLANNING:

How can I become more observant in my daily life? Are there any mysteries to be solved?

SECTION 5:
SUPERHERO GADGETS

Superpowers are rare, so you'll need some tech advantages if you can't fly or pick up cars. Sometimes a good gadget can get you out of dangerous situations. While grappling hooks and Batarangs may seem too good to be true, there are real life devices that can be used to help you become the superhero you're training to be. They may not be as physics-defying as shown in the comics, but these contraptions function in the real world and can give you an edge when facing down epic super-threats.

GRAPPLE GUNS

We're used to seeing heroes like Batman swing through cities using small pistols that shoot claws attached to cables. The problem is those small devices just aren't powerful enough in the real world to propel a line through the air and then pull a person behind it.

While these small versions aren't feasible, grapple guns do exist and allow soldiers to fire a line over impressive distances and then be pulled behind. One of those is the REBS Compact Launcher.

The *REBS Pneumatic Launcher* is an accurate, multi-shot, **pneumatic** (gas pressurized) cable shooter that allows military personnel to traverse distances up to 300 feet. The launcher uses unique spring arm grapnels to grip surfaces and hold firmly in place. This would allow you to climb buildings, cross expanses between skyscrapers, and even swing from one point to the next.

While not as compact as you would probably like if you had to chase villains across rooftops, this grapple gun would still be a powerful tool in your arsenal, particularly if you were planning an assault on an enemy lair.

Now, if you're willing to go less technological, standard grappling hooks can work very well and aren't as heavy as the machine versions. The hook lodges itself wherever you tossed it and you then climb up behind on the rope.

The only downside here is that the grapple can only travel as far as you can throw it, so you better get practicing.

INVISIBILITY

The power to become invisible is a fascinating idea, and one that has become more of a reality in the past ten years.

Canadian company *Hyperstealth* developed a light-bending material that can create a functioning invisibility cloak, like from Harry

Potter. The material, known as Quantum Stealth, bends light around the object or person behind it, leaving only the background visible. The material changes the light's frequency as it passes through, rendering objects invisible.

Now you see my head...now you don't!

Spectral cloaking effectively bumps light waves into a frequency that passes through the target object, then returns those light waves to their original state. What that means is you could place a basket of fruit behind the cloak, shine a flashlight on it, and the light would shine on the wall behind the basket as if it wasn't there at all. You just program the filter on the cloak to warp the appropriate colors.

While the technology isn't perfect, it shows the capability of becoming invisible. It will be years, even decades, before you could create an invisible suit that even slightly bends the light around a person, but it's still pretty cool.

ROBOT SUITS

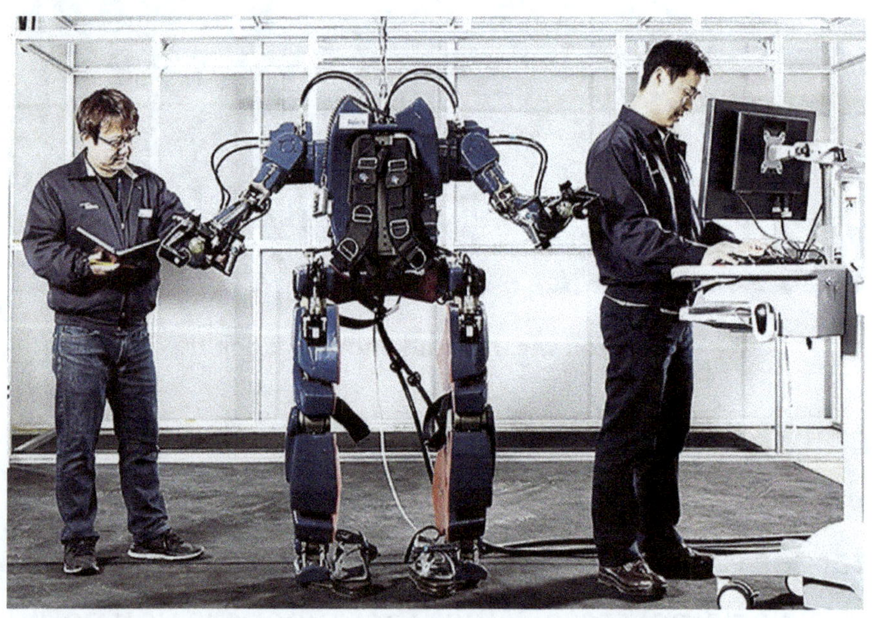

Scientists at Hyundai building a real exo-suit to help factory workers and military personnel.

We've all imagined flying around in our very own Iron Man suit. While that would be awesome, the technology to make that happen is still far in the future. Today though, exoskeletal suits are a reality. These

mechanical housings, or **exoskeletons,** are wearable devices that move with the body of the user, giving them added strength and agility, and in some cases allowing people with spinal cord injuries to walk again. Hydraulics, electric motors, and pneumatic levers all work together to give the user extra strength, but because of its size, no extra speed. In fact, the wearer will walk quite a bit slower, unfortunately.

Exoskeletons are placed on the user's body and act as amplifiers that augment, reinforce or restore human performance. They aren't as streamlined or efficient as what you see in movies and comic books (beginning to see a pattern here?), but they do work and can make an intimidating superhero suit.

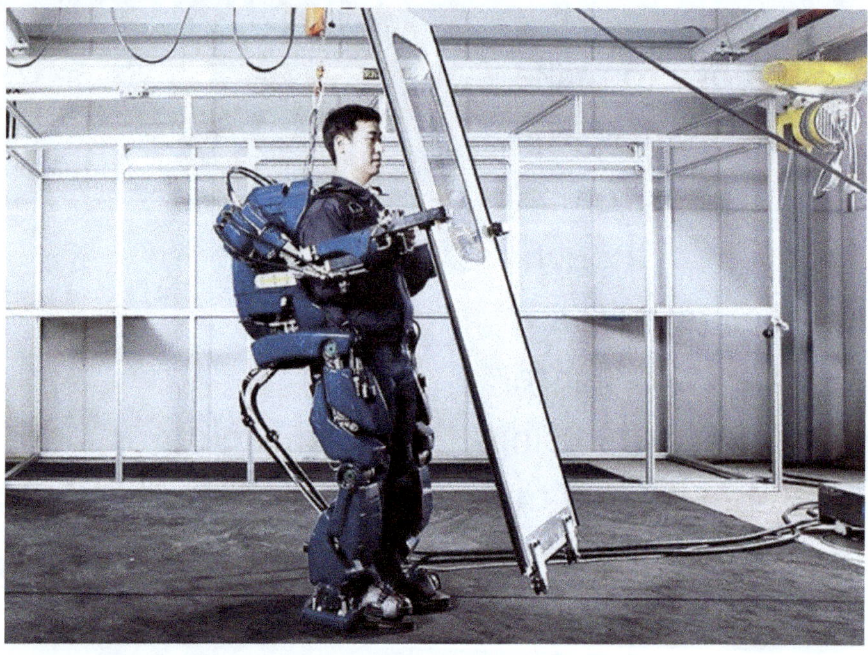

The exo-housings are balanced so the user can lift heavy objects without falling over. They're helpful in a factory environment, but it will probably be a few years before a good superhero version is in the works.

ARTIFICIAL INTELLIGENCE

Robots and androids are the future, right? Soon we'll have cybernetic overlords and protectors.

Well, not exactly.

The thing about intelligence is that it's incredibly complicated. Our brains are amazing! It's not a simple thing to create a computer that can learn and understand like our minds can.

That doesn't mean we haven't tried...and in some ways succeeded.

Siri debuted in 2011 from Apple and has since become a common feature in many homes across the world.

You may have a device like Siri in your home. Siri is an artificial intelligence (A.I.) designed to be a virtual assistant that listens, answers questions, and solves problems. It was developed with the purpose of being able to interpret voices and understand meaning just like our brains do.

Siri can't think for itself, however. Humans have created some pretty impressive A.I.s, but none of them are yet able to fully think for themselves.

Creating a body for such an intelligent robot is an entirely different problem to solve. Much like our brains, our bodies are incredibly complicated and intricate instruments that are not easily  copied. Walking is simple for us, but a robot? Not so much. Even grasping something with your hand is a difficult proposition for an android because we instinctively know how much pressure to apply to an object, so we don't break it. A robot doesn't have those natural sensors in their manufactured fingers.

While complicated self-thinking robots are still in the future, currently robots serve hundreds of functions in our everyday life, from building automobiles to exploring Mars! They are great for performing repeated simple tasks and never get tired.

Robot arms build a car in an automobile factory.

Even though robots aren't efficient enough yet to go stomping through the city, computer programs and robots don't get tired like human brains and muscles. In fact, a computer can cycle through programs and adjust parameters to calculate millions of scenarios to help us understand various outcomes. Humans would give up long before they could crunch all those numbers

A.I. may not be able to think for itself yet, but you could learn some simple programming logic and create subroutines to assist in your hunt for Dr. Deathmask.

SUPER JUMPS

You've probably jumped on a trampoline before and felt the effects as you're launched into the air. Now imagine you could attach miniature trampolines to your feet and high jump wherever you want.

It may sound impossible, but there are actually some simple devices that allow you to do just that!

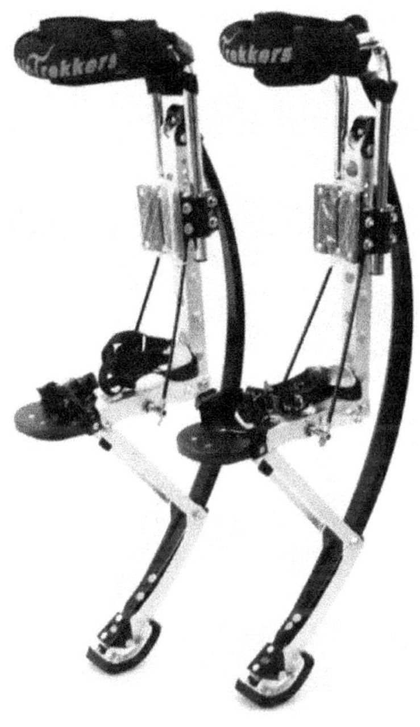

Jumping stilts are made from carbon fiber springs and are popular with acrobats. The stilts allow you to jump up to five feet in the air, run at speeds of 20 miles per hour, and take nine-foot strides while walking. They come in small sizes too, so kids can learn how to use them.

Another option is Kangoo Jump Boots. They work on the same principle as jumping stilts but use compression instead of springs. They don't allow you to jump as high, but they do cut down on the impact, so if you're jumping off a building, these would definitely help with the landing.

Kangoo Boots may not help you to jump super high, but they will help absorb impacts, so you don't hurt your knees and ankles.

BULLETPROOF CLOTHING

Unlike some of the other gadgets we've looked at, bulletproof clothing (vests, jackets, even business suits) are very real and work just as well as you see in movies and comics.

Even though something is bulletproof doesn't mean you're not going to get hurt if you are shot, though. Protective materials will keep the bullets from hitting your skin and killing you, but the force

from the impact still has the potential to break ribs and cause bruising, so be prepared!

Police and S.W.A.T. teams use body armor consisting of protective vests that can stop a bullet. These ballistic vests use layers of strong fibers, generally made from plastics and Kevlar, to "catch" and deform a bullet. By mushrooming the slug into a dish shape, it spreads the force of the projectile across a broader portion of the vest and thus keeps it from penetrating the textile mix.

Kevlar is five times stronger than steel and provides reliable performance and solid strength.

It's made from a mixture of chemicals that form thin sheets like silk. When laid together these sheets are fully bulletproof.

That fact allows for some pretty interesting wardrobe possibilities for the superhero-minded individual. The textile company *Garrison Bespoke* has actually created a pinstripe business suit that is fully bulletproof. Even the tie! The fabric is heavier than standard business attire, but it will stop a bullet.

This same fabric could be used in your superhero costume, but you need to keep in mind that the closer the fabric is to your skin, the more the bullet will hurt when it hits you.

Now that you have some options for protective clothing, we're able to move to the last section of our super-heroic journey where we will design our costumes and uniforms. You may want to add a few bulletproof layers to your cape just to be safe!

SUPERHERO PLANNING:

What real world gadget might work best with your superhero identity? Why?

SECTION 6:
SUPERHERO COSTUME DESIGN

Every guardian of greatness needs an outfit befitting the title they bear. Deciding on a super-suit is no trivial matter. The attire you sport says a lot about who you are and what you can do. One day your wardrobe may be copied by thousands of aspiring heroes on their path to prominence. Thus, you should don regalia appropriate for your high position.

Functionality Over Flash

It is important to design a costume that gives you a signature look; something simple and straight forward. You want to make an impression without having a costume that is too crazy or distracting. Your costume needs to compliment your superhero ability. Can you shoot fire from your hands? If so, you better get some flame-

retardant fabric. Are you a martial arts expert? Make sure to have a costume that allows you to move without restrictions. That said, anything fashionable from today, or decades past, can be modified and incorporated into the outfit of a superhero. Your personality should show through in your design. Have fun experimenting with colors, styles, patterns, and layers. **Be bold!**

Revealing Your True Colors

Different colors give an outfit a unique feel. Each color has various shades that can turn a bland design into an iconic look. It is essential to select colors that resonate with who you are and what you represent. If you're a dark, stalking hero, you  probably shouldn't design a bright yellow costume that draws attention. Conversely, if you're a cheerful and happy hero, blacks and grays probably wouldn't be the best choice either.

COLOR WHEEL

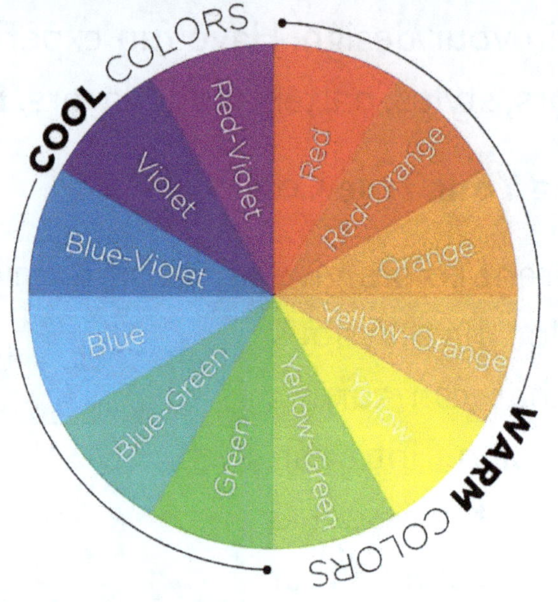

A color wheel is a simple tool that can help you figure out your color scheme. It includes all the major pigments and allows you to see which colors complement each other. For example, colors that are opposite each other on the color wheel (yellow and violet, or red and green) are colors that go well together. If you pair some of these colors, your costume will have a natural balance and will look pleasing to the eye. Aesthetics are important, even for superheroes.

These examples show how different color combinations can change the way you see a hero, and what you think that champion represents. If a hero dresses in red, white, and blue, you might think they are patriotic and work for the American government. A hero in all black might make you think they are dangerous and brooding. Play around with different designs until you find something that you not only like, but that shows the type of hero you want to be.

YOUR SUPERHERO NAME

This is the point where you need to have your superhero name nailed down. You can't figure out what your costume looks like until you know who you are.

Choosing your superhero name is a very personal thing. You may already know your superhero identity, but if you don't, there are a few tools you can use to help you figure out who you will become when you go out to save the world.

First, think about who you are. What do you like? What do you dislike? What's your favorite animal? Asking yourself questions will help you narrow things down. If your favorite color is red, you love gorillas, and you're super-strong, you could become the Crimson Ape.

Create a list and then choose what you feel will best characterize *you*. That's the most important part of becoming a superhero: representing who you are as a person.

DESIGNING YOUR EMBLEM

The most important aspect of your costume is your emblem, or logo. Think the Bat-symbol or Superman's stylized 'S.' Just like those well-known heroes, you need to have an emblem that tells people who you are.

Like your costume as a whole, make sure your symbol is simple. A great way to start is to decide whether you want to have your emblem inside a shape, like a circle, square, or diamond.

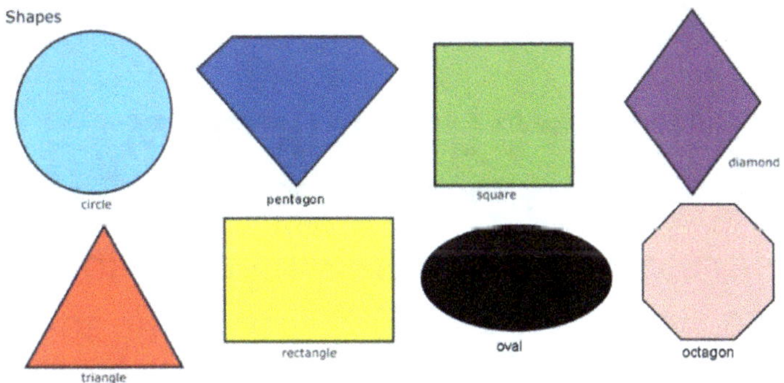

Do you want a letter inside your logo? An insignia? It's your choice. If your superhero name is Captain Sledgehammer, it might be good to have a straightforward drawing of a sledgehammer inside a circle. Are you the Emerald Cobra? A snake inside a green diamond would look cool.

Keep your emblem simple. If you have super strength, try to create something that will represent that in your logo.

DESIGNING YOUR UNIFORM

Before you can start sewing or building your costume, you first need to put your ideas on paper and draw them out. You don't have to be an artist to do this, so don't worry. Just draw your design, color it in, and then you'll have a base from which to work.

Try a few different designs and color schemes. This way you can see what you like best. Remember, this is a uniform you will wear while saving the world, so take your time to get it right. Ask your friends and parents what they think and listen to their feedback. They could have some good ideas. At the end of the day though, this is *your* uniform, so trust yourself and make it the way you want.

Once you have your basic design you can begin to create. If you're feeling really ambitions, and if you have access to a sewing machine, you could sew your costume from scratch. It's a lot of work, and you may not want to start out with this option, but it's fun nonetheless.

Sewing is the act of taking pieces of fabric and turning them into clothing. This is done using thread, needles, and patterns. In the old days all clothes were sewed by hand, but today we use sewing machines that make the work much easier and faster.

Needle and thread, along with a sewing machine.

If you choose to sew your uniform, you'll need to start out with a pattern. These can be found for free on the internet. Your parents can help you get what you need. The pattern shows how to cut the shapes that will eventually become your costume. You cut out the shapes from paper, pin them to your cloth, and then cut the fabric. Once the pieces are cut, they are then sewn together to make clothing, uniforms, whatever you need.

You can get colored fabric and create limitless combinations based off of simple patterns. You can even make your own patterns and do incredible designs that will make people's eyes truly go wide with amazement.

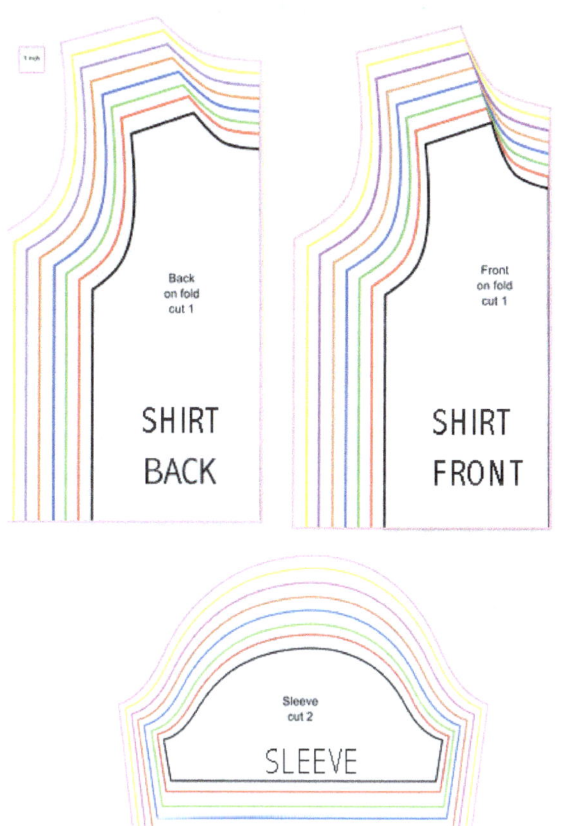

Now, for those of you who aren't feeling ambitious enough to sew your own costume, another great tool is fabric paint. Fabric paint is a type of liquid plastic that sticks to cloth and allows you to do fantastic designs. This is a great way to put superhero emblems onto tee-shirts if you want to keep things uncomplicated.

Fabric paint works the same way as regular paint, so you'll want to make sure to be careful you don't spill. Once you have your logo painted in place, leave the clothing out to dry over night and the next day you'll have your first superhero uniform ready to wear.

Fabric glue is another tool that allows you to do some interesting things with your costume. You can cut out symbols or swatches of color for accents and glue them to your uniform. It's easy and ends up looking pretty good.

Using fabric glue, you can add your symbol to your costume easily and effectively. It also allows you to combine layers of fabric to create different designs and accents.

ACCESSORIES

To cape or not to cape? That is the question. Capes look cool and also make you look bigger and more intimidating, but they can also cause problems during a fight or chase. If you're a flying hero, a cape is a good idea because it can make your take-offs and landings very dramatic, but if you're a ninja you'll probably need to avoid wearing one (sorry Batman).

Whether or not you want to wear a mask is another choice you'll need to make. Masks conceal your identity and protect the one's you love, but they can also impede your vision and make civilians less likely to trust you. It's a trade-off, so you'll need to think about it before your first adventure. Of course, masks look pretty cool too, so keep that in mind.

Creating a mask is pretty easy though. Take a long, thin strip of cloth and tie it around your face where you'll want the mask to be. Have a marker handy so you can mark where your eyes are. Then remove the fabric and cut circles out where you marked your eyes to be. It's that simple. You can also find templates on the internet if you want to get even more creative.

Belts are another accessory that may come in handy. You'll need to carry things while you're chasing Dr. Deathmask or Commander Chaos through the city. Will you be jumping from building to building? Where are you going to hold your grapple gun? A belt will solve some of these problems. Plus, you might want a snack while you're saving the day, so having a pouch full of granola bars would be great.

There are a lot of different types of tactical belts to choose from, so you'll want to see what will compliment your costume and help you while out on missions. You might not need something with a lot of pouches and holders, so think about what you'll need with you and plan accordingly.

You may also need to use different sized belts with bigger or smaller pouches depending on what type of mission you're about to pursue.

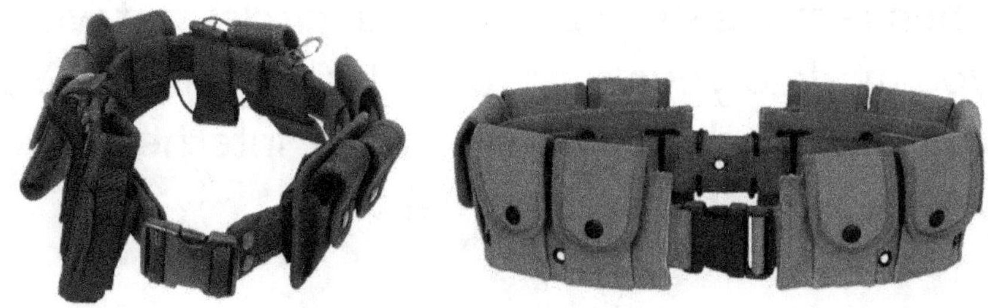

Different style utility belts

When it comes to creating your superhero costume and identity there's really no right or wrong way to do things. Being a superhero is about doing what is best and helping people in need. Your wardrobe is secondary.

Still, having a cool costume will make you feel confident, and you'll need that confidence if you're going to stand against the forces of evil and make the world a better place.

ACTIVITY:

Use this space to draw some designs for your superhero identity!

SUPERHERO PLANNING:

What is my superhero name? Why is this the best name for my superhero identity?

Epilogue

And there you have it! You've taken your first steps toward becoming a real-life superhero!

Congratulations!

Now that you have the knowledge, you need to continue to study, train, and work hard. Being a superhero requires all the diligence you can muster.

Villains, Like Dr. Deathmask, are becoming more devious when plotting their next evil plan. It will take smart superheroes to thwart their wicked schemes. This book is an introduction to the science that could save your life and the lives of countless innocents one day. Your journey has begun, it is up to you to walk the hero's path and take the next step. We are counting on you!

And perhaps one day you'll be so famous we'll be reading about your adventures in comic books all over the world.

BLUR
01
1ST ISSUE
CREATED BY
ZACH CIPRIANO
YELLOW
SOVEREIGN
25
No. 27
64 PAGES OF
thrilling action!
SEPTEMBER, 1939
HEUMANN
CIPRIANO
DEMON-BIRD
The Adventures of the Devil's Detective!
10c
Demon-Bird, the greatest, mysterious
hero of them all now featured in
your favrite comic magazine!
Be here each week!
1992
333
The AMAZING
DUNG-BEETLE
PURGE
450
PENANCE part 1
CAPTAIN FLEX
and the
HYZER BOMBERS
99
DEREK MANNING
STEVEN HEUMANN
ECLECTIC MAN
738
HEUMANN
CIPRIANO
BOOTH
WARRIOR
WOMAN
105
TITAN: PART 4
GEEK
REVENGER
SHP
ANNIVERSARY
ISSUE
FEB. 2014
225
GR

KEY TERMS AND DEFINITIONS

Antagonistic Pairs: Muscles transfer force to bones through tendons. In an antagonistic muscle pair as one muscle contracts the other muscle relaxes or lengthens. The muscle that is contracting is called the agonist and the muscle that is relaxing or lengthening is called the antagonist.

Atrophy: A wasting away of the body or of an organ or part, as from defective nutrition or nerve damage.

Bacteria: Ubiquitous one-celled organisms, spherical, spiral, or rod-shaped and appearing singly or in chains, comprising numerous and variously classified phyla: among the inestimable number of species are those involved in fermentation, putrefaction, infectious diseases, and nitrogen fixation.

Capillary Action: The movement of a liquid along the surface of a solid caused by the attraction of molecules of the liquid to the molecules of the solid.

Chain Reaction: A chemical reaction or other process in which the products themselves promote or spread the reaction, which under certain conditions may accelerate dramatically. The self-sustaining fission reaction spread by neutrons which occurs in nuclear reactors and bombs, or a series of events, each caused by the previous one.

Conduction: The transfer of heat between two parts of a stationary system, caused by a temperature difference between the parts.

Convection: The transfer of heat by the circulation or movement of the heated parts of a liquid or gas.

Deductive Logic: The process of reasoning from one or more statements (premises) to reach a logically certain conclusion.

Dehydrated: To deprive a chemical compound of water or the elements of water. To free (fruit, vegetables, etc.) from moisture for preservation; dry. To remove water from the body or a tissue.

Echolocation: the general method of locating objects by determining the time for an echo to return and the direction from which it returns, as by radar or sonar. The sonar-like system used by dolphins, bats, and other animals to detect and locate objects by emitting usually high-pitched sounds that reflect off the object and return to the animal's ears or other sensory receptors.

Electromagnet: A device consisting of an iron or steel core that is magnetized by electric current in a coil that surrounds it.

Endurance: The fact or power of enduring or bearing pain, hardships, etc. The ability or strength to continue or last, especially despite fatigue, stress, or other adverse conditions; stamina.

Evidence: That which tends to prove or disprove something; ground for belief; proof. Something that makes plain or clear; an indication or sign. In a judicial setting, evidence consists of objects, materials, fluids, that can be used against a person on trial for a crime.

Exoskeleton: An external covering or coating, especially when hard, as the shells of crustaceans. Exoskeletons can be natural and grow on a creature such as a snail or be scavenged and added to the body for protection, such as a Hermit Crab.

Ferromagnetic Metals: Ferromagnetism is the basic mechanism by which certain materials (such as iron) form permanent magnets or are attracted to magnets. Only a few substances are ferromagnetic. The common ones are iron, cobalt, nickel and most of their alloys, and some compounds of rare earth Metals.

Force Application: strength or energy; might; power. Exertion or the use of exertion against a person or thing that resists; coercion.

Fulcrum: The support, or point of rest, on which a lever turns in moving a body. Any prop or support.

Germ: A microorganism, especially when disease-producing; microbe.

Inclined Plane: An inclined plane, also known as a ramp, is a flat supporting surface tilted at an angle, with one end higher than the other, used as an aid for raising or lowering a load. The inclined plane is one of the six classical simple machines defined by Renaissance scientists.

Inductive logic: a method of reasoning in which the premises are viewed as supplying *some* evidence, but not full assurance, for the truth of the conclusion. It is also described as a method where one's experiences and observations, including what are learned from others, are synthesized to come up with a general truth.

Interrogation: The act of questioning a person, usually in the context of law enforcement and judicial circumstances.

Lift: The distance that anything rises or is raised. To move or bring (something) upward from the ground or other support to a higher position; hoist. To raise or direct upward.

Mass: A body of coherent matter, usually of indefinite shape and often of considerable size. The physical material comprising an object.

Molecule: The smallest physical unit of an element or compound, consisting of one or more like atoms in an element and two or more different atoms in a compound.

Pneumatic: A mechanism operated by air or by the pressure or exhaustion of air. Something filled with or containing compressed air, as a tire.

Radiation: The complete process in which energy is emitted by one body, transmitted through an intervening medium or space, and absorbed by another body, and the energy transferred by these processes.

Records: To set down in writing or the like, as for the purpose of preserving evidence.

Resultant Force: The single force and associated torque obtained by combining a system of forces and torques acting on a rigid body. The defining feature of a resultant force, or resultant force-torque, is that it has the same effect on the rigid body as the original system of forces.

Sew: To join or attach by stitches. To make, repair, etc., (a garment) by such means.

Voltage: electromotive force or potential difference expressed in volts.

Wedge: A form of the incline plane. A piece of hard material with two principal faces meeting in a sharply acute angle, for raising, holding, or splitting objects by applying a pounding or driving force, as from a hammer.

Yaw: (Of a moving ship or aircraft) twist or oscillate about a vertical axis.

PALMER HAWKINS

Palmer was often found organizing intergalactic superhero battles on his trampoline with neighborhood kids while in his youth. He developed a love for science and technology over the years which led to a career in engineering. Palmer has a passion for telling and hearing stories that are filled with action and adventure.

STEVEN HEUMANN

Steven spent his childhood recording stories into his sister's tape deck until she took it away in a huff. Even so, he wouldn't be stopped. After 15 years working as a writer and director in the television industry, he left it all behind to become a full-time novelist...with a wife and six kids. Seriously...

Other Novels by Steven Heumann

Paper Heroes: Stewart Mitchell is a corporate nobody. That all changes after he witnesses a terrorist attack that rocks the entire world. Was it chance, or did someone want him in the heat of the explosions? Nothing is what it seems when the heroes and villains share the same goal.

Gavin Baller Series: He's the number 1 A-lister in Hollywood, and as much as he thinks he's the greatest ever, Gavin is about to discover he's in fact the biggest disappointment in the galaxy. Adventure, intrigue, laughs, and maybe a bit of sewage awaits in this ongoing series of universal danger and high stakes acting. This isn't Luke Skywalker's galaxy far, far away!

Retooled: Sci-Fi Tales of Fairies & Folk: You only think you know the stories. Go down the rabbit hole like never before as you read lesser-known fairy tales with a dark sci-fi bent!

All novels and more stories available at
www.stevenheumann.com